BIOETHICS
and the Beginning of Life

BIOETHICS
and the Beginning of Life

An Anabaptist Perspective

Edited by
Roman J. Miller
and
Beryl H. Brubaker

HERALD PRESS
Scottdale, Pennsylvania
Waterloo, Ontario

Library of Congress Cataloging-in-Publication Data
Bioethics and the beginning of life : an Anabaptist perspective /
  edited by Roman J. Miller and Beryl H. Brubaker.
    p.   cm.
  Includes bibliographies and index.
  ISBN 0-8361-3502-4 (alk. paper)
    1. Human reproduction—Moral and ethical aspects. 2. Human repro-
ductive technology—Moral and ethical aspects. I. Miller, Roman J.,
1949-   . II. Brubaker, Beryl H., 1942-
QP251.B562   1989
176—dc20   89-15266
                                                                         CIP

The paper used in this publication meets the minimum requirements of American
National Standard for Information Sciences—Permanence of Paper for Printed Library Materials, ANSI Z39.48—1984.

BIOETHICS AND THE BEGINNING OF LIFE
Copyright © 1990 by Herald Press, Scottdale, Pa. 15683
    Published simultaneously in Canada by Herald Press,
    Waterloo, Ont. N2H 6H7. All rights reserved.
Library of Congress Catalog Card Number: 89-15266
International Standard Book Number: 0-8361-3502-4
Printed in the United States of America
Design by Gwen M. Stamm
Cover photo by Camerique Stock Photography
Art in Chapters 3 and 5 by Wade Lough
Art in Chapter 4 by Dennis Overman

1 2 3 4 5 6 7 8 9 10 96 95 94 93 92 91 90

Contents

   Biblical Perspectives   Dorothy Jean Weaver
   *In relationship to bioethics, a fundamental idea in Scrip-
   ture is that God is the Giver of life. Scripture teaches
   that God is actively involved in the problem of infertility
   and in the development of the unborn.*

   A Theological Approach   John Richard Burkholder
   *Basic theological assumptions shape responses to bioethi-
   cal issues. Anabaptist-Mennonite assumptions prevent an
   absolutist position on issues surrounding the unborn and
   emphasize the importance of the church community in
   discernment.*

   Overview of Human Reproduction   Gary J. Killian
   *Human reproduction involves hormonally controlled pro-
   duction of the male and female sex cells, as well as a series of biological events to ensure the success of conception. Fertilization results in the formation of a single cell,
   the zygote, that contains genetic material from both parents.*

   **Overview of Human
      Embryonic Development**   Dennis O. Overman
   *Successful early biological development of the human
   organism begins with a single cell, the zygote, and involves the process of growth, implantation, formation of
   basic cell layers, establishment of the organ systems, and
   further maturation until the moment of birth. Environ-*

mental influences and biotechnological advances may alter this normal developmental sequence.

Through research and development, humans have learned to control the possibility of conception. Additionally, we have the potential to alter the nature of the embryo by selecting its gender and genetic characteristics.

Our moral deliberations in attempting to resolve ethical dilemmas involve several levels of reasoning. The ethical principles and rules that we select reflect our acceptance of a particular ethical theory.

Moral reasoning may begin from the perspective of the individual or the community. Even more important is the particular community that forms one's perspective. Christian communities with the guidance of the Scriptures and the Holy Spirit have the power to resolve individual bioethical dilemmas and to provide healing for those hurt by biotechnology.

Attitudes of Jews and early Christians toward the unborn and abortion contrasted sharply with those of most Greeks and Romans. Although Protestants have been less vocal than Catholics about the morality of abortion, the church as a whole has historically condemned abortion.

Pregnancy and its termination have profound psychological effects on women—effects that vary depending on the circumstances surrounding the pregnancy. Intense attachment to the baby and fantasies about its nature are frequent maternal responses during pregnancy.

Acknowledgments

The editors wish to acknowledge the following persons and groups who provided financial support for the bioethics forum and the publication of this book:

Mennonite Central Committee, U.S. Peace Section
Mennonite Mutual Aid
Dr. and Mrs. G. Edward Chappel, Harrisonburg, Virginia
Dr. and Mrs. Vernon H. Kratz, Sellersville, Pennsylvania
Orie Miller Global Village Center, Eastern Mennonite College
Daniel B. Suter Biology Program Endowment, Eastern Mennonite College
Division of Academic Affairs, Eastern Mennonite College
Departments of Biology, Nursing, Psychology, Sociology and Social Work, and Bible and Religion, Eastern Mennonite College

Appreciation is also extended to the following persons who reviewed drafts of some of the chapters: Myron S. Augsburger, J. Mark Brubaker, Richard C. Detweiler, Stephen F. Dintaman, John W. Eby, Valda Garber-Weider, Ray C. Gingerich, William J. Hawk, Beulah Hostetler, Carl S. Keener, Albert N. Keim, Gayle Gerber Koontz, Ernest N. Kraybill, Joseph L. Lapp, John H. Lederach, Naomi K. Lederach, Robert Shabinowitz, Donald E. Showalter, Edward B. Stoltzfus, Gary L. Stucky, Daniel B. Suter, Willard M. Swartley, Dale Thomson, J. Denny Weaver, Delbert L. Yoder, and Susan H. Yoder.

The editors wish to extend a special thanks to Lila B. Collins, who efficiently typed and retyped the many manuscript drafts and who worked through the many indexing problems.

Foreword

Howard W. Jones

Howard W. Jones
Professor of obstetrics and gynecology at Eastern Virginia Medical School. He is also founder and president of the Howard and Georgeanna Jones Institute for Reproductive Medicine in Norfolk, Virginia. He initiated the first clinic for in vitro fertilization in the United States in 1982.

REPRODUCTIVE concerns have a special ethical sensitivity. This book will be of interest not only to those in the Anabaptist tradition, but also to those of alternate persuasions who are interested in how to make ethical decisions in this area.

Those outside the Anabaptist heritage may be unsure of their knowledge of this tradition. The Anabaptist movement had its origin in the sixteenth-century Reformation in Europe. Convinced that baptism in the New Testament was for believers only, they concluded that infant baptism was unscriptural. They therefore rebaptized themselves as adult believers. Hence, the name: the prefix *ana* in *Anabaptist* means "again." They have, of course, many other tenets. Nonresistance and the separation of the church and state are two of the better known.

Among the contemporary descendants of the Anabaptist tradition in North America are the Mennonites and the Hutterites. Both of these groups have views about reproduction which in some matters

9

are quite conservative, but in others can be considered liberal. This need not be surprising. Rome's view on reproductive matters have changed little since pre-Reformation days.

As the chapters of this book indicate, the Anabaptists of the Mennonite tradition are certainly prepared to examine reproductive options. They consider these options not only from the perspective of history, but also in the light of applied bioscientific developments.

It would be inappropriate to mention in this foreword the ethical tilt of the various chapters on such matters as contraception, abortion, and assisted reproduction—that is, *in vitro* fertilization and its allied techniques. To do so would be akin to giving away the ending to the latest mystery novel in *its* foreword.

The ethical discussions in this book will generally satisfy the intellectual. In keeping with good ethical tradition, they are careful not to be too directive one way or the other.

Ethicists, theologians, philosophers, legislators, and others have pondered long and learnedly about the relative weight to be given to personal, familial, and governmental interests in reproductive matters. Their counsel is often ignored. As a clinician with more than forty years experience, I have listened to hundreds of patients with reproductive concerns. Many from very conservative religious traditions quickly cut through those traditions and give priority to personal, familial interests. Others are greatly troubled by what they learn of their tradition and seek help in solving ethical dilemmas.

Those who are genuinely concerned about the ethical dilemmas represented by the new options made available through bioscientific technologies will find this book invaluable. Fortunate indeed are those who belong to a tradition which is prepared to examine reproductive priorities in contemporary terms!

Preface

Roman J. Miller

Roman J. Miller
Ph.D. in physiology, Kent State University. Bioethics forum organizer; recipient of Daniel B. Suter Biology Chair Endowment; associate professor of biology, Eastern Mennonite College, Harrisonburg, Virginia.

Beryl H. Brubaker
Doctor of Science in nursing, University of Alabama at Birmingham. Department Head and professor of nursing, Eastern Mennonite College, Harrisonburg, Virginia.

RAPID ADVANCES in biotechnology have given our society new capabilities in various areas of human reproduction. These new capabilities have brought with them dilemmas regarding the possibility of their use. Should an infertile couple attempt to use in vitro fertilization technology in order to conceive, or should they simply accept their situation as the plan of God? What about manipulating the molecules of our heredity through genetic engineering? Is it morally acceptable to replace a defective disease gene but immoral to replace a gene that may cause baldness? Does God implant a soul into a fertilized egg, making an abortion for any reason a mortal sin? Questions abound. Since they reflect real-life human dilemmas, they are important questions. Are there answers? How does a Christian find guidance to deal with these issues?

Three years ago for the first time I taught an embryology course to a group of premedical students at Eastern Mennonite College. In addition to my problem of struggling through some new material, I quickly became aware that in the study of human development and the advancement of modern biotechnology lay a host of issues that involve critical decision making on the part of the future health-care worker. As a Christian educator on the one hand and a Christian research scientist on the other, I felt compelled to raise student awareness of these life issues, to demonstrate the complexity of the problems, and at the very least to offer some Christian perspectives that may help to solve these dilemmas. The two weeks that we spent in that class directly dealing with bioethics at the commencement of life were helpful but in retrospect were not totally adequate.

As an educator I began to read the popular and more technical literature in an attempt to form a consistent Christian perspective on the issues. Especially on the topic of abortion, I quickly found a lot of things written from Catholic, Reformed, Evangelical Protestant, and Fundamental Christian positions. Less material was available on the topics of artificial insemination, genetic engineering, in vitro fertilization, or embryo transfer. With the exception of a few articles in church periodicals, I was surprised to find that little had been written in this area from an Anabaptist perspective. Yet, as affirmers of life, Anabaptist theologians and ethicists have written and struggled with other life-oriented issues—war, capital punishment, death and dying, hunger, and poverty. Numerous books and pamphlets have been published about these topics. However, I could not find one entire book dealing with issues at the commencement of life from an Anabaptist perspective. Only a few articles discussing the problem of abortion from an Anabaptist perspective were found in a couple of religious periodicals.

As a community of kingdom builders who attempt to follow the "Jesus way," why have we not been more concerned and involved in issues at the beginning of life? Is it due to our lack of awareness of the potentiality that exists with the use of modern tools of biotechnology? Maybe a partial answer lies in the fact that too often our theology and ethical theories have been reactionary toward solving a specific problem. For example, abortion has been a common practice in our society for over twenty years, while only during the past few years has in vitro fertilization moved from the experimental laboratory to the clinical laboratory. Consequently, Christians are more likely to have an opinion about the practice of abortion than about the morality of surrogate motherhood or embryo freezing. Thus, many Mennonites who strongly believe that abortion is wrong have no thoughtful opinion about genetic engineering.

During the late fall of 1986 and early spring of 1987, a group of Eastern Mennonite College faculty from the departments of biology, nursing, Bible and religion, sociology and social work, and psychology formed a committee to develop a forum on bioethical issues at the commencement of life. A group of highly qualified Christian experts from the fields of biomedicine, ethics, history, philosophy, theology, psychology, sociology, law, nursing, and education were assembled on the Eastern Mennonite College campus on November 20, 1987. Their goal was to present multidimensional aspects of bioethical issues in order to aid in analyzing bioethical dilemmas. Additional effort was made to determine if any insights from a distinctive Anabaptist Christian perspective might be helpful in this decision-making process.

During this one-day forum several presentations detailed the biological bases for recent developments in medicine and technology in the area of conception and development. Other talks presented various perspectives and provided examples of how bioethical issues have been handled in the past. Theological and ethical frameworks for Anabaptist-Christian decision making were described. Finally, the role of the Christian church/community for aiding persons who struggle through the process of ethical decision making and for bringing healing to persons who are physically, emotionally, or spiritually hurt by the forces of biotechnology was presented.

This book contains the presentations of that forum. Chapters 1 and 2 describe some scriptural and theological principles important in developing a Christian perspective when dealing with bioethics. Chapters 3 and 4 give the biological basis for human reproduction and development. Chapter 5 builds on that knowledge by explaining how current biotechnology can alter reproductive and developmental processes that affect the unborn. Chapter 6 introduces how the field of bioethics provides a means of working with the dilemmas of decision-making. Chapter 7 points out the possibilities of using the Christian community to affect decision making. Chapters 8-11 provide additional perspectives on the unborn—historical, maternal, psychological, and legal—that help the Christian community maintain clarity and accountability in responsible decision making. Chapters 12 and 13 further enlarge on the ability and responsibility of the Christian community to function as channels of the grace of Christ in bringing help, strength, and power to resolve bioethical problems. Grace enables the people of God to faithfully follow a directional pathway through the maze of bioethical dilemmas.

Bioethics and the Beginning of Life is written for students who are interested in bioethical issues and are attempting to form a Christian Anabaptist understanding about them. Additionally, health-care professionals, pastors, church leaders, guidance counselors, social workers, parents, and other responsible members of the Christian community will find this material helpful. These pages do not contain simple answers. Much of the information portrays the complexities of bioethical issues. However, some guidelines are suggested to help us as the people of God in our communal response to the dilemmas of bioethics. May you, the reader, find this book to be a source of information and insight in dealing with issues that affect us at the beginning of life.

Chapter 1

Biblical Perspectives

Dorothy Jean Weaver

Dorothy Jean Weaver
Ph.D. in New Testament studies, Union Theological Seminary in Virginia. Assistant professor of New Testament, Eastern Mennonite Seminary, Harrisonburg, Virginia.

TO ASK ABOUT biblical perspectives on the unborn is to reach into a vast undercurrent of thought that pervades the biblical materials from Genesis to Revelation but is seldom in itself the primary focus of attention. At the same time notable passages throughout both Old and New Testaments focus significantly on unborn children. The approach of this chapter will be (1) to group the biblical evidence of all types—passing references as well as larger passages—according to the form of the materials or the thematic motifs that they reflect and (2) to identify the perspectives on unborn life that emerge from each of these groupings.

God as Life-giver

Without question one of the most fundamental motifs that runs throughout the biblical materials is that of God as Life-giver. This motif is introduced in the first chapters of Genesis (Gen. 1:1—2:25), where God is portrayed as Creator of the heavens and the earth (Gen. 1:1),[1] and carried through to the final chapters of Revelation (Rev. 21:1—22:21), where John depicts God as Creator of a new heaven and a new earth (Rev. 21:1). Arguably, the most foundational confession within the Judeo-Christian Scriptures is that God is Creator of all that exists and Life-giver to all that lives.

Within this framework, therefore, it comes as no surprise to discover that human procreation is viewed not only as a gift but likewise as a command of the Creator God. In the account of Genesis 1:1—2:4 God concludes the creative activities of the sixth day by instructing the created human beings to "be fruitful and multiply, and fill the earth and subdue it" (Gen. 1:28). Apparently in accordance with this view of human procreation as both divine gift and divine imperative, the judgment meted out to Eve for her share in the primal rebellion of Eden (Gen. 3:1-24) relates to her role in the procreative process: "I will greatly multiply your pain in childbearing; in pain you shall bring forth children" (Gen. 3:16). Within the Hebraic worldview God is clearly the ultimate source of life, and all human procreation is therefore both gift and mandate from the life-giving God.

The imagery of God as Life-giver shows up in differing types of biblical materials. One of these consists of metaphorical references to God as the one who gives birth. In the song that Moses addresses to the Israelites before they cross the Jordan (Deut. 32:1-43), he says of them: "You were unmindful of the Rock that begot you, and you forgot the God who gave you birth" (Deut. 32:18). In Isaiah 66:9 the word of the Lord with reference to Zion comes in the form of a question: "Shall I bring to the birth and not cause to bring forth? says the LORD; shall I, who cause to bring forth, shut the womb? says your God."

Elsewhere, God is depicted as the one who bestows fertility on human beings. In Jacob's final testament to his twelve sons (Gen. 49:1-27) he declares to Joseph that "God Almighty . . . will bless you with blessings of heaven above, blessings of the deep that crouches beneath, blessings of the breasts and of the womb" (Gen. 49:25). Throughout Deuteronomy God is depicted as one who will reward the faithfulness of the Israelites with fertility for themselves, their livestock, and the ground they till:

> And because you hearken to these ordinances, and keep and do them, the LORD your God will keep with you the covenant and the steadfast love which he swore to your fathers to keep; he will love you, bless

you, and multiply you; he will also bless the fruit of your body and the fruit of your ground, your grain and your wine and your oil, the increase of your cattle and the young of your flock, in the land which he swore to your fathers to give you. You shall be blessed above all peoples; there shall not be male or female barren among you or among your cattle.[2]

(Deut. 7:12-14)

A third type of reference to God as Life-giver appears within the framework of the biblical birth narratives. Within these passages both the narrator of the events and the characters living out the events speak of God as one who has power to close and to open the womb. When women are barren, it is God who has brought this barrenness upon them. Sarai observes to her husband, Abram, "Behold now, the LORD has prevented me from bearing children" (Gen. 16:2). When Rachel demands that Jacob "give her children," he responds in anger, "Am I in the place of God, who has withheld from you the fruit of the womb?" (Gen. 30:1-2). Elsewhere the narrator explains that Elkanah, who gave portions of meat to his wife, Peninnah, and her children when he sacrificed, would give only one portion to his wife, Hannah, "because the LORD had closed her womb" (1 Sam 1:4-6).[3]

But if it is God who closes the womb, it is also God who opens it. A variety of phrases are used by the narrator to describe this action on the part of God: God "heals" the wife and the female slaves of Abimelech "so that they [bear] children" (Gen. 20:17); the Lord "visits" Sarah and "does to her as he had promised" (Gen. 21:1); God "grants prayers" (Gen. 25:21), "remembers" women (Gen. 30:22; 1 Sam 1:19), "hearkens" to them (Gen. 30:17, 22), and "opens the womb" (Gen. 29:31; 30:22).

Likewise, the women themselves give witness to the belief that it is God who has given them the children that they bear. Typically, the mother gives expression to this belief in an explanation of the name of her child[4] that at the same time serves as a confession of faith in the God who has given her the child:[5]

I have gotten a man with the help of the LORD (Cain, Gen. 4:1).
God has made laughter for me (Isaac, Gen. 21:6).
Because the LORD has looked upon my affliction (Reuben, Gen. 29:32).
Because the LORD has heard that I am hated (Simeon, Gen. 29:33).
This time I will praise the LORD (Judah, Gen. 29:35).

God has judged me, and has . . . given me a son (Dan, Gen. 30:6).
God has given me my hire . . . (Issachar, Gen. 30:18).
God has endowed me with a good dowry . . . (Zebulun, Gen. 30:20).
May the LORD add to me another son (Joseph, Gen. 30:24).
I have asked him of the LORD (Samuel, 1 Sam 1:20).

A further expression of the belief in God as Life-giver lies in references to the power of God to work the seemingly impossible within the womb of a barren woman. In response to the derisive laughter of Sarah (Gen. 18:12), the Lord says to Abraham her husband, "Why did Sarah laugh, and say, 'Shall I indeed bear a child, now that I am old?' Is anything too hard for the LORD?" (Gen. 18:13-14).[6] Similarly, the angel Gabriel explains to Mary that "your kinswoman Elizabeth in her old age has also conceived a son; and this is the sixth month with her who was called barren. For with God nothing will be impossible" (Luke 1:36-37).

The implications of these texts as a group are threefold: (1) God is Creator of all that exists and Life-giver to all that lives; (2) God has mandated that humankind shall participate in the act of creation and life-giving, and God has gifted them to do so through the process of human procreation; and (3) God both wills and empowers human procreation not only where it occurs in the natural course of human events, but also where it is humanly impossible.

Barrenness as a Curse

Integrally linked to the belief in God as Life-giver is the corresponding belief in barrenness as a curse. The motif of barrenness as a curse is closely interwoven with that of God as Life-giver throughout the biblical materials to the extent that barrenness provides the primary backdrop against which God's life-giving powers become visible.

One level on which the tension between barrenness and the life-giving powers of God is played out is that of narrative plot. Throughout the Old and New Testaments the barrenness of women is introduced numerous times as the driving motif of a narrative or sequence of narratives: Gen. 11:30 and 16:1 —Sarah; Gen. 20:18—the women of the house of Abimelech; Gen. 25:21—Rebekah; Gen. 29:31 and 30:1—Rachel; Judg. 13:2—the wife of Manoah; 1 Sam. 1:2, 5, 6—Hannah; Luke 1:7—Elizabeth. But nowhere is barrenness the final word. To the contrary, barrenness is introduced precisely in order to serve as a foil for the life-giving power of God. In each of these instances the curse of barrenness ultimately gives way to the blessing of conception and childbearing.[7] And in this narrative fashion—no less than through propositional or poetic statements concerning barrenness—the narrator expresses the firm conviction that barrenness is a curse that God through life-giving power and will chooses to transform into the blessing of childbearing.

A second level on which the motif of barrenness as a curse finds expression is that of language itself, the literary contexts that surround the concept of barrenness and give it a field of meaning. At the primary level of meaning, *barrenness* stands paired with the ideas of sadness, mourning, loss, and incompleteness; it stands in contrast to ideas of joy, rejoicing, fulfillment, and plenty:

> Sing, O barren one,
> who did not bear;
> break forth into singing and cry aloud,
> you who have not been in travail.
> For the children of the desolate one will be more
> than the children of her that is married,
> says the LORD. (*Isa. 54:1*)

> Who is like the LORD our God,
> who is seated on high,
> who looks far down upon the heavens and the earth?
>
> ° ° °
>
> He gives the barren woman a home,
> making her the joyous mother of children.
> Praise the LORD! (*Ps. 113:5, 9*)

> Those who were full have hired themselves out for bread,
> but those who were hungry have ceased to hunger.
> The barren has borne seven,
> but she who has many children is forlorn. (*1 Sam. 2:5*)

> The leech has two daughters;
> "Give, give," they cry.
> Three things are never satisfied;
> four never say,"Enough":
> Sheol,
> the barren womb,
> the earth ever thirsty for water,
> and the fire which never says, "Enough." (*Prov. 30:15-16*)

Even more specifically, however, barrenness is set up in pointed contrast to the blessing of fertility and fruitfulness:

> You shall serve the LORD your God,
> and I will bless your bread and your water;
> and I will take sickness away from the midst of you.
> None shall cast her young or be barren in your land;
> I will fulfill the number of your days. (*Exod. 23:25-26*)[8]

On the secondary level of meaning, *barrenness* stands as a metaphor for bereavement, loneliness, and desolation on the national level and with reference to national disaster:

> Surely your waste and desolate places
> and your devastated land—
> surely now you will be too narrow for your inhabitants,
> and those who swallowed you up will be far away.
> The children born in the time of your bereavement
> will yet say in your ears:
> "The place is too narrow for me;
> make room for me to dwell in."
> Then you will say in your heart:
> "Who has borne me these?
> I was bereaved and barren, exiled and put away,
> but who has brought up these?
> Behold, I was left alone;
> whence then have these come?" (*Isa. 49:19-21*)

> Ephraim's glory shall fly away like a bird—
> no birth, no pregnancy, no conception!
> Even if they bring up children,
> I will bereave them till none is left.
> Woe to them when I depart from them!
> Ephraim's sons, as I have seen, are destined for a prey;
> Ephraim must lead forth his sons to slaughter.
> Give them, O LORD—
> what wilt thou give?
> Give them a miscarrying womb and dry breasts. (*Hos. 9:11-14*)

In a striking reverse formulation of this motif—barrenness as a curse—Jesus indicates that a time of tribulation is coming in which barrenness will be viewed as a blessing: "For behold, the days are coming when they shall say, 'Blessed are the barren, and the breasts that never gave suck!'" (Luke 23:29).[9] The overall impact of even this statement, however, is to confirm the basic viewpoint that barrenness is a curse. The fact that barrenness is unexpectedly acclaimed a blessing serves no other purpose than to point to the extreme desperation of the circumstances under which this will be true.

A similar sort of "backwards confirmation" of the motif of barrenness as a curse lies in the passages in which curses or woes are called down upon the day or the fact of an individual's birth (Job 3:1-19; 10:18-19; Jer. 20:14-18; Mark 14:21//Matt. 26:24). In these instances, as with Jesus' blessing on barrenness, the circumstances under which these curses or woes are pronounced are extreme and extraordinary. In such circumstances normal values are turned upside down.

By cursing the day of his birth Job overturns conventional evaluations of day and night, light and darkness:

After this Job opened his mouth and cursed the day of his birth.
And Job said,
"Let the day perish wherein I was born,
and the day which said, 'A man-child is conceived.'
Let that day be darkness!
May God above not seek it,
nor light shine upon it.
Let gloom and deep darkness claim it.
Let clouds dwell upon it;
let the blackness of the day terrify it.
That night—let thick darkness seize it!
let it not rejoice among the days of the year,
let it not come into the number of the months.
Yea, let that night be barren;
let no joyful cry be heard in it.
Let those curse it who curse the day,
who are skilled to rouse up Leviathan.
Let the stars of its dawn be dark;
let it hope for light, but have none,
nor see the eyelids of the morning;
because it did not shut the doors of my mother's womb,
nor hide trouble from my eyes." (*Job 3:1-10*)

Jeremiah invokes the language of military crisis in decrying the announcement of his birth:

Cursed be the day on which I was born!
The day when my mother bore me, let it not be blessed!
Cursed be the man who brought the news to my father,
"A son is born to you," making him very glad.
Let that man be like the cities which the Lord overthrew without pity;
let him hear a cry in the morning and an alarm at noon,
because he did not kill me in the womb;
so my mother would have been my grave,
and her womb for ever great.
Why did I come forth from the womb to see toil and sorrow,
and spend my days in shame? (*Jer. 20:14-18*)

Jesus is speaking of the extreme event of his own death when he comments, "The Son of man goes as it is written of him, but woe to that man by whom the Son of man is betrayed! It would have been better for that man if he had not been born" (Matt. 26:24//Mark 14:21).

The bottom line with reference to barrenness, however, points neither to the desolation of childlessness nor to its obverse, the curse of being born, but rather to the power of God to reverse the situation of barrenness. The fundamental affirmations here are that God is able to reverse the curse of barrenness and that God wills to do so: "Is anything too hard for the LORD? At the appointed time I will return to you in the spring, and Sarah shall have a son" (Gen. 18:14).[10] "And behold, your kinswoman Elizabeth in her old age has also conceived a son; and this is the sixth month with her who was called barren. For with God nothing will be impossible" (Luke 1:36-37).[11] Ultimately, the motif of barrenness as a curse does no less than once again reaffirm the character and the role of God as Life-giver.

Birth Predictions

A further corollary of the belief in God as Life-giver is the belief that God not only opens the womb but also breaks into the world of human events to announce that fact. Birth prediction narratives constitute the single most prominent category of biblical narratives dealing with unborn children. No less than nine major narratives throughout the Old and the New Testament focus on the announcement that a child will be born: Gen. 16:1-14 (Ishmael); Gen. 17:1-21 (Isaac); Gen. 18:1-15 (Isaac); Judg. 13:2-25 (Samson); 1 Sam. 1:1-20 (Samuel); 2 Kings 4:11-17 (son of the Shunammite woman); Luke 1:5-25 (John the Baptist); Luke

1:26–38 (Jesus); and Matt. 1:18-25 (Jesus). Less extensive birth predictions are found within 2 Sam. 7:1-17//1 Chron. 17:1-15 (Solomon);[12] 1 Kings 13:1-3 (Josiah); Isa. 7:10-25 (Immanuel);[13] and Isa. 9:1-7 (ruler on the throne of David).[14]

These birth predictions exhibit certain differences. First, they are communicated to the individuals concerned by a variety of agents: the Lord (Gen. 17:1-21; 18:1-15); an angel of the Lord (Gen. 16:1-14; Judg. 13:2-25; Luke 1:5-25; Luke 1:26-38; Matt. 1:18-25); a priest (1 Sam. 1:1-20);[15] and a prophet (2 Sam. 7:1-17 and parallels; 1 Kings 13:1-3; 2 Kings 4:11-17; Isa. 7:10-25; Isa. 9:1-7).

Second, these birth predictions speak to a broad range of experiences. The women who are about to bear children represent widely differing circumstances. These circumstances include a woman who has already conceived (Gen. 16:1-14), women for whom there appears to be no natural hindrance to conception (Judg. 13:2-25; 2 Sam. 7:1-17 and parallels; 1 Kings 13:1-3; Isa. 7:10-25;[16] Isa. 9:1-7), women identified or implicitly depicted as barren (Gen. 17:1-21; Gen. 18:1-15; 1 Sam. 1:1-20; 2 Kings 4:11-17; Luke 1:5-25), and a woman who is a virgin (Luke 1:26-38; Matt. 1:18-25).[17]

The birth predictions also differ in the kind and amount of information given. To the Shunammite woman (2 Kings 4:11-17) comes only the information that she will bear a son within the next year.[18] Elsewhere the predicted child is frequently given a name (Gen. 16:1-14; Gen. 17:1-21; 1 Kings 13:1-3; Isa. 7:10-25; Luke 1:26-38; cf. 2:21; Matt. 1:18-25) and sometimes a character description (Gen. 16:1-21; 1 Kings 13:1-3; Isa. 7:10-25). On the other end of the spectrum from the account of the Shunammite woman lie those accounts in which the children to be born have their vocation identified for them prior to the moment of birth: Nazirite (Judg. 13:2-25; cf. 16:17; 1 Sam. 1:1-20[19]), messianic forerunner (Luke 1:5-25), and king or messianic ruler (2 Sam. 7:1-17 and parallels;[20] Isa. 9:1-7; Luke 1:26-38; Matt. 1:18-25).

But beyond their differences the fundamental statements that these birth prediction narratives make as a group constitute their primary significance. In the first place these texts reaffirm the role of God as Life-giver. Regardless of the agents through whom they are made, God is without question their ultimate source. These predictions also depict God as one who not only knows the shape but also controls the direction of human history. The God of the birth prediction narratives is one who is actively at work within the world of human events to enact plans for human history through the conception and birth of children. The implications are clear: The God who opens and closes the womb is *in so doing* the God who controls all of human history.

While the birth prediction narratives as a group speak about the nature of God, they likewise speak about the nature of human life. Although varying amounts of information are conveyed by these predictions, their commonality lies in the fact that they refer to specific individuals—individuals with birth dates, names, character traits, and vocations. Long before these children of promise are born—in some cases even before they are conceived—they are already viewed as human beings and invested with human characteristics. Nor is that all. These children yet to be born are also invested with a divine calling. The affirmation that God is shaping history through their conception and birth indicates that all these children—not merely those whose vocations are identified—have a significant role to play in the history that God is designing.

Life Within the Womb

Moving beyond statements that merely predict the conception and birth of children are those statements that contain descriptions of life within the womb. This category of texts can be subdivided according to the types of affirmations that are made with reference to life and activity within the womb of the pregnant woman.

The fundamental affirmation is that God is at work within the wombs of pregnant women. This affirmation takes a variety of forms. God is depicted, first of all, as the one who is intimately involved in the process of creating life within the womb:

> If I have rejected the cause of my manservant or my maidservant,
> when they brought a complaint against me;
> what then shall I do when God rises up?
> When he makes inquiry, what shall I answer him?
> Did not he who made me in the womb make him?
> And did not one fashion us in the womb? (*Job* 31:13-15)

> For thou didst form my inward parts,
> thou didst knit me together in my mother's womb.

∘ ∘ ∘

Thou knowest me right well;
my frame was not hidden from thee,
when I was being made in secret,
intricately wrought in the depths of the earth. (*Ps. 139:13, 14b-15*)

As you do not know how the spirit comes to the bones
in the womb of a woman with child,
so you do not know the work of God
who makes everything. (*Eccles. 11:5*)[21]

The affirmation of God's activity within the womb takes other forms as well. God gives names to individuals while they are yet in the womb or even before they are conceived: "Listen to me, O coastlands, and hearken, you peoples from afar. The LORD called me from the womb, from the body of my mother he named my name" (Isa. 49:1). God determines the lifespan of the individual while he or she is still an infant within the womb: "Thy eyes beheld my unformed substance; in thy book were written, every one of them, the days that were formed for me, when as yet there was none of them" (Ps. 139:16). God announces the establishment of a covenant with an individual who has not yet been conceived: "But I will establish my covenant with Isaac, whom Sarah shall bear to you at this season next year" (Gen. 17:21).

Perhaps the most striking of the affirmations made with reference to God's activity in the womb has to do with vocation. God is identified as one who calls individuals and sets them apart for their lifework even before they are born:

And now the LORD says,
who formed me from the womb to be his servant,
to bring Jacob back to him,
and that Israel might be gathered to him . . . . (*Isa. 49:5*)

Now the word of the LORD came to me, saying,
"Before I formed you in the womb I knew you,
and before you were born I consecrated you;
I appointed you a prophet to the nations." (*Jer. 1:4-5*)

But when he who had set me apart before I was born,
and had called me through his grace. (*Gal. 1:15*)

A second type of affirmation relates to the immediacy of the relationship between the mother and the child within the womb.

In announcing to the wife of Manoah that her son will be a Nazirite, the angel of the Lord says to the woman herself, "Therefore beware, and drink no wine or strong drink, and eat nothing unclean" (Judg. 13:4; cf. 13:7, 13-14). To fulfill the Nazirite vow of her son in the womb, the wife of Manoah herself must abstain from those things prohibited to a Nazirite.[22]

A third type of affirmation has to do with the personhood of the unborn child. Children within the womb are described as individuals who give evidence of their personality by taking action themselves and interacting with each other:

> And Isaac prayed to the Lord for his wife, because she was barren;
> and the LORD granted his prayer, and Rebekah his wife conceived.
> The children struggled together within her;
> and she said, "If it is thus, why do I live?"
> So she went to inquire of the LORD.
> And the LORD said to her,
> "Two nations are in your womb,
> and two peoples, born of you, shall be divided;
> the one shall be stronger than the other,
> the elder shall serve the younger." (*Gen. 25:21-23*)

> When [Rebekah's] days to be delivered were fulfilled,
> behold, there were twins in her womb.
> The first came forth red,
> all his body like a hairy mantle;
> so they called his name Esau.
> Afterward his brother came forth,
> and his hand had taken hold of Esau's heel;
> so his name was called Jacob.
> Isaac was sixty years old when she bore them. (*Gen. 25:24-26*)[23]

> When the time of [Tamar's] delivery came,
> there were twins in her womb.
> And when she was in labor,
> one put out a hand;
> and the midwife took and bound on his hand a scarlet thread,
> saying, "This one came out first."
> But as he drew back his hand,
> behold his brother came out;
> and she said, "What a breach you have made for yourself!"
> Therefore his name was called Perez.
> Afterward his brother came out with the scarlet thread upon his hand;
> and his name was called Zerah. (*Gen. 38:27-30*)

Even beyond mere actions and interactions, unborn children are described as entering into relationship with God through the actions that they take within the womb. In Hosea 12:2-3 Jacob's action of grabbing his brother's heel is portrayed as a sin parallel to that of "striving with God": "The LORD has an indictment against Judah, and will punish Jacob according to his ways, and requite him according to his deeds. In the womb he took his brother by the heel, and in his manhood he strove with God."[24] And in Luke 1:41 the gymnastics of John the Baptist within Elizabeth's womb are clearly depicted as Spirit-filled action: "And when Elizabeth heard the greeting of Mary, the babe leaped in her womb; and Elizabeth was filled with the Holy Spirit."[25]

A final type of affirmation witnessing to the personhood of the infant within the womb comes from language describing the fate of the child who dies at the moment of birth or is miscarried in untimely fashion. In picturing the circumstances of "death at birth" Job describes the dead child as associating in death with other human beings who have died:

Why did I not die at birth,
come forth from the womb and expire?
Why did the knees receive me?
Or why the breasts that I should suck?
For then I should have lain down and been quiet;
I should have slept;
then I should have been at rest
with kings and counselors of the earth,
who rebuilt ruins for themselves,
or with princes who had gold,
who filled their houses with silver.
Or why was I not as a hidden untimely birth,
as infants that never see the light?
There the wicked cease from troubling,
and there the weary are at rest.
There the prisoners are at ease together;
they hear not the voice of the taskmaster.
The small and the great are there,
and the slave is free from his master. (*Job 3:11-19*)

From every angle of consideration, therefore, life within the womb of the pregnant woman is viewed as human life. The infant within the womb is a human being whom God is creating, naming, and calling and a human being who is already responding to God in acts portrayed as sinful or Spirit-filled. The infant within the womb is depicted as one who acts and interacts with others already before birth and who will associate with others after death even if death precedes or accompanies the moment of birth. Within the Hebraic mentality the unborn child is viewed as an unborn human being.

Legal and Societal Status of the Unborn Child

The biblical materials provide very little evidence relating to the legal and societal status of the unborn child. Exodus 21:22-25 provides the single legal ruling that speaks, albeit in oblique fashion, of the legal status of the unborn child. This text implies that the accidental death of an unborn child is not to be viewed with the same degree of seriousness as other physical harm inflicted on the mother of the child:

> When men strive together,
> and hurt a woman with child, so that there is a miscarriage,
> and yet no harm follows,
> the one who hurt her shall be fined,
> according as the woman's husband shall lay upon him;
> and he shall pay as the judges determine.
> If any harm follows,
> then you shall give life for life,
> eye for eye, tooth for tooth,
> hand for hand, foot for foot,
> burn for burn, wound for wound, stripe for stripe. (*Exod. 21:22-25*)

A single narrative dealing, also in oblique fashion, with the physical fate of an unborn child is found in Genesis 38. Here Tamar is condemned to death (though not finally executed) not only while she is carrying a child in her womb, but because she is carrying that child:

> About three months later Judah was told,
> "Tamar your daughter-in-law has played the harlot;
> and moreover she is with child by harlotry."
> And Judah said,
> "Bring her out, and let her be burned." (*Gen. 38:24*)

Both of these passages appear to leave the legal and societal status of the unborn child in an ambiguous, if not altogether tenuous, position. At the same time, however, there is other evidence that points unambiguously to the significance and sanctity of life within the womb. This evidence lies in the formulaic language used to describe the ultimate outrage carried out by military conquerors, the action of "ripping up women who are with child." This brutal action appears to symbolize the most heinous crimes with which military forces can be charged and for which they will be judged by God:

> And Hazael said,
> "Why does my lord weep?"
> He answered,
> "Because I know the evil that you will do to the people of Israel:
> you will set on fire their fortresses,
> and you will slay their young men with the sword,
> and dash in pieces their little ones,
> and rip up their women with child." (*2 Kings 8:12*)[26]

> Thus says the LORD:
> "For three transgressions of the Ammonites, and for four,
> I will not revoke the punishment;
> because they have ripped up women with child in Gilead,
> that they might enlarge their border." (*Amos 1:13*)[27]

The New Testament has no specific reference to the legal or societal status of the unborn child. The only potential evidence with reference to this question lies in texts that condemn the use of "magic" (*pharmakeia*: Gal. 5:20; Rev. 18:23) and "poison" (*pharmakon*: Rev. 21:8; 22:15) as well as persons who deal in such things, the "magician" (*pharmakos*: Rev. 9:21) and the "mixer of poisons" (*pharmakeus*: Rev. 21:8). Possibly, this constellation of vocabulary was associated with the practice of abortion within the pagan society of the first-century Mediterranean world.[28] If this is true, then the New Testament writers clearly stand against the practice of abortion and firmly support the sanctity of life within the womb.

✻ ✻ ✻

> Then the king of Egypt said to the Hebrew midwives,
> one of whom was named Shiphrah and the other Puah,
> "When you serve as midwife to the Hebrew women,
> and see them upon the birthstool,
> if it is a son, you shall kill him;

but if it is a daughter, she shall live."
But the midwives feared God,
and did not do as the king of Egypt commanded them,
but let the male children live.

        ° ° °

So God dealt well with the midwives;
and the people multiplied and grew very strong.
And because the midwives feared God
he gave them families. (*Exod. 1:15-17, 20-21*)

Questions for Reflection and Discussion

1. In discussing the ethics of human procreation, many Christians
   begin with the assumption that humans are created in the image of God. How does reflection beginning from that assumption differ from reflection beginning from the assumption that
   God is Life-giver?
2. Does barrenness have meaning from a theological perspective
   today? Why or why not?
3. How do examples from Scripture give us insight about God's
   activity during the development of the unborn?
4. When humans use in vitro fertilization, are they usurping the
   role of God as Life-giver?

For Further Reading

Gorman, Michael J.
    1982 *Abortion and the Early Church: Christian, Jewish and Pagan Atti-
         tudes in the Greco-Roman World.* Downers Grove, Ill.: Inter-
         Varsity Press.

Chapter 2

A Theological Approach

John Richard Burkholder

John Burkholder
Ph.D. in religion and society, Harvard University. Interim professor of ethics and director of peace studies, Associated Mennonite Biblical Seminaries, Elkhart, Indiana.

THIS CHAPTER introduces several theological approaches to bioethics and ends with an Anabaptist perspective. My approach is suggestive, showing first how theology may serve the bioethical agenda, then setting forth some implications of certain theological assumptions for bioethical questions. A review of Anabaptist distinctives leads to comments on the present situation among heirs of that tradition. I conclude with some rather personal suggestions.

How Does Theology Intersect with the Bioethical Agenda?

Most Christians would claim that all serious questions are ultimately of a religious character. They would thus insist that theology must be the foundation from which to understand what is going on in the bioethical field. But others, including some Christians, would be suspicious of such a self-serving stance on the part of the theologian.

Our first task, then, is to ask how theology approaches the complex questions raised in a book on bioethics. The chapters in this book, while all written by Christians, are developed from a number of viewpoints: biological, social, ethical, psychological, maternal, legal, and pastoral—along with the theological and biblical. How do these views fit together, or don't they? Which perspective has priority? What distinctive contribution can the theologian make to this discussion?

Of course, in a book sponsored by a church-related college, we really do not need to justify the presence of a theological perspective. In a broader social context, however, it is important to note the continuing problems that religious convictions provoke in the public debate on bioethical matters. For example, Christian opposition to legalized abortion has been challenged by "pro-choice" advocates as an improper intrusion of religion into the realm of politics. In response, one needs only to observe that religiously motivated groups have taken stands on virtually every kind of social issue, from affirmative action to the Vietnam War to immigration policy. That obvious reality, however, does not exempt those matters from public legislation or turn them into "theology."[1]

An important foundational role for theology is suggested by Stanley Hauerwas in his recent contribution to medical ethics, *Suffering Presence*.[2] Hauerwas proposed that the flourishing of medical ethics (or bioethics) today is due not only to the questions raised by complex technological advances, but also to the confused moral world in which we live. The real problem is that in today's pluralistic situation, the purpose of the practice of medicine is no longer clear.

Hauerwas observes that our traditional Western understandings about the practice of medicine are grounded in the historical linkage between the physician's Hippocratic Oath and the classic Christian convictions about caring for the weak and ill. This view, however, is threatened by the direction being taken in bioethics today. To illustrate, Hauerwas cites the recent work of H. T. Engelhardt, who argues that the obvious need to develop a biomedical ethic for a pluralistic secular society will increase the tension between the public morality, which by definition is secular, and the more particularistic moralities of religious communities. Recognizing that the core value of American public morality is *freedom*, the primary ethical task of the physician, according to Engelhardt, becomes simply a matter of informing the client about the likely consequences of various choices, enabling a maximization of individual freedom. Increasingly, physicians and others who hold particular religious convictions will need to live in two moral worlds, subordinating their private convictions to the public ethos of freedom.

Hauerwas does not like this state of affairs. (Nor do I!) His work is an attempt to present an alternative view. He argues that medicine is and must be a moral art and that the morality of caregiving, as embodied in the Hippocratic-Christian tradition, cannot logically be sustained in Engelhardt's scenario. Although Christian theology is not the only basis for an ethical view of medicine, Hauerwas argues that some kind of moral community, "sectarian" if it must be, is required to form and undergird the convictions needed for a health care profession that truly cares for the ill. This community-forming function of Christianity, enabling not only physicians but all of us to live out an ethic of caring, is perhaps the most important contribution that theology can make to bioethics.

A further preliminary observation has to do with the way in which different modes of ethical reasoning are characteristically associated with theological views, or the absence of such. A distinctive ethical orientation usually accompanies a primarily *secular* worldview. The secular viewpoint, limited by self-definition to a "this-worldly" view of reality, is concerned almost exclusively with the well-being or happiness of existing human life, life within history. Thus, a secular ethic will tend to be teleological and utilitarian, concerned with consequences and outcomes for the good of individuals and the society.

A theological outlook, however, must incorporate another dimension—the transcendent, the eternal. In that view, human life is contingent upon and responsible to some kind of absolute, which may be expressed directly by a divine command or in theories of natural law. Such views tend to give more importance to deontological ethical formulations, that is, concerns for fulfilling duties and obligations.

Theological Perspectives on Bioethics

My assignment, however, is not primarily to do ethical analysis, but rather to provide a survey of theological approaches to bioethical questions concerning the unborn. One way to do this would be to trace the distinctive aspects of the theological positions represented under such conventional labels as Lutheran, Reformed, Methodist, or Catholic.

Instead of following the trail of traditions, however, I want to set forth several basic bioethical questions in theological perspective. This brief exercise calls for rather bold generalizations, without making the necessary qualifications that more careful work would demand. I simply want to illustrate how theological assumptions shape answers.

The meaning of "human life." One of the recurring questions in bioethics, especially in the abortion controversy, is simply, "What makes human life human?" Typically, the debate involves discussion about when human life begins, about such terms as the "sanctity of life" and the "quality of life," and about how to value the human person. Three examples will illustrate how basic theological assumptions make significant differences.

The first example is the biblical understanding of life. Biblical thought is God-centered. Biblical writers approach human life, not on its own terms, but totally in relation to God. Life is a gift of the Creator God, who is the source of all life. In both its origin and its manifestation, life is dependent on God: It is God's Spirit that sustains life. The human being who is created in the image of God is set apart from other forms of life, inbreathed with God's own Spirit, and protected by God's commandment, "Thou shalt not kill."[3]

Human life, however, is more than physical viability. In the biblical understanding, the quality of humanness is the capacity for *relationship,* with God and with other humans. Life is the sum total of activities and experience. It is not something that one "has" but rather what one *is* or *does.* "The person is a psychosomatic whole, not an embodied mind or an imprisoned soul."[4] Further, in the New Testament witness, life gains a new dimension in Christ. The promise of "eternal life" is more than mere duration. It is a different quality of life, a participation in the fullness of God.

The second example is natural law. A significant stream of Christian theology has relied on this philosophical tradition, which was developed in its classic form by Thomas Aquinas from Aristotelian notions. This view has been characteristic of Roman Catholicism, of some orthodox Protestant thought, and of evangelicals such as Francis Schaeffer. All such views begin with an assumption that human nature in its givenness is the source of moral value. The human person as a whole has a natural meaning and natural purpose. From that order of nature, moral principles may be derived. For example, a morality grounded on this basis could claim that the natural function of the reproductive system is to produce children; therefore, sexual activity for any other reason is questionable, even immoral.[5]

Natural law tends to begin with physical and biological data, rather than with the historical drama of the biblical material. The problem, however, is that when "life" is defined in basically physical terms, its meaning is dependent to some degree on the scientific knowledge of the times, whether fifth century B.C. or twentieth century A.D. When such a concept then becomes the norm for the theological and ethical judgments, the judgments appear to be legalistic and arbitrary, removed from the particulars of actual life stories. The problem many critics find in the classic natural law and Roman Catholic formulations is that theological-ethical norms come to depend on judgments made on nontheological grounds.

The third example relates to social value. Christians must also take into account the meaning and value of life as framed by the modern secular worldview, with its utilitarian and pragmatic bias. The issue may be stated thus: "Is the value of human life a given, or is it dependent on the socially determined value of a given life?" To value life only for its social utility opens the door to all kinds of potential abuses. Stanley Hauerwas argues that we must learn to regard "life as good because it has being, not because it is useful."[6]

None of this really answers the question at the center of the abortion debate: Is the fetus "human life" or isn't it? My view is that a satisfactory answer cannot be constructed on either biological or theological assumptions alone. Although theological grounding is fundamental, answers will vary widely, depending on how the characteristics of humanness are understood and what weight is given to the many elements.

To be sure, the natural law logic tends toward a fixed assumption, that essential humanity is present at the very beginning in the fertilized ovum. Others prefer to speak in more developmental terms, seeing the fetus as a *potential* human person. Among the writings of scholars more or less identified with conservative Protestantism, the work of Paul Simmons, a Southern Baptist seminary professor, is notable for its rejection of the view that the fetus is a fully human person. Simmons develops a concept of "anticipatory personhood," building on a distinction between the *vitality* of the fetus and its *humanity*. Vitality is biological, based on "vital signs" such as heartbeat and respiration. Humanity is grounded in relationships. It has to do with acceptance, respect, affirmation, and love from other humans. Humanity is thus developmental, dependent to some degree on the attitudes of the (potential) mother and the family.[7]

Is God's will grounded in nature or history? For another theological perspective on basic bioethical issues, we must examine briefly two different understandings of the way God acts in the world, with particular reference to how God's will is expressed in the human community. These two classic views may be described as the tension between nature and history, between creation and redemption, and even between the preferred use of organic or covenantal metaphors.[8]

From one perspective, which we are calling the *natural*, God is understood primarily as "the creator and the conserver of order." This, of course, is congruent with the static view of natural law and has huge consequences for sexual morality and medical ethics. "When natural ends, by appeal to God's creative wisdom, are viewed as inviolable, then certain conclusions follow rather quickly. Thus no contraception no matter what. Thus no artificial insemination by husband no matter what. These are seen as illicit tamperings with nature."[9]

Strictly interpreted, any medical or surgical procedure that interfered with "nature," the normal course of human life, would be an unwarranted intervention. Over the years, however, those who hold this view have worked out elaborate arguments to allow for many instances of medical activity, such as amputations and life-saving surgery; yet the basic idea that any intervention must be carefully justified still prevails.

The opposing view starts with a dynamic idea of *history* as the realm of God's activity, a history in which the future is open and human responsibility is expressed in freedom to choose. Humans are not passive creatures, but co-creators with God who "have a share in shaping an as yet fluid and plastic world—a world in which the most fluid entity is human nature itself."[10] Human beings make meaningful choices, use nature for their own purposes, and thus shape their own destinies in the course of history—the history in which God acts to reveal God's will and purpose.

Although questions revolving around the "meaning of life" are particularly important to the ethics of abortion, the attitude toward "intervention in nature" is relevant in shaping norms for the various technologies dealing with fertility. I have tried to outline how these basic theological orientations determine our understanding of ethical choices. Are all human decisions judged in advance by fixed categories given in nature? Or is there an openness to a future in which humans participate with God in carrying out God's purposes in the world? These classic questions present theological issues that extend far beyond our present concerns, but they must be recognized as necessary reference points.

Perhaps more important for our bioethical thinking as Christians is another important dimension: the special role of the *church* as a context for character formation and decision making. Hauerwas puts it succinctly: "The primary function of religious belief is not to describe the world or to determine the rightness or wrongness of particular actions, but to form a community that understands itself as having a particular mission in the world."[11] That community is what we know as church. We turn now to a particular story of church—the Anabaptist account.

Anabaptist-Mennonite Theology and Bioethical Problems

Does the Anabaptist story have anything distinctive to contribute to the theological foundation for bioethics? One recent writer notes that Mennonites are giving increasing attention to bioethical issues,

... but no clear pattern of response has yet emerged. Because of their biblicism, their continuing preoccupation with ethical minutiae, and their concern for purity, Mennonites find these issues, like divorce and homosexuality, extraordinarily difficult to deal with. Hence they are tempted to ignore them.

This quotation comes from Walter Klaassen's chapter on "The Anabaptist Tradition" in an excellent book, *Caring and Curing: Health and Medicine in the Western Religious Traditions*, with some twenty chapters outlining the views of major religious groups.[12]

Anabaptist themes. Klaassen begins his historical account by noting that the Anabaptists generally accepted the major doctrines of the common Christian faith. Two distinctive emphases, however, shaped their attitudes toward health and healing: (1) a view of the church as community, with the congregation as the visible presence of the kingdom; and (2) the conviction that good deeds are the necessary evidence of faith.

Another Mennonite historian, J. Denny Weaver, sets forth his version of the famous "Anabaptist vision" in his recent book, *Becoming Anabaptist*. He proposes three "first-level principles" to identify the believers church tradition: (1) Jesus as the norm of truth and life—*discipleship*; (2) the church as new social reality—*believing community*; and (3) nonresistance and peace—the *rejection of violence*. Weaver calls these "regulative principles" that are to function as "a stance, an outlook, an attitude, a way of living in the world."[13]

What aspects of this foundational "vision" are relevant for the bioethics of the unborn? Along with the obvious implications of the *pacifist* ethic, the *discipleship* norm suggests both a compassionate caring for human life and a readiness to suffer for one's convictions. *Community* becomes a resource for developing and sustaining disciples, as well as a context for ethical decision making.

Mennonite teaching. From the roots of sixteenth-century Anabaptism, we take a leap to twentieth-century Mennonitism, specifically to a normative bioethical statement. In 1975 the Mennonite Church General Assembly adopted a one-page "Summary Statement" on abortion, accompanied by six pages of supplementary study material. The statement begins:

> Because we believe that the Bible teaches that persons are created in God's image, that human life is a gift from God to be held in high esteem, and that God's interest in individuals begins before their birth with His desire that they develop into knowledge of and faith in Him: We believe that—1. Abortion violates the biblical principles of the sanctity and value of human life.[14]

The document continues in point two to deplore societal erosion regarding sanctity of life, but acknowledges in point three that "we do not legislate morality for society." Point three goes on to call for making alternatives available, and point five counsels sensitivity and compassion for those who differ with this view. In relation to guidance on bioethical decision making, point four is most interesting: "When very difficult decisions must be made about the life of the mother or the unborn child, Christians should prayerfully seek the guidance of the Holy Spirit with a group of believers committed to discerning the Lord's leading."

Here, in apparent recognition of situational complexity and consequent moral ambiguity, the approach allows for openness in decision making. The whole statement, admirably brief, suggests a nonjudgmental attitude and avoids making any clear identification of abortion as murder. The document appears to reflect a consensus that bridges the range of views expressed at several Mennonite conferences on abortion.[15]

Mennonite experience. In addition to these normative statements, we must examine some descriptive data from the sociological survey of Mennonite attitudes in Kauffman and Harder, *Anabaptists Four Centuries Later*.[16] The rightness or wrongness of abortion was tested with two items in the 1972 survey of five denominations. The percentage distribution shows that a significant majority of Mennonites would allow for therapeutic abortions (at least 60 percent saying it is "never wrong" or only "sometimes wrong").

Mennonite Responses to Abortion

	Always Wrong	Some- times	Never Wrong	Uncertain
Therapeutic Abortion (for mother's health)	10	27	36	27
Nontherapeutic (at mother's wish)	57	23	4	16

Kauffman and Harder comment: "Clearly the majority opinion is against nontherapeutic abortion as currently approved by the Supreme Court and most state laws. The sizable minority which is 'uncertain' reflects the complexity of the issues and the confusion that many people consequently feel."[17]

Compare these data with the fact that these same Mennonites are strongly opposed to war.[18] Something in the Mennonite worldview apparently distinguishes war and abortion. Notably, these Mennonite attitudes are the reverse of Catholic and conservative evangelical thinking. Most American Christians in those bodies oppose abortion much more vigorously than they do war.

Making sense out of Mennonites. Observers of the peace churches have been troubled by this apparent inconsistency. To begin with, a thoroughgoing pacifist theology would seem to point in one direction only: prohibition of all killing. How then does one account for the reluctance we have noted, both in the survey data and the official statement, to take an absolutist position on abortion, parallel to the rejection of killing in warfare? The following observations, admittedly based more on speculation than careful research, may suggest some reasons.

Until recently for most Mennonites abortion was simply not on the ethical agenda. Mennonite views have not been the result of the kind of systematic ethical reflection found in other religious groups or the various careful efforts of scholars to trace the parallels between just war thinking and reasons for abortion.[19] Most Mennonites were content with a folk wisdom that kept the topic in an offstage gray area.

Several aspects of this traditional Mennonite view may be suggested:

(1) The fetus was often not considered a real human being. Miscarriages, and in some cases even premature stillbirths, were not ceremonially buried, but simply discarded. The conventional wisdom in Mennonite families of the past generation was that the baby as a person was not really "there" until late in pregnancy. This "gut feeling" has probably been altered by increasing awareness of more recent scientific findings on the human qualities of the fetus.

(2) Many Mennonites have not seen abortion as equivalent to murder because it is not as obvious a wrong as killing on the battlefield. The typical unreflective view has been that it is a kind of surgical procedure, an unseemly "medical violence," but not quite like the butchery of war.

(3) These views may well be linked, in a folk culture, to the traditional medieval teaching that animation or "ensoulment" occurs sometime after conception. The Anabaptist insistence on believers baptism may implicitly reinforce this apparent "less than human" status of the unborn. If the infant is not really a responsible soul in God's sight, how much less the fetus?

Toward an Anabaptist Ethic for the Unborn

These speculative hunches about the reasons behind the ambiguity in Mennonite thought do not really give us much ethical guidance, however. My work thus far has been mostly descriptive. Now I want to move toward some normative implications. What have we learned that will help Mennonites think about bioethical issues?

How is the Anabaptist vision still relevant? Even if the basic principles summarized by Denny Weaver continue to function as recognized norms among Mennonites, considerable tension and disagreement about their meaning and relevance can be anticipated. The *community* ideal is threatened by social mobility and urbanization, as well as the corroding effects of such contemporary values as personal freedom and individual rights. *Discipleship* must contend today with the temptations of materialism, egocentrism, and even a counter-gospel of wealth and success. The language of self-denial, suffering, and the way of the cross is challenged by much of modern American religiosity.

However, the most intriguing ambiguities in Mennonite bioethical attitudes revolve around the *pacifist* commitment. Common-sense logic would seem to argue that, as pacifists, Mennonites should be absolutists with regard to the protection of the life of the unborn. We have noted, however, that both the intuitions of folk wisdom and the nuances of the official statement reveal a reluctance to advocate an absolutist position.

Perhaps an alternative ethic is emerging among progressive Mennonites, one which would undergird these implicit views with a more forthright "developmental theology of human life" along the lines proposed by Paul Simmons. Such an ethic might employ concepts of community to take into account *all* the lives involved in the abortion situation: not only the fetus, but the life of the mother, the needs of others in the family, the implications of overpopulation, and so on. Added to such considerations would be the relatively recent but strong concerns for women's rights and justice for the poor and oppressed. Together, these themes would mitigate the absoluteness of a total condemnation of abortion.

Further, current Anabaptist thought can make creative use of the traditional two-kingdom theology in its public policy implications. Although we may strive to uphold absolutist norms for our own behavior as Christians, we are hesitant to impose those norms on others. In a pluralistic society we are willing to allow others to do what we would not do ourselves.

I make these suggestions with a great deal of hesitancy, because I continue to believe that the choice of abortion is almost always a *tragedy,* if not necessarily the *sin* of murder. I share John H. Yoder's view that the Bible calls into question our modern Western emphasis on the *individual* and his or her rights. The biblical alternative begins with the moral authority of the *community.* The important questions then become "what that infant contributes to the identity of the community, what it does to the viability of the community to hold a cheap view of the life of the child, what it does to the whole fabric of community existence to consider life as something we may dispose of."[20]

What about the ethics of intervention? Most of our attention thus far has been given to the questions related to abortion. But we must also ask, what criteria from the Mennonite ethos are applicable to the new technologies surrounding the unborn? I am referring to such things as artificial insemination, in vitro fertilization, embryo transfer, sperm or ovum donation, surrogate motherhood—a whole class of exotic and sophisticated methods designed to "cure" infertility.

With reference to the nature versus history debate above, good Mennonite theology would certainly be on the side of openness to change, of genuine choice and freedom. Thus, there would be no *a priori* prohibition of medical intervention if the procedures are justified on other grounds. Intervention has been around for a long time. So has surrogate motherhood, as the Old Testament accounts of the role of handmaidens may remind us!

For Anabaptists, however, the real problem with these technologies is not the question of intervention against natural order. Although sophisticated techniques to "cure" infertility may not be wrong per se, what about the high price of these expensive procedures? Can an Anabaptist disciple casually accept this kind of allocation of scarce medical skills and resources? We must begin to ask hard questions about our health care priorities—as individuals, as medical professionals, as a church, indeed as a whole society!

Other serious theological and moral concerns grow out of our emphasis on community, relationships, meanings, and social consequences. New procedures raise basic questions about the nature of the family and about social roles and responsibilities. As self-determining agents active in history and responsible before God, *we must ask again about our reasons for having or not having children.*[21] And that leads me to my final point.

A paradoxical conclusion. In the course of thinking about these issues, I have discovered a curious paradox, an ironical state of affairs in our current situation with regard to the unborn. Stated bluntly, in fact overstated and exaggerated for emphasis: *The fertility intervention techniques would not be needed if our society didn't have abortions on demand!*

There is something ridiculous, pathetic, perhaps downright immoral about the American situation regarding childbearing. Look at our social setting. In one arena we have the great public debate over abortion. Tremendous amounts of moral and political energy are expended by both sides. The pro-choice slogan is attractive: "No woman should ever have an unwanted child." So hundreds of thousands of presumably unwanted children are thus being aborted. Yet, all but the most extreme abortion advocates recognize that abortion is seldom a happy choice.

On another stage, we have thousands of people who are willing to pay thousands of dollars for a baby; but because very few babies are available for adoption, huge amounts of medical resources are expended to deal with the problem of infertility. This approaches a kind of social pathology. *Babies are desperately wanted, yet babies are being aborted.*

Is there no way to bring these two scenarios together? Can we as a society, and especially as Christians, find ways to make it possible or even desirable for more healthy women to bear their babies and then give them up for adoption to families who genuinely want a child? - not so easy an answer
  - what about need to "replicate self"?

Questions for Reflection and Discussion
1. How might acceptance of abortion affect the identity of the Christian community?
2. Why do you think some sincere Christians have not taken an absolutist position on abortion and other beginning-of-life issues?
3. How should morality and science interrelate in the practice of medicine?
4. Is the role of health care professionals merely to provide information about consequences of choices and allow clients to make their own decisions? If not, what is their role when issues of the unborn arise?
5. What difference does it make in decision making about the unborn when life is understood in relation to God? When humans are viewed as cocreators with God?

6. What does a theology that emphasizes stewardship have to say about the high price of procedures to achieve fertility or child-bearing?

7. How should the desire for children be viewed by a theology that emphasizes discipleship, rejection of violence, and the believing community?

For Further Reading

Alderfer, Edwin, and Helen Alderfer, eds.
1974 *Life and Values.* Scottdale, Pa.: Mennonite Publishing House.

Brenneman, George
1979 "Abortion: Review of Mennonite Literature, 1970-1977." *Mennonite Quarterly Review*, 53 (2): 160-172.

Burtchaell, James T.
1982 *Rachel Weeping and Other Essays on Abortion.* Kansas City: Andrews and McMeel, Inc.

Friesen, Duane K.
1974 *Moral Issues in the Control of Birth.* Newton, Kans.: Faith and Life Press.

Hauerwas, Stanley
1981 *A Community of Character: Toward a Constructive Christian Social Ethic.* Notre Dame, Ind.: University of Notre Dame Press.

_____.
1974 *Vision and Virtue: Essays in Christian Ethical Reflection.* Notre Dame, Ind.: Fides Publishers, Inc.

Koontz, Ted
1978 "Hard Choices: Abortion and War." *The Mennonite.* 93 (February 28): 132-34.

Lammers, Stephen E., and Allen Verhey, eds.
1987 *On Moral Medicine: Theological Perspectives in Medical Ethics.* Grand Rapids: Eerdmans.

Numbers, Ronald L., and Darrel W. Amundsen, eds.
1986 *Caring and Curing: Health and Medicine in the Western Religious Traditions.* New York: Macmillan. (The book is a project of the Lutheran General Health Care System and Park Ridge Center.)

Sider, Ronald J.
1987 *Completely Pro-Life: Building a Consistent Stance.* Downers Grove, Ill.: InterVarsity Press.

Simmons, Paul D.
1983 *Birth and Death: Bioethical Decision-Making.* Philadelphia: Westminster Press.

Chapter 3

Overview of Human Reproduction

Gary J. Killian

Gary Killian
Ph.D. in reproductive physiology, Pennsylvania State University. Associate professor of animal science and coordinator of Pennsylvania State University's Dairy Breeding Research Center, University Park, Pennsylvania.

REPRODUCTION in humans is comprised of a fascinating series of biochemical and physiological events that culminate in the birth of a child. In biological terms, human reproduction is sexual, involving male and female, with each producing a specific sex cell, that is, sperm or egg. Successful sexual reproduction is dependent upon the union of sperm and egg at fertilization and the embryonic development of the resulting fertilized egg. Although reproductive organs are not considered vital organs for the survival of an individual, they are necessary for the continued survival of humankind.

Successful reproduction is also dependent on events occurring in the right sequence and timing. Fertilization will occur only if sperm and egg are in the right place at the proper time. This is important to remember when considering how humans might manipulate reproduction, either through contraception or in the correction of infertility.

The purpose of this chapter is to pro-

45

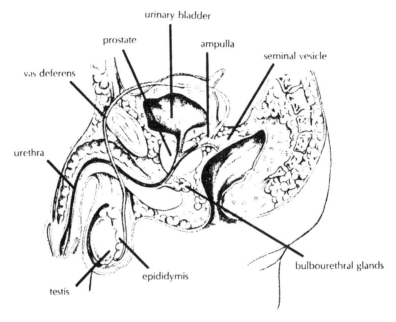

Figure 1
Human Male Reproductive System. Sperm form in the seminiferous tubules of the testis and are stored in the epididymis. At ejaculation, sperm move through the male reproductive tract, mix with secretions from the seminal vesicle and prostate, and are expelled from the male reproductive tract as semen.

vide a general overview of major events in human reproduction. Such an overview provides a basis for understanding how biotechnology might be used to alter or mimic reproductive events.

Male Reproductive Anatomy

The male reproductive system consists of three major components (Figure 1). The testes produce sperm and secrete male hormones called androgens, including testosterone. The excurrent ducts convey the sperm from each testis through the penis to the outside of the body. These ducts consist of the efferent ducts, epididymis, vas deferens, and the urethra. The seminal vesicles, prostate, and bulbourethral glands are located around the junction of the vas deferens and the urethra. These glands produce secretions that are mixed with the sperm to form semen at ejaculation.

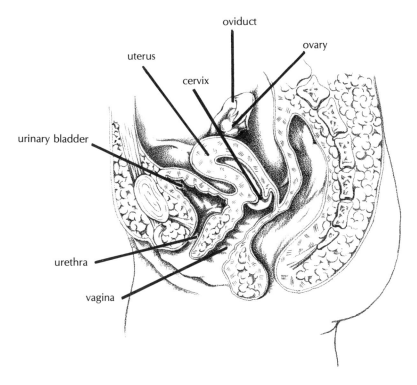

Figure 2

Human Female Reproductive System. An ovulated ovum moves from the ovary and passes to the oviduct. If sperm are present in the oviduct, fertilization may occur. The fertilized ovum moves down the oviduct and enters the uterus. In some cases the fertilized ovum will attach to the wall of the uterus, embed itself into the uterine lining (implantation), and continue its development as an embryo; in other cases, the fertilized ovum will fail to implant and be discharged.

Female Reproductive Anatomy

The female reproductive system (Figure 2) is comprised of both gonads and ducts as in the male. The ovaries produce ova and the hormones estrogen and progesterone. The system of ducts consists of the vagina, cervix, uterus, and oviducts. The vagina serves both as a site for semen deposition and a birth canal. The cervix, uterus, and oviducts convey sperm from the vagina to the site of fertilization in the oviduct. The oviduct also conveys the early embryo to the uterus where implantation and fetal development occur. During pregnancy the cervix secretes material to fill its lumen and produce a "sterile" barrier to seal off the uterus from the vagina.

Hormonal Control of Reproduction

The reproductive function of men and women is under the precise regulation of hormones. The general scheme for this regulation is pictured in Figure 3.

The hormonal control of reproduction is initiated at puberty through a process not fully understood. A specialized part of the brain called the hypothalamus increases the secretion of a protein "releasing" hormone (RH). This RH is carried a short distance by the blood circulation from the hypothalamus to the pituitary gland where it stimulates the synthesis and secretion, or "release," of two other hormones important to reproduction.

Both of these hormones, follicle stimulating hormone (FSH) and luteinizing hormone (LH), were first studied in females and were named to describe events that they stimulated. Although scientists later discovered that the male had pituitary gland hormones that were chemically identical to those secreted by the female, the hormones have retained their initial names.

Following stimulation of the pituitary gland by RH, FSH and LH are secreted into the circulatory system and carried to the ovaries or testes. Here their function is to stimulate the production of sex cells and to stimulate the synthesis and secretion of androgens or estrogens. Another hormone called inhibin is produced along with the sex cells. Androgens or estrogens secreted locally within the gonad enhance sex cell production. Androgens and estrogens that are secreted into the bloodstream initiate a variety of effects throughout the body. Physical and behavioral attributes of "maleness" and "femaleness" are associated with these male and female hormones.

The organs comprising the male and female reproductive systems are dependent on adequate levels of androgens and estrogens in the blood to function normally. Too little or too much of a hormone results in inadequate or excessive responses by the "target" organs or tissues that respond to the hormone. The control system that maintains the proper level of hormone in the blood involves a negative feedback loop. This hormone-regulating mechanism operates like many heating systems operate in homes. The

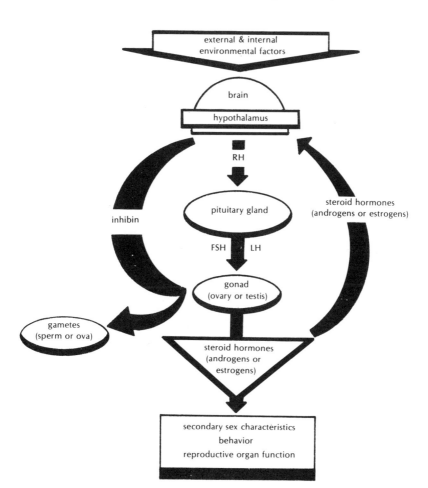

Figure 3
Hormonal Control of Reproduction.

desired temperature is set on the thermostat. The furnace is switched on when the temperature of the house drops below the temperature setting on the thermostat. Heat produced by the furnace then raises the temperature in the house. When the temperature reaches the level set on the thermostat, a signal is sent from the thermostat to turn off the furnace. In this example a negative feedback loop is established between the furnace and the thermostat. The heat produced by the furnace not only produces the desired effect of a warm house, but also serves as the messenger to the thermostat to indicate exactly how warm the house is. Obviously, without a feedback loop, the furnace would not be turned on or off and the house would not be maintained at the desired temperature.

Referring again to Figure 3, we can see that negative feedback loops exist between the testes or ovaries and the hypothalamus. In this context the testes or ovaries are analogous to the furnace in the home, the hypothalamus is analogous to the thermostat, and the products of the sex organs that "feed back" to the hypothalamus are like the heat. If blood levels of androgens, estrogens, or inhibin drop below normal, the hypothalamus responds by releasing more RH. This, in turn, stimulates the pituitary gland to release more FSH and LH. Both FSH and LH then stimulate the sex organs to produce androgens, estrogens, and inhibin. When these hormones reach normal levels in the blood, their feedback to the hypothalamus turns off the secretion of RH. When hormonal blood levels drop, on the other hand, the mechanism is switched on again.

The hormonal control of reproduction that has been described thus far has been presented in a general way to apply to both men and women. However, an important distinction exists between men and women regarding the pattern of hormone secretion.

Levels of reproductive hormones in men are quite constant from day to day. A relatively constant daily production of RH by the male hypothalamus accounts for this consistency. Women, however, are different in this regard. The secretory pattern of RH and pituitary hormones in women undergoes cyclic increases and decreases about once a month. These differences bring about cyclic changes in function of the reproductive organs that are evidenced by the menstrual cycle. The importance of these cyclic changes will be discussed later.

Production of the Sex Cells

The combining of genetic material of both parents at fertilization enables some genetic characteristics of each parent to be passed to the next generation. This process, called meiosis, involves cell division and also determines the sex of the offspring. The sex cells derived from each parent contain one half the ge-

seminiferous tubule

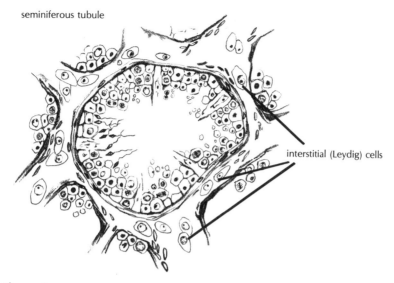

interstitial (Leydig) cells

Figure 4a
Production of Sperm in the Testis. Sectional cut through a seminiferous tubule.

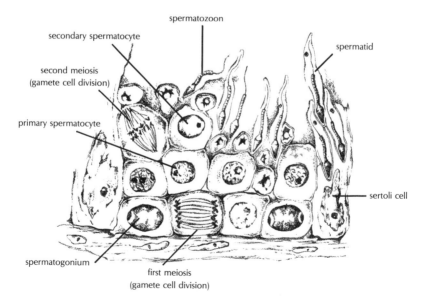

spermatozoon

secondary spermatocyte

spermatid

second meiosis
(gamete cell division)

primary spermatocyte

sertoli cell

spermatogonium

first meiosis
(gamete cell division)

Figure 4b
Spermatogenesis Occurring in a Section of the Seminiferous Tubule Wall.

netic material of a parent so that the total amount of genetic material, or chromosomes, in the offspring will equal that of the parent. If this were not the case, the amount of genetic material in the offspring of each generation would be double that of the parent and the characteristics of a given species could change dramatically. Human cells each contain 44 non-sex chromosomes and two sex chromosomes for a total of 46.

The process of meiosis in males is called spermatogenesis. It takes place in the seminiferous tubules of the testes under the control of the pituitary gland hormones FSH and LH. The process begins with spermatogonial cells that line the tubules (Figure 4). Some spermatogonia begin meiosis and divide. After two meiotic cell divisions, four spermatids result, each having one-half the normal number of chromosomes as the original spermatogonium. At this point, however, the spermatids are round cells and do not resemble sperm in the least. The round spermatids must undergo additional structural changes in the seminiferous tubules to transform the round cells into highly specialized spermatozoa.

As spermatogenesis proceeds, the spermatogenic cells are moved slowly toward the lumen of the tubule until they are released and carried away in fluid to the epididymis. For man the process of spermatogenesis takes about 64 days from start to finish. The development of spermatozoa to spermatids does not occur synchronously throughout the entire testis. Development among different groups of spermatogenic cells is staggered to ensure a continuous supply of spermatozoa throughout the postpubertal years of men.

The human male produces about 150 million sperm per day. Although some decline in sperm production by the testes occurs with age, men appear capable of fathering children throughout their lifetime. Lest one thinks that the production of 150 million sperm per day by the human male is a big deal, note that by animal standards this is not the case. Male rabbits produce about the same number of sperm; yet they have a body weight of only 10 lbs. The male pig holds the record, however, by producing about 16 billion sperm per day or more than 100 times that produced by men.

After sperm complete spermatogenesis, they are carried from the seminiferous tubules to the epididymis. The human epididymis is a convoluted duct that when unraveled is about 20 ft. long. In man 3-4 days are required for sperm to reach the distant end of the epididymis where they are stored until ejaculation. When sperm enter the epididymis, they are incapable of swimming properly or fertilizing an ovum (female egg). Only after sperm pass through the epididymis do they acquire these traits. Therefore, the epididymis can be thought of as a "finishing school" for sperm, as well as a storage organ.

Sex cell production in women is considerably different from that of men. One obvious difference is that while men produce millions of sperm each day, women typically release one ovum every 28 days. For the average reproductive life span of a woman from puberty to menopause, about 400 ova are released. These ova are produced from oogonia cells in the ovaries by the process of meiosis. Unlike spermatogonia of the male, oogonia do not undergo continual proliferation throughout life. All proliferation of oogonia and the initiation of meiosis take place during fetal development. Although the ova await maturation, at birth the ovaries contain all the ova a woman will ever have. If these ova are destroyed by irradiation, for example, they will not be replaced and the woman will be infertile.

Normally one ovum is released each month by an ovary (Figure 5) as a result of changes in levels of pituitary hormones in the blood. During each menstrual cycle, FSH and LH stimulate several ova and the cells that surround them to begin follicular growth. Although a group of follicles begin to develop each month, typically only one follicle will progress to a mature size and release an ovum. The follicles that do not reach mature size degenerate. Follicular development each month can be likened to a marathon race where many runners leave the starting line, many drop out along the way, and only one finishes the contest. Nevertheless, the follicles that undergo some development each month secrete increasing amounts of estrogen. Estrogen is important to prepare the uterus and oviducts for events associated with fertilization.

At about the middle of the menstrual cycle, a sharp but brief increase in LH and FSH secretion from the pituitary gland occurs in response to the increasing blood levels of estrogen originating from the developing follicles. This promotes the final ripening of the most mature follicle and the subsequent "release" or ovulation of the ovum contained within. Although under natural circumstances usually only one ovum is released, women treated therapeutically with hormones such as LH and FSH may ovulate

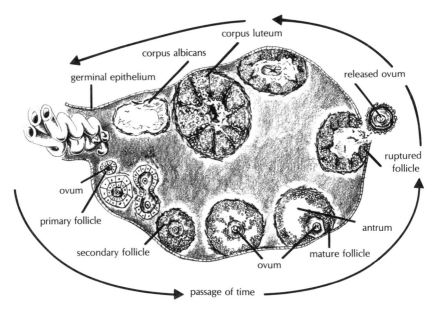

Figure 5
Production of Ova in the Ovary. Follicle growth, maturation, and ovulation are illustrated. Corpus luteum formation and subsequent regression (corpus albicans) are also shown.

several ova. We are occasionally reminded of this in newspapers when the birth of quadruplets or quintuplets is reported.

After the release of the ovum, the empty follicle collapses and undergoes structural and functional reorganization to form a corpus luteum. The corpus luteum secretes progesterone that prepares the female reproductive tract to accept and nurture an embryo. If fertilization does not occur, the corpus luteum degenerates and another menstrual cycle ensues with the development of another group of follicles.

The Menstrual Cycle

The biological role of the male in mammalian reproduction is to produce an adequate number of spermatozoa (sperm) and deliver them to the female reproductive tract. The role of the female in reproduction, however, is much more complex. A woman not only produces ova, she also provides a place for fertilization to occur. As if that were not enough, she also provides a protective, nourishing environment in which the embryo will develop for nine months. This multipurpose role of the reproductive system of the woman is made possible by the changes that take place in the reproductive organs during the menstrual cycle.

In a functional sense, the menstrual cycle is divided into two parts (Figure 6). The first half involves follicular development and estrogen production and culminates with the release of an ovum. The second half involves production of progesterone by the corpus luteum. The predominance of estrogen during the first half of the cycle has distinct effects on a woman's reproductive organs. These effects favor the production of ova, the transport of sperm, and fertilization. In addition, the lining of the uterus proliferates in preparation for support of embryo development should fertilization occur. During the second half of the cycle, the influence of progesterone on the reproductive system favors movement of the embryo from the oviduct to the uterus, embryo nourishment, and development of the placenta.

After the embryo implants in the uterus, a hormone produced by the placenta enters the blood and signals the brain that pregnancy has occurred. The brain responds by ensuring that hormone patterns of FSH and LH secreted by the pituitary sustain embryonic development. If fertilization does not occur, there is no embryo to implant in the uterus, and the uterine lining is shed as menses, along with some blood from ruptured vessels. The menstrual cycle then repeats itself to provide yet another opportunity for ovum production, fertilization, and embryo development to occur.

Events Associated with Fertilization

Fertilization normally takes place in the upper third of the oviduct, close to the ovary. In order for fertilization to occur, however, sperm must be present in the oviduct at the time the ovum is released and carried into the oviduct. Thus, the timing of intercourse is very important to the success or failure of fertilization.

After semen is deposited in the vagina, some sperm move into and through the cervix to the uterus. Sperm are observed in the oviduct within a few minutes of intercourse. This rapid transport of sperm to the site of fertilization is accomplished through wavelike muscular contractions of the uterus and oviduct. Al-

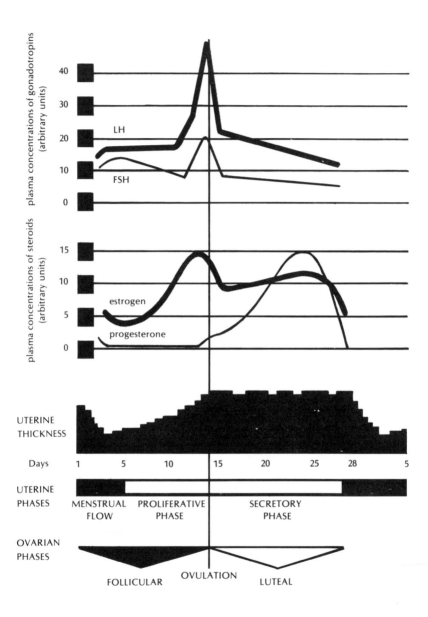

Figure 6
Blood Concentrations of Hormones during the Normal Female Sexual Cycle.
The time line of the menstrual cycle correlates hormonal changes with events in
the ovary and uterus.

though millions of sperm are deposited in the vagina, only a few hundred sperm reach the vicinity of the egg in the oviduct at one time. Some sperm appear to be retained in the crevices and folds of the cervix. These sperm apparently are released gradually over the next one or two days to provide a constant supply of sperm in the oviduct to await the arrival of the ovum.

The female reproductive system also plays a role in bringing spermatozoa to a state of readiness or "capacitation" to fertilize the ovum. When sperm are simply combined with ova in a test tube, fertilization does not occur unless biochemical conditions that mimic effects of the female reproductive system are present. As a result of capacitation (involving a series of biochemical reactions), the sperm membranes covering the head are modified and the sperm are brought to a frenzy of activity. These events are believed to occur when sperm are in the vicinity of the ovum and are necessary prerequisites for fertilization.

The ovum presents a formidable barrier to penetration by the sperm (Figure 7). Hundreds of cells from the follicle (cumulus oophorus cells) are carried with the ovum at ovulation and surround the ovum while it is in the oviduct. Another structure, the zona pellucida, also encapsulates the ovum. When sperm encounter the ovum, they appear to swarm over it and "attack" it as hornets attack people who have disturbed their nest. The frenzied activity of the sperm is thought to aid fertilization by mechanically propelling the sperm through the follicular cells and the zona pellucida. The membrane changes that occurred on the sperm head apparently release and expose enzymes that help digest a path to the ovum. These combined mechanisms enable the sperm to make contact with the cell membrane of the ovum. The sperm and ovum then fuse and form a unique single cell called the zygote. During the next 20 hours the genetic materials of the sperm and the ovum combine, and embryonic development is initiated.

Of more immediate concern, however, is the fact that many other sperm are still in the process of penetrating the ovum. If more than one sperm penetrates the ovum, the embryo will surely die. How then will the attempts of other sperm to penetrate the ovum be foiled? After the first sperm enters the ovum, both the zona pellucida and the cell membrane of the ovum are rapidly modified chemically. Their new chemical structure prevents additional sperm from entering the ovum, similar to changing the locks on a house. The old key will not work in the new lock.

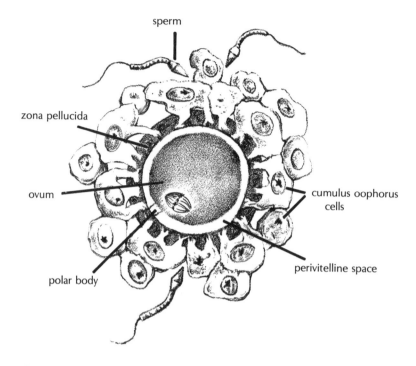

Figure 7
Barriers to the Sperm in Fertilizing the Ovum. A sperm must traverse the cumulus oophorus cells, the zona pellucida, and the perivitelline space in order to activate and fertilize the ovum.

As a consequence of fertilization, the number of chromosomes is restored to that of the parents, the sex of the offspring is determined, and embryonic development is initiated. The single-celled zygote repeatedly subdivides, forming an embryonic ball of cells. During the next 3-4 days, this embryo, a tiny speck to the human eye, moves through the oviduct to the uterus where it will make its home for the next 9 months.

Questions for Reflection and Discussion
1. By using the diagrams in Figures 1 and 2 can you explain why vasectomy and tubal ligation are effective in preventing conception?

2. How does the pattern of releasing hormone (RH) by the hypothalamus differ between men and women?
3. What event separates the menstrual cycle into two parts?
4. In what body organ is the zygote normally found?
5. How do the events and products of spermatogenesis and oogenesis fundamentally differ?
6. How do the effects of FSH and LH differ between males and females?
7. What forms of birth control are considered natural? What forms are considered artificial? Are some forms more acceptable ethically than others? Why?

For Further Reading

Lamb, J. F., C. G. Ingram, I. A. Johnston, and R. M. Pitman
  1980 *Essentials of Physiology.* Boston: Blackwell Scientific Publications.
Guyton, A. C.
  1986 *Textbook of Medical Physiology.* 7th ed. Philadelphia: W. B. Saunders.
Page, E. W., C. A. Villee, and D. B. Villee
  1976 *Human Reproduction: The Core Content of Obstetrics, Gynecology and Perinatal Medicine.* 2nd ed. Philadelphia: W. B. Saunders.

Chapter 4

Overview of Human Embryonic Development

Dennis O. Overman

Dennis Overman
Ph.D. in anatomy, University of Michigan. Associate professor of anatomy and associate professor of orthodontics, School of Medicine and School of Dentistry, West Virginia University, Morgantown, West Virginia.

ONE OF THE most active times of our lives occurred when we existed but were not yet born. Important to understanding ourselves is an appreciation for the process of development, of how we got to be the way we are. This chapter is a review of the important stages of human development and maturation. The chapter includes a discussion of the influence of environmental factors on the developmental process.

Outline of Very Early Embryology

Union of the male and female sex cells at fertilization results in the restoration of the full chromosome number and the formation of the first cell or zygote (Figure 1a). This single large cell, surrounded by the zona pellucida, contains all the genetic information that will determine the course of development, the sex, the appearance, and even many aspects of behavior of the individual. Fertilization occurs in the oviduct at some distance from the uterus, and a trip of about four

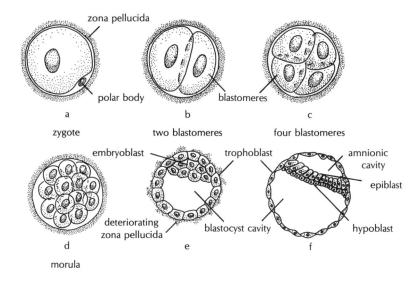

zona pellucida

polar body

blastomeres

a

zygote

b

two blastomeres

c

four blastomeres

embryoblast

trophoblast

amnionic cavity

epiblast

deteriorating zona pellucida

blastocyst cavity

hypoblast

d

morula

e

f

Figure 1
Early Developmental Stages. (a) Zygote surrounded by zona pellucida on the day of fertilization. (b and c) 2-cell and 4-cell stages. (d) Morula stage, still within zona pellucida on third day after fertilization. (e) Early blastocyst formation with deteriorating zona pellucida, outer layer of trophoblast cells, and inner cell mass (embryoblast) on fourth day after fertilization. (f) Embryo at bilaminar disc stage showing epiblast of taller cells near the small amnionic cavity and hypoblast of shorter cells adjacent to large blastocyst cavity. Time is about 6 days after fertilization, and the embryo is ready to implant into the wall of the uterus.

days is required before the very early embryo reaches the site of implantation in the wall of the uterus. During these several days the zygote begins the process of cleavage, dividing first into two cells (Figure 1b), then four (Figure 1c), then eight, and so on, with the division occurring within the bounds of the zona pellucida. With each succeeding generation the new cells are smaller than the preceding ones. The future embryo arrives in the uterus as a clump of 12 to 16 cells (Figure 1d) resembling a little mulberry, and for this reason it received the name morula, after the Latin word for mulberry.

Shortly after entering the uterus, the zona pellucida surrounding the morula breaks down and disappears, allowing the cells of the morula to contact the lining of the uterus. At the same time the cells continue to divide, forming a hollow ball of cells from what was originally a solid mulberry-like clump. This hollowing process is the result of the accumulation of fluid among the cells. The resulting structure (Figure 1e) is called the blastocyst. The cells forming the blastocyst are not distributed uniformly. Rather, they contain an outer zone of cells called the trophoblast and an inner clump of cells called the inner cell mass or embryoblast, which is located at one end. The word trophoblast means "the cells forming the nutritive or feeding structures." In other words, the trophoblast will form the placenta, as well as other embryonic membranes. The term embryoblast refers to the cells that will form the embryo.

As the blastocyst begins to invade the nutritive lining of the uterus, the cells that will form the embryo begin to separate from the trophoblast. This is a very important step in development, because up to now the future embryo has been simply a clump of cells with no apparent direction or orientation. Now the embryo is a clump of cells with a top and a bottom. To be more precise, the embryo at this point is a flat disc of two layers of cells (Figure 1f). The space above the new embryo is the amnion, the fluid-filled sac that will ultimately surround and protect the embryo for the next months, in fact until just hours or minutes before birth.

Because these cells that form the embryo, placenta, and amnionic sac all develop from the original single zygote, they all have identical genetic makeup or chromosomes. This fact is the biological basis of prenatal diagnostic techniques such as amniocentesis, in which sample cells are removed from the amnionic fluid, and chorionic villi sampling, in which a few cells are removed from the placenta. The removal of cells with the same genetic makeup as the embryo allows for the diagnosis of genetic conditions that can be identified on the basis of inspection of the chromosomes, and of metabolic diseases that can be identified on the basis of examination of the metabolic products of cells grown in culture in the laboratory.

The embryo, after the formation of the amnionic cavity, resembles a flat disc consisting of two layers of cells, an upper epiblast and a lower hypoblast. As the embryo matures, some of the cells of the top layer begin to migrate through a groove called the primitive streak to a new location between the original two cell layers (Figure 2). This cell migration results in the formation

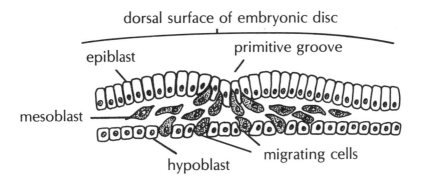

Figure 2

Formation of the Three Germ Layers. Some cells from the upper epiblast migrate to a new location between the epiblast and the hypoblast, forming a middle mesoblast. With additional migration of some mesoblast cells into the hypoblast, the endoderm is formed. The middle layer then becomes the mesoderm and the upper layer the ectoderm. This happens about 15 or 16 days after fertilization; the embryo is now deeply implanted in the wall of the uterus.

of a new middle layer of cells called the mesoblast. Most of the cells of the mesoblast remain in this location between the other layers, but some continue to migrate and join the hypoblast. The final three layers of cells are called the embryonic germ layers. The top layer is the ectoderm, the middle layer is the mesoderm, and the bottom layer is the endoderm. All parts of the body can trace their origin back to one or sometimes a combination of these three embryonic germ layers.

Embryo Folding and Establishment of the Organ Systems

At the point of establishment of the germ layers, approximately two and one-half weeks of age, the embryo is still in the form of a flat disc. Then a time of very rapid growth in size of the embryo begins. However, space is limited within the confines of the developing membrane structures. As a result, rapid growth in the width of the embryo results in a lateral curvature so that the embryo is no longer shaped like a flat disc, but is more like a tube. Concurrently, rapid elongation of the embryo from head to tail results in additional curvatures, one at the head end (the cranial fold) and another at the tail end (the caudal fold). As a result of cranial and caudal folding, the tubular embryo is shaped somewhat like the letter C, and the embryo maintains this C-shaped tubular form for the duration of its formation.

Although during development a great many events are occurring at the same time, it is only possible to describe them one at a time. Returning, then, to the three-layered embryo, the fate of each of the three embryonic germ layers will be described. The ectoderm is the top layer of the three-layered embryo. As a result of embryonic folding, the ectoderm covers the outside of the C-shaped tubular embryo. Therefore, the epidermis of skin, covering the entire outside of the body, is derived from this ectodermal layer. All the structures that are derived from the skin (hair, nails, sweat glands, and other glands of the skin) are formed from the ectoderm. The ectoderm, by a complex process of folding, also gives rise to the entire nervous system, the lens of the eye, and the inner ear. Of special interest to dentists, the teeth and other oral structures arise from the ectoderm.

The middle layer, the mesoderm, is still located in the middle after all the folding of the embryo has occurred. The mesoderm produces the skeleton, muscles, cardiovascular system, and most of the urogenital system.

The endoderm, which in the flat disc embryo was on the bottom, forms the inside lining of the folded tube, so it becomes the inside lining of the embryo. This layer forms the gastrointestinal system, including the various glands associated with it, such as the liver and pancreas. The endoderm also forms the respiratory system, which buds off from a portion of the developing gastrointestinal tract.

Many structures develop as the result of interaction between germ layers. The limbs form by interaction between the ectoderm and the mesoderm. The mesoderm contributes to the formation of most of the organ systems that develop from ectoderm and endoderm.

The establishment of the various organ systems is a major step in development and one that occurs very rapidly during the first trimester of pregnancy. All the organ systems are established, in immature form, by the end of the first trimester.

Maturation of the Organ Systems

Human development is a process that begins with a very undifferentiated cell, the zygote. Development proceeds through the formation of the various cells, tissues, and finally organs that make their appearance in an undifferentiated and immature condition. Before birth, the relatively undifferentiated cells and tissues must mature to the point of being able to live independently outside the maternal environment. Even at birth the maturation process is not complete, and, in fact, continues for many years. The second and third trimesters of pregnancy are devoted primarily to the growth and maturation of tissues and organ systems that were already present at the end of the first trimester. Meanwhile, some embryonic organ systems attain a high degree of differentiation and are able to function at a surprisingly early age. For example, the nervous system, the body's major controlling and coordinating system, develops early so that it can begin to exert a controlling influence over the process of development at an early age.

Over the years, researchers have had the opportunity to examine and study living human embryos and fetuses that have been recovered surgically for medical reasons. Surprisingly, embryos of only seven weeks old respond to stimulation of the skin in the area around the mouth by flexing the neck and moving the upper part of the body. At this age, the embryo is just beginning to look human. Within only a few weeks the response to stimulation becomes much less generalized. By about twelve weeks, the end of the first trimester, the fetus responds to touch stimulation by turning the head to face the stimulus and moving the limbs independently.

Potential ethical situations appear because of the relatively undifferentiated state of embryonic and fetal tissues and organs in comparison to their adult counterparts. We are familiar with tissue and organ transplantation to replace body parts damaged or destroyed by trauma or disease. We are also familiar with the importance of tissue matching in terms of blood type and other immune characteristics in order to prevent rejection of the transplant by the host whose body recognizes the presence of foreign material. Because embryonic tissues, in a primitive state of differentiation, are less readily recognized as foreign by an organism into which they might be transplanted, they are not as readily rejected. In addition, if cells and tissues are being transplanted in order to take over the function of some damaged structure, undifferentiated embryonic or fetal tissues are better suited than adult tissues for this purpose. Embryonic tissues adapt more easily to a new location.

We are continually learning more every week about the transplantation potential of various tissues for the correction of chemical problems. For example, a number of patients with Parkinson's disease have received transplants into their brains of cells taken from their own adrenal medulla. Hopefully, these transplanted cells in their new environment will take over the function of damaged or missing cells from the brain by producing a chemical messenger lacking in patients with this condition. Experimental evidence from laboratory animals indicates that actual brain cells would work better than adrenal medulla cells and that fetal brain cells work better than adult cells. Similar evidence exists in the treatment of leukemia. Normally bone marrow is the source of new blood cells in children and adults, but in people having leukemia their bone marrow cannot produce new blood cells. Leukemia is treated by replacing the abnormal bone marrow with bone marrow transplants from a normal individual. In the fetus, the blood-forming organ is the liver. Experimental evidence indicates that the transplantation of fetal liver cells is less likely to lead to transplant rejection than transplantation of adult bone marrow cells.

The preceding information raises an ethical question. Is it ethical to use cells or tissues obtained from human fetuses for transplant purposes? If we normally throw human fetal tissue in the garbage, should we retrieve some of those cells and transplant them into another person before discarding the rest? In at least one case a woman suggested that she become pregnant and then have an abortion in order to provide a source of fetal cells for transplantation to her father who suffers from Parkinson's disease. Her plan, incidentally, was rejected by other people concerned. We consider it ethical, desirable, and an example of good Christian stewardship to donate one's organs for the benefit of others in case of accidental death. However, the use of fetal cadaver tissue raises additional unanswered questions. This is an example, one of many, in which technology is moving faster than either law or philosophy.

Environmental Influences on Development

Environment plays a significant role in the development and differentiation of embryonic and fetal tissue. Teratogens, environmental factors that adversely influence development, may result in physical developmental defects (malformations) or behavioral deficits. Whether or not any particular environmental influence causes a malformation depends on the state of differentiation of the embryo. For example, certain drugs may cause the arms and legs to fail to develop. If an embryo is exposed to one of these drugs after the limbs have already formed, however, the drug will have no effect on limb formation. During development, sensitive periods for the action of teratogens exist. The developing human is most sensitive to environmental influences during the first trimester of pregnancy. This first trimester is the time when the various tissues and organ systems are first making their appearance and are most rapidly developing. For example, the brain develops early in the first trimester, so teratogens can have their greatest influence on the brain early in the first trimester. The urogenital system develops late in the first trimester, so environmental influences will have their greatest effect on the formation of this system at that later time.

Many environmental agents are known to cause malformations in experimental animals, and several are capable of inducing malformations in humans. Some malformations are hereditary and can be traced back through family histories. Some are due to chromosomal aberrations that can be observed and identified, although the cause of the chromosome defect may not be known. Among the environmental agents known to cause malformations in humans are X-rays and other ionizing radiation. Consequently, we take precautions against any unnecessary exposure to irradiation of the embryo, and even of the ovaries and testes. Some infections are known to induce malformations in humans, the most notable one being rubella, or German measles. Exposure of the embryo to the rubella virus early in the first trimester most often leads to heart defects. Exposure late in the first trimester results in deafness or other ear problems. This is a good example of different organ systems having different periods of sensitivity to the same environmental agent.

Some drugs are teratogenic in humans. The most famous of the teratogenic drugs is thalidomide, developed in Europe as a sedative and presumed to be safe for use during pregnancy on the basis of laboratory tests. Unfortunately, its action in humans was not comparable to its action in laboratory animals, and pregnant women who used this drug during the sensitive period for limb development gave birth to infants with absent or seriously deformed arms and legs. More recently some drugs that were developed as anticonvulsants for the treatment of epilepsy have been found to induce malformations in humans in a small but significant percentage of cases. This raises another problem for the physician and the mother. The drug is required for the epileptic mother to maintain her own health, but its continued use during pregnancy has the possibility of causing birth defects in her unborn child. Together the physician and mother must weigh the consequences of either course of action.

Other environmental factors are suspect in the induction of human malformations. Yet, in spite of what we have learned and what we are continuing to discover, at best only half of the birth defects appearing in humans can be explained on the basis of heredity, chromosomal problems, or environmental influences. Estimates of serious birth defects reach as high as three out of every one hundred births. Although our environment is becoming more complex in terms of the drugs, types of radiation, chemicals in food and water, and pollutants in the air, the incidence of malformations has stayed fairly constant over the years. However, as infant death from other causes decreases, birth defects become increasingly important as a cause of infant death in comparison to other factors.

The birth of a malformed infant can place extraordinary strain on a marriage, particularly in the absence of a satisfactory medical explanation for its occurrence. The lack of a medical explanation can lead to unresolved feelings of guilt as the parents ask themselves, "Is it something we did during pregnancy? Is God punishing us for our sins by giving us this child?" This situation leads the medical profession to feel that the prenatal diagnosis of malformations is important.

Recent technological advances make it possible to diagnose more and more types of malformations at earlier and earlier ages. Amniocentesis and chorionic villi sampling were mentioned previously as examples of prenatal diagnostic techniques that take advantage of the genetic properties of cells of the various fetal membranes to provide information about fetal chromosomal and metabolic conditions. Abnormal blood levels of some proteins, which are also revealed by amniocentesis, can be another indication of maldevelopment. These abnormal levels of fetal blood proteins can sometimes be detected by sampling maternal blood.

Fetoscopy is an invasive procedure that uses a fiberoptic fetoscope introduced through an abdominal opening to observe the fetus directly and sample actual fetal tissues if necessary. This particular technique is of relatively higher risk than the other procedures. Ultrasound visualization of the fetus is now routinely practiced in conjunction with invasive diagnostic techniques in order to determine the orientation of the fetus. In addition to serving as an aid to the other techniques, ultrasound can directly detect numerous malformations, both internal and external.

Some people oppose the widespread and routine use of prenatal diagnostic procedures on the grounds that the finding of abnormalities will lead to a more frequent use of abortion as a solution to the problem. Others point out that since the majority of high-risk pregnancies are uneventful, prenatal diagnosis for malformations will most often reveal normal fetuses and save the lives of infants who might have been aborted for fear of the unknown.

The period from fertilization to birth is a time of dramatic change for the unborn. For those of us who are already born, the present is another time of drastic change. Advances in our understanding of the process of development and differentiation are occurring so rapidly that it is becoming almost impossible to keep up with them. How we deal with this time of change will depend as much on our understanding and appreciation of the bioethical issues as it will on our understanding of the medical aspects of human development.

Questions for Reflection and Discussion
1. Normally about how many days pass after fertilization until the developing embryo is implanted in the uterus?
2. When the embryo changes from a two-layered embryonic disc into a three-layered embryo, what is the new cell layer that is formed?
3. At what point of development are all the major organ systems established?
4. What ethical problems may arise if fetal tissues are used in organ transplantation?
5. What value is there in determining if an unborn fetus is developing normally? Is abortion the only "corrective" course in the case of a diagnosed malformation?
6. What responsibility do we bear in the birth defects resulting from environmental pollutants?

For Further Reading

Hooker, D.
  1952 *The Prenatal Origin of Behavior*. Lawrence, Kans.: University of Kansas Press.
Moore, K. L.
  1988 *The Developing Human*. 4th ed. Philadelphia: W. B. Saunders Co.
Persaud, T. V. N., A. E. Chudley, and R. G. Skalko
  1985 *Basic Concepts in Teratology*. New York: Alan R. Liss, Inc.
Sadler, T. W.
  1985 *Langman's Medical Embryology*. 5th ed. Baltimore: Williams & Wilkins.

Chapter 5

Biotechnological Advances

Gary J. Killian

Gary J. Killian
Ph.D. in reproductive physiology, Pennsylvania State University. Associate professor of animal science and coordinator of Pennsylvania State University's Dairy Breeding Research Center, University Park, Pennsylvania.

ALTHOUGH THE TERM *biotechnology* has become a buzz word of the 1980s, the application of technology to control or modify reproduction in humans and domestic animals is not new. The first reported use of artificial insemination in dogs was nearly 200 years ago. Embryo transfer was first described for rabbits 100 years ago. Humans have used the techniques of genetic selection and controlled matings for hundreds of years to produce livestock of great utility.

One of the most striking examples of benefits derived from the use of biotechnology in reproduction of livestock involves the use of semen dilution, cryopreservation, and artificial insemination in dairy cattle. These techniques have made possible the extensive use of genetically superior sires for breeding, far beyond what would be possible by natural mating. Through dilution and freezing of semen, sperm from a single ejaculate of a genetically superior bull are often diluted into as many as 800 insemination doses. After

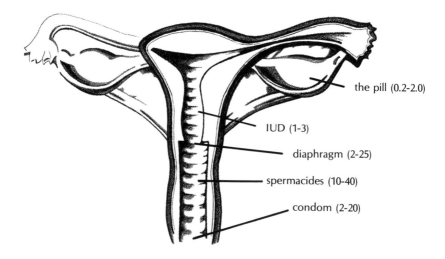

Figure 1
Contraceptive Devices and Pregnancy Rates. Numbers in parentheses indicate the number of pregnancies occurring per 100 woman years of reproductive activity.

freezing, sperm may be stored indefinitely and shipped for use throughout the world. As a result of the application of this technology, the genetic quality of dairy herds has improved considerably over the past 30 years, and the average milk production per cow has nearly doubled.

The desire of humans to control their own fertility dates back to antiquity. Early Egyptian writings, as well as later Greek and Roman writings, describe various potions used by women as contraceptives. Coitus interruptus was apparently used in biblical times as a contraceptive technique, because the practice is mentioned in Genesis 38:8-9.

Infertility has also been of concern throughout history. Infertile women have been treated with herbs, spells, and even snakebites to reverse their condition. Barren women have been viewed with both sorrow and scorn, exemplified by the biblical account of Sarai, Abram's wife.

In addition to a desire to control fertility, humans have also attempted to control the sex of their progeny. Many cultures of the world have in the past controlled the sex ratio of their children through infanticide.

The continued interest in the control of fertility, sex ratio, and genetic characteristics of economically important animals has generally resulted in the new technological advances associated with reproduction. Some of these techniques have been adapted and further modified for use with humans. The intent of this chapter is to provide an overview of biotechnology currently in use with humans as it relates to contraception, development, and correction of infertility. In addition, biotechnology that is currently experimental but may find its way into human medicine will be described.

Reproductive Biotechnology Applied to Humans to Reduce Fertility

Current applications of biotechnology to regulate human reproductive processes are largely concerned with either reducing fertility or correcting infertility. Three methods of controlling fertility are sterilization, contraception, and abortion.

Elective sterilization of men is normally achieved by vasectomy. This operation is performed under local anesthesia and involves removing a segment of the vas deferens to interrupt the flow of sperm from the epididymis to the urethra. Women electing sterilization undergo tubal ligation. In this operation segments of the oviduct are tied off and removed or destroyed. This procedure prevents sperm passage from the uterus to the ovum and prevents transport of ova through the oviduct into the uterus. Although recent technological advances have made it possible to reverse these conditions by surgery or in vitro fertilization (IVF), the success rates are low. Individuals choosing sterilization as a method of reducing fertility are advised to consider it permanent and irreversible.

Contraception is the method most couples choose in the United States to control fertility. With the exceptions of coitus interruptus and the condom, the various contraceptive methods available have been devised for use by women. The sites in the reproductive system that are affected by the contraceptive devices are depicted in Figure 1, along with the success rate of the method. The purpose of this discussion is not to debate the merits or disadvantages of each method, but simply to describe how they work.

Spermicides that come in the form of foam, jelly, or cream are placed in the vagina prior to intercourse. When ejaculation occurs, sperm are killed by the spermicide while they are in the vagina.

Two barrier methods of contraception are available to couples: the condom and diaphragm. The condom is a latex receptacle that is worn over the penis during intercourse and ejaculation. The semen technically never enters the female reproductive system. The diaphragm is a latex disc that is positioned in the vagina over the opening to the cervix. Sperm deposited in the vagina are prevented from moving to the site of fertilization because they are unable to pass through the cervix. Both the condom and the diaphragm are used in combination with spermacide for maximum effectiveness.

The intrauterine device, or IUD, is made of a substance that is foreign to the body. Several types are plastic with copper wire wrapped around them. A physician inserts the IUD into the uterus through the cervix. The precise mechanism by which the IUD works is not known. The IUD may alter the intrauterine environment so that the early embryo, arriving from the oviduct, will not be implanted.

Oral contraceptives, commonly known as the "pill," employ a hormonal approach to block ovulation. The pill is presently the most effective contraceptive device available. The pill usually consists of both estrogen and progesterone and is taken daily for 21 days. The estrogen and progesterone contained within the pill inhibit the production of FSH and LH by the pituitary gland. This in turn inhibits follicle growth and ovulation. An interval of seven days is allowed between each 21-day segment of taking the pill. During this time a menses results because of the withdrawal of the estrogen and progesterone, as is seen during the normal menstrual cycle.

Another contraceptive approach is the rhythm method, which attempts to control fertility by abstinence from intercourse around the time of ovulation. In order to be effective, the time of ovulation must be known. Methods of determining when ovulation occurs involve monitoring changes in basal body temperature and the viscosity of cervical mucus. Unfortunately, these methods are of more value in predicting when ovulation *has occurred*, than when it *will occur*. As a result, many couples using the rhythm method of contraception become parents.

Sterilization and contraceptive devices interfere with fertility by preventing conception. Abortion, on the other hand, reduces fertility by terminating pregnancy after conception. Abortion during the first trimester is usually done by a "D and C" (cervical dilation and uterine curettage) or vacuum aspiration. In the former method, an instrument is inserted through the cervix into the uterus and the lining of the uterus, along with the fetus, is scraped off. During vacuum aspiration, a vacuum tube is inserted into the uterus via the cervix and the fetus and placenta are sucked out.

Abortions at later stages of pregnancy are more difficult and involve increased risks to the mother. One commonly used approach is to inject hypertonic saline into the amniotic fluid. The hypertonic fluid draws water out of the fetal and placental tissues, in a way not unlike pickling procedures using brine. The consequences of this treatment irritate the uterine lining, and premature labor results. Another method of inducing abortion after the first trimester of pregnancy involves injection of prostaglandins into or around the amniotic sac. Prostaglandins are hormones that have a variety of effects in different tissues. When injected into the uterine lumen, they induce strong contractions of uterine muscle and result in premature labor and fetus expulsion.

Application of Reproductive Biotechnology to Reverse Human Infertility

Approximately one in four married couples in which the wife is of childbearing age suffer from reduced fertility. The reasons for reduced fertility include both male and female factors. Forty to 50 percent of the fertility problems in couples are associated with women, about 40 percent are traced to men, and the remainder are due to combined male and female factors.

A variety of diagnostic tests and evaluation procedures are currently in use and under development to ascertain the causes of infertility in men and women. Many of these diagnostic tools involve the use of biotechnology. Information gained during the evaluation to establish the cause of infertility is invaluable in determining a course of action. Although the likelihood of correcting the infertility varies with the diagnosis and the hospital or clinic involved with the treatment, a great many couples gain fertility through biotechnology.

Male Infertility

Male infertility is usually associated with four principal causes. The testes may not produce adequate numbers of sperm. The ducts carrying sperm away from the testes (the epididymis or vas deferens) may be blocked or impaired. Semen quality or sperm motility may be poor. Finally, the delivery of semen to the vagina may be hindered by an inability to ejaculate or maintain penile erection.

Poor semen production by the testes is sometimes correctable by drug therapy, although several months of treatment are required before the success of the treatment is known. Blockage or impairment of the epididymis or vas deferens is sometimes alleviated by surgery. Impotence may be treated by drug therapy, surgery, or psychotherapy.

Artificial Insemination

The use of artificial insemination (AI) is indicated when the husband's semen is of poor quality or contains few sperm. The couple may choose AI because other therapies have failed or because AI represents a less drastic and expensive form of treatment. The procedure of AI is relatively simple. The husband provides a semen sample by masturbation. The semen may or may not be treated in the laboratory before a physician transfers it to a site in the woman's reproductive system.

How does using AI increase the chances of conception when semen quality is poor? The answer to this question is twofold. Treatment of the semen in the laboratory provides an opportunity to improve its quality. Chemical substances may be added to the semen to improve sperm motility or quality. Dead sperm, poorly motile sperm, and debris may be removed so that the sperm actually inseminated are of better quality. Artificial insemination also offers the advantage of strategically placing the semen in the female reproductive system to minimize losses. Most of the sperm deposited in the vagina during coitus either drain out of the body or are killed within 1 or 2 hours by the inhospitable environment provided by the vagina. During AI, semen is commonly injected into the cervical opening with a plastic tube. Alternatively, it may be placed in a plastic cap, which is then positioned over the opening to the cervix. In some instances the semen may be injected through the cervix directly into the uterus. All three methods of insemination reduce the loss of semen and tend to compensate for semen with reduced sperm numbers or quality.

Artificial insemination with donor semen is sometimes elected by a couple when the husband's semen does not contain sperm or when other therapeutic approaches have failed. Donors are carefully screened for semen quality and medical history. Donors are screened for hepatitis and genetic diseases and periodically checked for venereal diseases. Many donors are medical students or physicians who have previously demonstrated fertility. The physical characteristics of the donor are often matched with those of the husband. The anonymity of the donor is absolute, as is that of the couple who use the donor semen.

Semen from a donor may be inseminated fresh or after freezing for a period of time. The procedure for freezing human sperm was modeled after that developed in the cattle industry for freezing bull sperm. Sperm are cooled at a controlled rate to extremely low temperatures in the presence of glycerol, a cryopreservative. Typically, frozen sperm may be stored indefinitely at -324F in liquid nitrogen. The freezing procedure is designed to minimize damage to sperm that might occur as ice crystals develop.

As a result of the freezing and thawing process, as many as 50 percent of the sperm may be killed. For donors with normal fertility, this still leaves more than enough sperm for insemination. For a husband with low sperm numbers, however, freezing several semen samples to accumulate an adequate number of sperm to inseminate does not often meet with success. The low numbers of sperm initially, along with the high sperm loss during freezing, appear to counter the benefit of combining semen samples.

The question is often asked, does using frozen sperm and AI increase the chances of spontaneous abortions or birth defects? No evidence exists to suggest that the occurrence of these events is increased when frozen semen and AI are used. In fact, some evidence suggests that the number of spontaneous abortions and birth defects may be slightly less than that associated with natural pregnancies.

Several advantages exist for using frozen donor semen for AI. The same donor's semen may be used repeatedly if several inseminations are performed around ovulation. Using frozen sperm also allows a complete and thorough work-up of medical tests on the donor at the time when the semen was obtained and with adequate time to obtain test results prior to insemination. The need for a current medical assessment of the donor at the time the semen is obtained is important to prevent disease transmission through semen. This need has become increasingly apparent when considering ways to prevent the spread of acquired immune deficiency syndrome, commonly known as AIDS. In the future, few inseminations of donor semen will be done with fresh semen.

Thus far we have described how AI is used to accomplish pregnancy for a couple when the husband is subfertile or infertile. AI may be used when the husband is fertile, but the wife is infertile. In this instance, a surrogate mother can be inseminated at ovulation by AI with the husband's semen. Some couples choose this option over adoption if a surrogate mother is available, so that the genetic characteristics of the father will be present in the child. However, the legal and emotional difficulties that may arise from this arrangement are much more complicated than the use of a "surrogate" father through donor insemination.

In Vitro Fertilization and Embryo Transfer

The birth of a baby conceived by in vitro fertilization (IVF) was first reported by scientists in England in 1978. Although the procedure was developed for use in patients with disorders of the oviduct, it has since been used for ovulation disorders as well. Because IVF requires fewer sperm for conception than are necessary under natural conditions, it has also been used when the husband has reduced sperm numbers or quality.

The success of the procedure was actually made possible by combining several technologies with IVF to bypass events that normally take place in the oviduct. Simply stated, the procedure involves egg recovery, IVF and embryo development in vitro, and embryo transfer to the uterus (figure 2).

During the menstrual cycle one egg is normally produced every 28 days. To increase the chances of recovering more eggs, patients for IVF are stimulated with drugs or hormones that mimic the effects of FSH and LH. The supplemental hormones usually stimulate several follicles to develop on the ovary and increase the chances of recovering several eggs. The eggs must be recovered after adequate follicular development has occurred, but before ovulation. Therefore, follicular development is monitored by measuring the output of estrogen in the urine, because estrogen is secreted in increasing amounts by the developing follicles. Follicular development may also be monitored by ultrasound scan-

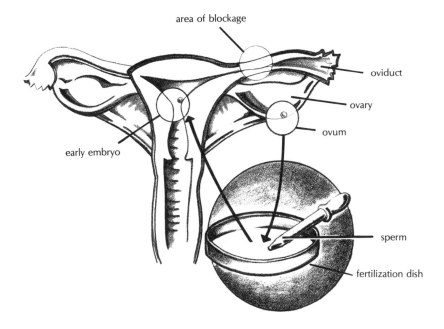

Figure 2
In Vitro Fertilization Technique. The egg is surgically removed from the ovary (thus bypassing the area of oviduct blockage) and combined with sperm in a glass dish. After fertilization has occurred, the developing embryo is implanted into the uterus.

ning techniques that enable the visualization of the ovaries and measurement of follicular size.

Once the follicles have attained the proper size—hopefully a few hours before ovulation—the eggs are ready to be recovered. The apparatus to recover eggs consists of an aspirating needle connected to a suction pump and a collecting chamber between the two. The needle is used to puncture the follicle. Then the egg, fluid, and some cumulus oophorus cells contained within the follicle are drawn into the collecting chamber.

The physician recovers the eggs from the ovaries with the aid of a laparoscope (Figure 3). A laparoscope is a fiberoptic device that illuminates an area and allows the area to be viewed at the same time. The laparoscope is inserted into the abdominal cavity through a one-inch incision made below the navel. The

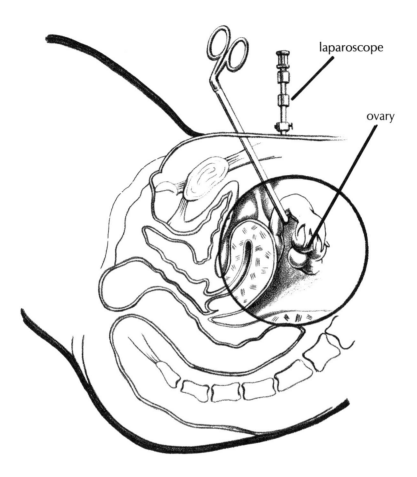

laparoscope

ovary

Figure 3
Ova Recovery from Human Ovary.

abdominal cavity is inflated with carbon dioxide to permit easy
viewing of the ovaries. Another small incision is made above the
pelvis so that the aspirating device can be guided to the follicles
with the laparoscope. Although less successful, eggs may also be
recovered with the aid of ultrasound scanning. In this method the
aspirating needle is placed in the abdominal cavity through a
small incision made in the vagina. The needle is then guided to
the follicle with ultrasound scanning.

After collection, eggs are removed from the collection chamber and transferred to culture medium containing some of the mother's blood serum. Here the eggs are maintained at constant temperature (98F), pH, and osmolarity. Depending on how ripe the eggs appear, sperm may be added to the eggs immediately or as much as a day later. In most instances, however, they are added after six hours.

Sperm are prepared for insemination by replacing the fluid part of the semen with artificial medium and holding them at room temperature for a few hours, which increases their fertility. In the case of subfertile men additional steps may be taken to concentrate and stimulate the motile sperm, as well as to remove the dead cells and debris.

After the preceding steps, several thousand sperm are placed in droplets of culture medium and eggs are transferred into the droplets. The eggs are examined after about 24 hours to determine the rate at which fertilization occurred, which under normal conditions will exceed 75 percent.

The fertilized egg, or embryo, is then cultured for an additional one to two days to assess whether cleavage and development are normal. The embryo should develop to four or eight cells before it is placed in the uterus. This stage should be attained within two or three days after fertilization.

The placement of the embryo in the uterus is the simplest part of the procedure. A catheter is directed through the cervix and into the uterus where the embryo is deposited. No anesthesia is required for the procedure.

What is done with any excess embryos? The answer to this question depends on the policy of the clinic involved and the wishes of the parents. Many clinics transfer three to four embryos at one time. The chances of pregnancy are increased as the number of embryos transferred is increased. The pregnancy rate can be more than doubled by increasing the number of embryos transferred from one to three. This gain in pregnancy rate is also accompanied by a slight increase in twinning rate. Therefore, the advantages of transferring more than three or four embryos at a time must be weighed against the increased risks that accompany triplet or quadruplet pregnancies.

The recent development of techniques to freeze human embryos has provided another option for excess embryos. Embryos may be frozen and stored in liquid nitrogen indefinitely. Whether or not pregnancy results from the first transfer, frozen embryos could be thawed and transferred at a future date. This would make it unnecessary for the couple to again endure the discomfort, stress, and expense of the entire in vitro fertilization procedures. If the parents did not care to use the embryos themselves, they could donate them to a couple who are unable to produce their own. In this case the embryos could remain frozen until the "adoptive" mother was physiologically prepared to receive them. Alternatively, the parents of the embryos may choose to donate them to a clinic or laboratory for scientific investigation.

Gamete Intrafallopian Transfer (GIFT)

An alternative approach to in vitro fertilization for treating infertility has recently been developed. The term *gamete* means "male or female sex cell," that is, a sperm or egg (ovum). Gamete intrafallopian transfer (GIFT) can be used for treating many of the same types of infertility as IVF, except the woman must have at least one functional oviduct. The major difference between the IVF and GIFT procedures is that with GIFT fertilization takes place within the oviduct. Eggs, recovered from follicles, and sperm are prepared for insemination similarly in both procedures. However, in the GIFT procedure eggs and sperm are introduced separately into the oviduct, via laparoscopy, and fertilization is allowed to take place naturally. The embryo then moves to the uterus for implantation as it would under natural conditions. Embryo transfer is not involved with the GIFT procedure.

How Successful Is Human IVF and Embryo Transfer?

Now that many clinics have been performing IVF for several years, sufficient data have been accumulated to evaluate the success of these procedures. Established clinics report that live births occur at a rate of from 10 to 30 percent of the number of IVF procedures performed. Note that these rates are expressed on the basis of the number of IVF procedures performed. As mentioned earlier, success rates for each procedure are improved when more than one embryo is transferred. Because many clinics routinely transfer up to four embryos during each procedure, the live birth rate per embryo transferred is approximately from 5 to 15 percent.

One may think that this success rate is very small, but it must be viewed in proper perspective. In normal human reproduction live births occur only at a rate of 35 percent of the eggs fertilized. More than 60 percent of the embryos conceived are lost by the sixth week of pregnancy. Furthermore, success rates for natural human reproduction are much lower when subfertile individuals or older women are involved.

The reason for the high rate of embryonic loss in normal human reproduction is not fully understood, but much of the loss appears to be associated with genetic defects. Pregnancy seems to be a screening process that prevents most genetically defective embryos from going to term. At the present time with only limited data available it is not possible to assess whether IVF procedures affect the incidence of genetic defects or embryonic loss. However, IVF procedures probably do not have a profound negative effect on these factors, because it would have been apparent in the thousands of births that have already resulted from the use of IVF.

Future Developments in Reproductive Biotechnology

Contraception. Contraceptives currently in use likely will become safer in the future, and entirely new approaches will be available. The hormonal approach to contraception will be further developed. The "morning after" pill currently available abroad will no doubt become available in the United States. Longer-acting hormonal contraceptives that do not require daily attention are undergoing development and testing. Some of these require only three or four injections a year. The Population Council in New York is developing a contraceptive designed to last five or more years. Small tubes made of silastic are filled with levonorgestrel, sealed, and inserted beneath the skin. The hormone is then released gradually over five years but in sufficient quantities to interfere with the menstrual cycle.

Other approaches to contraception in the future will likely involve immunology. Possibly a woman could be immunized against the zona pellucida that surrounds her egg. Studies with animals have shown that the presence of antibodies to the zona pellucida blocks fertilization from occurring. Another immunological approach may be to immunize a woman against pregnancy. A few days after the embryo is implanted in the uterus it produces a unique hormone called human chorionic gonadotropin (hCG), which signals the mother that she is pregnant. If a woman were immunized against hCG, her antibodies would inactivate the hormone and prevent it from signaling the brain that implantation occurred. As a result, pregnancy would not be sustained and menses would occur. Whether either of the immunological approaches to contraception would be reversible is not known at present.

Contraceptive approaches for men are likely to remain limited in the future. Use of the strategy of the female pill to block secretion of pituitary hormones has been successful in turning off sperm production by the testes. However, because male sex hormone secretion is diminished as well, libido is also lost. Recently, the discovery in China that gossypol, a derivative of cotton seed oil, was effective as a reversible male contraceptive was viewed with great interest. However, further investigation revealed that the incidence of serious side effects was unacceptably high. Thus far, chemical analogs of gossypol synthesized in the laboratory have not reduced the adverse effects. The epididymis has also been viewed as a possible target organ for contraceptives that would prevent sperm maturation. Although alpha-chlorohydrin reversibly blocks sperm maturation in rats, this family of chemicals is highly toxic in humans.

The concept of a reversible vasectomy has been considered for some time. Small valves could be placed in the vas deferens and opened or closed depending on whether one wished to be fertile or infertile. In the modern age of electronics one could envision the use of radiotelemetry to open and close the valve, not unlike the functioning of an electric garage door opener. However, the user would have to be careful that a neighbor did not operate his transmitter on the same frequency.

Sex selection. In mammals, the male is the heterogametic sex. This means that the male produces two types of gametes, one carrying the X sex chromosome, the other carrying the Y sex chromosome. All eggs contain only X sex chromosomes. At fertilization, when sperm and egg combine, the two possible normal combinations occurring in the embryo are XX or XY. Embryos with the XX combination develop into females, whereas those with the XY develop into males.

The development of technology to select the sex of the offspring has been focused in several areas. One strategy of sex selection is to separate X- and Y-bearing sperm and then inseminate with only the type of sperm that will produce the desired sex in the offspring. Research in this area has been conducted for more than 25 years, but little progress has been made. Although techniques have been developed to identify X- and Y-bearing sperm, no reliable and practical way has been developed to separate them, with two possible exceptions. One method for humans uses albumin, a blood protein, to increase the number of Y-bearing sperm. Limited results indicate that for this method 75 percent of the offspring are males. Another approach for human sperm separation uses column filtration. Some have claimed that 80 percent of the offspring resulting from this method are females.

A second strategy for developing technology to aid in controlling the sex of the offspring involves identifying the sex of the embryo and transferring only those embryos that are of the desired sex. This approach could be used in conjunction with IVF and embryo transfer. The sex of an embryo can be distinguished quite early in its development, because male embryos have a specific protein, the H-Y antigen, which is not present in females. Antibodies to the H-Y antigen are labeled with a fluorescent dye and are then incubated with the embryos. Under a fluorescent microscope, male embryos tagged with the antibody become fluorescent, while female embryos do not. This approach has been tested in laboratory animals and farm species and on the average is able to predict the sex of the embryo correctly about 80 percent of the time.

A third strategy for controlling the sex of the offspring involves testing at later stages of embryonic development. In this approach a few cells are removed from the embryo or placental membranes while it is in the uterus. These cells are tested for H-Y antigen or the presence of Y chromosomes. If the embryo turns out to be of a sex not desired, abortion can be induced.

Research currently conducted in the area of sex determination is primarily directed toward agricultural applications. The potential economic benefits to dairy farmers of having mostly female calves are staggering. Beef cattle ranchers would also benefit greatly if more male calves were produced. The economic incentive to animal agriculture is likely to continue to foster research on controlling the sex of the offspring until a practical method is developed.

Genetic evaluation, selection, and therapy. If there is a higher than average risk for a genetic defect to occur, parents are usually offered the opportunity for a genetic diagnosis of the fetus during the woman's pregnancy. Current procedures involve amniocentesis to sample the amniotic fluid surrounding the fetus at about 16 weeks gestation, during the second trimester of pregnancy. The amniotic fluid is analyzed biochemically, and the cells contained within the fluid are analyzed for chromosomal makeup. These analyses may determine if abnormalities indicative of a genetic defect exist. Fetal diagnosis earlier in pregnancy is currently being tested by sampling placental tissue at 8-12 weeks gestation. Although early results indicate that the technique is relatively safe, further study is needed to accurately assess the risks.

Given the rapid advances occurring in genetic engineering and analysis, possibly within 10 years the entire human genome will be mapped. The chromosomal location of many genetic traits and diseases will be known. Likely, further advances in the field of reproductive biotechnology will enable cell sampling of the early embryo during IVF procedures. Combining these two technologies in the future may make it possible to predict many of the genetic traits of IVF embryos before they are transferred to the uterus. The diagnosis of most genetic diseases in embryos should be possible while they are still in a culture dish. This technology will also raise other possibilities. In the future, parents with normal fertility could use IVF and genetic evaluation to select for transfer only those embryos that have the "right" eye color, height, or intelligence.

On the other hand, the identification of genetic defects in preimplantation embryos may provide an opportunity to correct the defects. Some progress has been made in the area of gene cloning and transfer of genes to mammalian embryos. Current techniques involve injection of genes into a pronucleus (nucleus of a fertilizing sex cell) or a zygote (fertilized egg), after fertilization but before the first cleavage (Figure 4). Genes coding for growth hormone have been injected into embryos of mice, rabbits, pigs, and sheep to produce "transgenic" animals. Except for sheep, genes for growth hormone were incorporated and expressed in some animals of all species tested. With future developments in this rapidly progressing field, technology will likely be developed someday to correct genetically defective embryos by replacing defective genes with normal genes.

A major goal of genetic engineering and biotechnology as it relates to animal agriculture is to improve domestic animals for the production of food and fiber. Efforts will likely be made to use genetic engineering to modify existing breeds of animals to

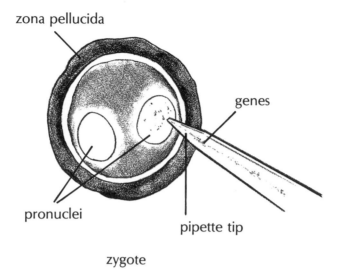

zona pellucida

genes

pronuclei

pipette tip

zygote

Figure 4
Gene Injection.

make them more resistant to disease, better adapted to regional climates, and more efficient in producing milk, meat, eggs, or fiber. This philosophy of improving domestic animals and plants to benefit humankind is deeply rooted in the history of agriculture. Over the centuries selective breeding in agriculture has dramatically changed the characteristics of domestic animals as compared to their wild ancestors. Time brings change. The tool of scientists to improve animal agriculture in the 21st century will be biotechnology. The development of biotechnology to improve the genetic characteristics of agriculturally important species may suggest and reinforce the technical feasibility of using biotechnology to alter the genetic characteristics of humankind.

Embryo Manipulation Techniques
Nonsurgical embryo recovery. A procedure routinely used in the embryo transfer industry for cattle involves the nonsurgical recovery of embryos. This technique enables genetically superior cows to produce many calves each year by transferring the recovered embryos to surrogate mothers. Donor cows are treated for

several days with hormones to stimulate follicular growth and superovulation. Artificial insemination is then used to fertilize the eggs. After allowing seven days for the embryos to move from the oviducts to uterus, the embryos are recovered. Nonsurgical embryo recovery is accomplished by "flushing" the uterus with a physiological medium. The medium is introduced into the uterus by a catheter that is passed through the cervix. The medium is then recovered from the uterus through the same catheter. This filling and emptying of the uterus is repeated several times. Embryos are carried out of the uterus as the fluid is emptied and are recovered by a filtering process. The number of embryos recovered by this procedure for cattle is variable and depends primarily on the ability of the cow to respond to the hormone treatment. At our facility at Pennsylvania State University, the number of recovered embryos has ranged from 0 to 40 per cow with an average of 8.

The nonsurgical embryo recovery technique has been performed with some success on a limited basis in women. However, the uses of the technique in women have yet to be fully defined. Some women may choose to become embryo "donors" for couples unable to produce their own. Couples may use this technique instead of IVF for genetic evaluation of the embryos, because it is less expensive and physically less traumatic. Those embryos having genetic defects or that are not of the "right" sex would not be returned to the uterus to complete embryonic development.

Another possible use for the nonsurgical embryo transfer technique might be for a career-oriented couple who wishes to delay having a family until after they had reached 40 years of age. A woman's fertility decreases with age, and the incidence of genetic defects in her eggs increases with age. To reduce the possibility of defects occurring in their children, embryos from a couple in their twenties could be collected and frozen for eventual transfer 15-20 years later. Of course, the possibility exists that during the interim the couple could be separated by divorce or death. What then is done with the embryos becomes a sticky problem and one that is likely to recur frequently with increased long-term frozen storage of human embryos.

Embryo splitting. Methods involving embryonic manipulation by the transfer of genes to alter the genetic characteristics of the offspring have already been outlined. However, reproduction can be controlled using other types of embryo manipulation. One ap-

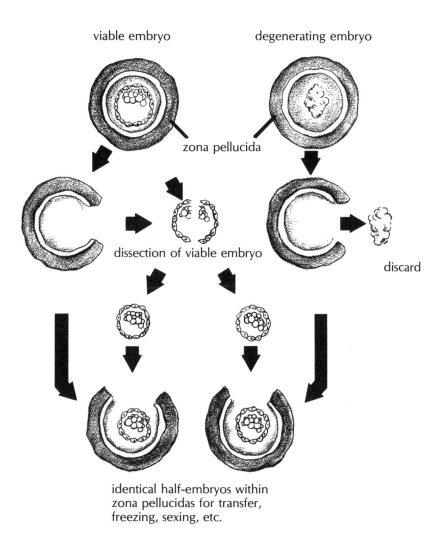

viable embryo   degenerating embryo

zona pellucida

dissection of viable embryo

discard

identical half-embryos within
zona pellucidas for transfer,
freezing, sexing, etc.

Figure 5
Embryo Splitting.

proach involves embryo "splitting" to produce genetically identical offspring. As embryos progress through early cleavage up to the 8-cell stage, each cell (blastomere) apparently has the potential to develop normally into a separate individual. Thus, an 8-cell embryo could theoretically be divided into eight separate embryos, which would develop into eight genetically identical individuals. In actual practice, the eight separated blastomeres must be combined with "carrier" cells that promote development but do not form part of the embryo. The resulting embryos are then transferred to surrogate mothers to complete development. Using the described embryo-splitting technique, five genetically identical lambs have been produced from one 8-cell sheep embryo.

As cleavage divisions of the embryo continue past the 8-cell stage, groups of blastomeres rather than single cells must be split from an embryo to produce several genetically identical individuals. Currently, the latter approach of embryo "splitting" is used commercially in the cattle industry to produce identical twins (Figure 5).

The availability of genetically identical animals is important for scientific research because animal-to-animal variation is reduced and fewer animals are needed to test hypotheses. Moreover, the use of genetically identical animals in research allows a distinction to be made between factors in an animal's response that are associated with genetics from those that are determined by the environment.

Cloning, selfing. Although the production of genetically identical individuals by embryo "splitting" is a type of "cloning," relatively few offspring can ultimately be produced. Techniques for larger-scale cloning have not been successfully developed for mammals, although they are still theoretically possible. One suggested approach for cloning involves removing the nucleus from an unfertilized egg and replacing it with the nucleus of a cell from a fully developed animal. When the embryo is activated to divide, the replacement nucleus would direct development and differentiation to produce an animal identical to that of the animal providing the nucleus. Because the animal providing the nucleus has millions more like it, repetition of this method could produce virtually limitless numbers of identical offspring.

The technical difficulty with the preceding cloning procedure is that although transfer of a cell nucleus from an adult animal to an embryo is possible, the embryo fails to differentiate. Only nuclei from embryonic cells (or tumor cells) appear to be capable of directing differentiation.

Nuclear transplantation procedures make it theoretically possible to combine genetic material from only one parent (selfing) or two parents of the same sex. For example, the female pronu-

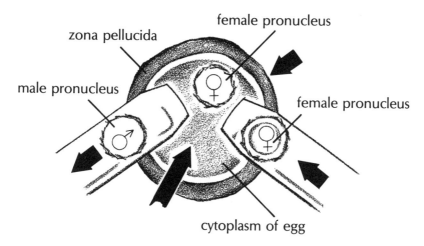

Figure 6
Transferring Nuclei in a Previously Fertilized Egg. Step 1: The male pronucleus is removed from the one-cell fertilized egg by pipette suction. Step 2: Using a second pipette, a female pronucleus is injected into the fertilized egg. Step 3: The two female pronuclei combine to form a female embryo.

cleus of one egg could be transferred to "fertilize" another egg (Figure 6). A female progeny would result with one or two mothers (depending on whether the eggs came from one or two females) and no father. Likewise, the female nucleus of an egg could be removed and replaced with two sperm, one bearing an X chromosome and the other a Y chromosome, to produce a male offspring with one or two fathers but no mother.

In more conventional thinking nuclear transfer may soon have a role in treating male infertility where men have very few sperm or sperm without motility and are unable to fertilize an egg. In these instances eggs from the spouse could be "fertilized" in vitro by microinjection of a sperm head.

Chimeras. If the cells from two different cleavage stage embryos are combined, they will form a single embryo called a chimera. This embryo technically has four parents (Figure 7). Chimeras are an excellent research tool to study regulatory processes and factors involved in embryonic differentiation, as well as gene expression. As the chimera undergoes differentiation, some of the cells from one embryo will develop into certain tis-

sheep blastomeres

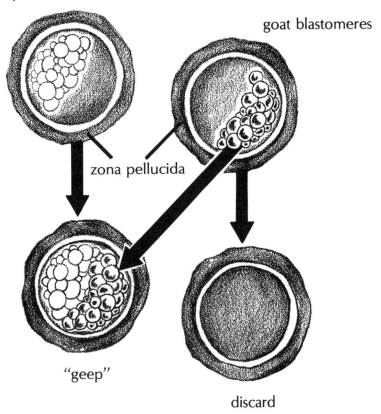

goat blastomeres

zona pellucida

"geep"

discard

Figure 7
Formation of a Chimera.

sues, while cells from the other embryo produce other tissues. The chimeric animal represents a composite of the genetic make-up of both embryos (genotypes); yet the genotypes are regionally distinct within tissues of the animal. An analogy that might describe this is mixing chocolate and vanilla cake batters together. If you mix them thoroughly, you get a light brown cake. If you fold one batter into the other, you get marble cake, or a chimera.

The word chimera is of Greek origin and was originally used

to describe a mythological fire-spouting monster with a lion's head, a goat's body, and a serpent's tail. Interspecies chimeras have been produced by mixing blastomeres of cleavage stage embryos from, among other things, goats and sheep. The resulting "geeps" are somewhat bizarre in appearance and display physical characteristics of both sheep and goats.

Combining embryos later in development at the trophoblast stage involves a somewhat different procedure. At the trophoblast stage some differentiation has taken place, so that the inner cell mass will become the fetus and the cells surrounding it will develop into the placenta. Chimeras may be made by combining two inner cell masses within one trophoblast.

The trophoblast stage embryo also has the potential to be used as a tool to permit the transfer of embryos of one species into a surrogate mother of another species. Normally, interspecies embryo transfers are only rarely successful, because the transferred embryo is recognized as foreign and is rejected by the surrogate. Nevertheless, transfer of endangered wildlife embryos to surrogates of related species could provide a way to rapidly increase the population of the endangered species. The technical feasibility of this approach has been demonstrated by removing the inner cell mass (embryoblast) from a trophoblast of a goat and replacing it with the inner cell mass of a sheep (Figure 8). If this trophoblast is placed in a goat surrogate, it will be accepted and the goat will give birth to a sheep. In simple terms the goat has been tricked into carrying a sheep embryo, because the trophoblast is "a sheep in goat's clothing."

Are interspecies surrogates a technical possibility for humans? One can only speculate. Current research with animals suggests that surrogate relationships are successful only between closely related species. Therefore, a cow surrogate would probably not accept a human embryo, even though the length of pregnancy is about the same for both. What about subhuman primates? Maybe.

One final thought on surrogates. Many women who have experienced pregnancy have jokingly said to me that they wished their husbands could "share" more of the experience. Theoretically, this is possible. In rare instances women may experience an ectopic pregnancy where the embryo escapes from the oviduct and is implanted outside of the reproductive system. Usually the embryo is implanted in the mesentaries supplying blood to the in-

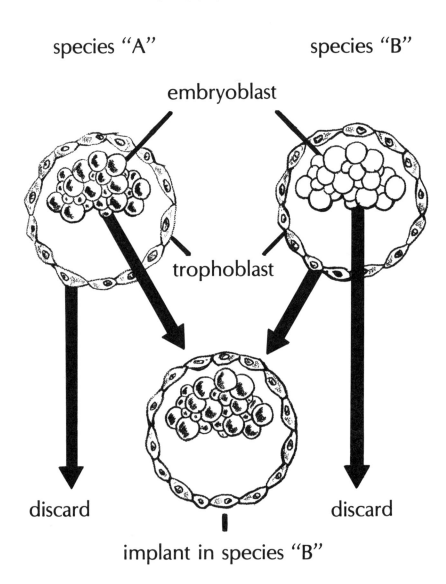

Figure 8
Preparation of Embryos for Interspecies Transfer.

testines. In the few instances where ectopic pregnancies continue to term, they require complex and high-risk surgery to remove the baby and placenta. Although no physician in his right mind would attempt it, possibly an embryo transferred by laparotomy to the intestines of a man could become implanted. Male "pregnancy" could be sustained by injection of progesterone and delivery accomplished surgically.

My goal in writing this chapter has been to present an overview of reproductive biotechnology that is either currently available or in experimental stages. As a scientist, I am concerned that some readers might react to this technology and its possible use with humans by calling for all research in this area to cease. Hopefully, the need to continue this research and technology development in most of these areas is apparent. This research is essential to increase our understanding of reproduction in order to treat human infertility and develop contraceptives. Research is also needed to improve production of food and fiber by domestic animals to meet the challenge of human population increases in the future. Although this research will undoubtedly produce new methods to manipulate the biological substance of life, we should not assume that procedures that are technically feasible with animals will be implemented with humans. Humans have the ability to make a choice. My hope is that we will assume this responsibility.

Questions for Reflection and Discussion
1. List three general methods used to prevent fertility. Do any of these methods present ethical dilemmas? Why?
2. Is artificial insemination by donor (AID) inherently adulterous or simply a medical procedure?
3. What should be done with the leftover embryos resulting from an in vitro fertilization attempt? Should they be discarded? All implanted into the mother? Frozen for a second implantation attempt if the first one is unsuccessful?
4. How do ethical considerations differ between in vitro fertilization (IVF) and intra-fallopian transfer (GIFT) procedures?
5. Is it unethical for a couple who desperately want a male child that they use some of the available sex-selection technologies? Why or why not?
6. Do you think human chimeras are a future possibility? What about interspecies surrogates? What should be the Christian's response to this technology?

7. Should reproductive research and reproductive technologies be limited for humans? For agricultural animals? In what ways can the Christian community act responsibly in this area?

For Further Reading

Austin, C. R., and R. V. Short, eds.
  1986 *Reproduction in Mammals 5: Manipulating Reproduction.* 2nd ed. New York: Cambridge University Press.

Evans, J. W., and A. Hollaender, eds.
  1986 *Genetic Engineering of Animals: An Agricultural Perspective.* New York: Plenum Press.

Fredericks, C. M., J. D. Paulson, and A. H. DeCherney
  1987 *Foundations of In Vitro Fertilization.* Washington: Hemisphere Publishing Corporation.

Gwatkin, R. B. L., ed.
  1986 *Developmental Biology.* Vol. 4, *Manipulation of Mammalian Development.* New York: Plenum Press.

Rossant, J., and R. A. Pedersen, eds.
  1986 *Experimental Approaches to Mammalian Embryonic Development.* New York: Cambridge University Press.

Chapter 6

Survey of Bioethical Systems

James F. Childress

James Childress
Ph.D. in religious studies, Yale University. Kyle Professor of Religious Studies and professor of medical education; chairman, department of religious studies, University of Virginia, Charlottesville, Virginia.

ENCOUNTERING A moral dilemma is not like stepping into a mud puddle or bumping into a wall. Instead, dilemmas are de-pendent on the moral principles and values we affirm. As a character in Tom Stoppard's play *Professional Foul* notes, "There would be no moral dilemmas if moral principles worked in straight lines and never crossed each other." But moral principles do cross each other and thus create dilemmas.

This point really impressed me during a trip to the People's Republic of China in 1979 with an interdisciplinary, interprofessional delegation that was exploring ethics and public policy in health care. We frequently asked our Chinese hosts how they handled some of our problems and dilemmas, such as an adult refusing life-sustaining treatment. The most common response was, "That's not a problem here; it simply doesn't exist here." Sometimes that response reflected a different stage of technological development; the Chinese lacked some of our technologies for sustaining life and intervening in other ways.

I want to emphasize, however, that technologies do not create moral dilemmas; they simply provide the arena for the conflict of moral principles and values. Most often the Chinese response seemed to reflect a different emphasis in principles and values. In particular, the Chinese were puzzled by our individualism and by our constant reference to such values as personal autonomy and privacy. One Chinese host said, "Well, in the rare event that an adult refused life-sustaining medical treatment against the wishes of the professionals and the family, he would simply be persuaded to change his mind."

In a similar way, a family reluctant to donate the organs of a dead or dying relative might be persuaded to donate those organs, or a woman pregnant for the second time might be persuaded to have an abortion. These persuasions posed no problem for Chinese health professionals, family members, and policymakers. However, to visitors who had been influenced by Western liberalism, such tactics seemed to approximate coercion, manipulation, and undue influence.

My point is a simple one: What is perceived as an ethical dilemma and how it will be resolved depends on the principles and values that are affirmed. We could eliminate many of our moral dilemmas in science, medicine, and health care, as well as elsewhere, if we were not blessed—or burdened—with the moral principles and values we affirm, both in our religious traditions and in our society.

Many of our images for debates about developments in the life sciences and technologies have been shaped by Aldous Huxley's negative utopia, *Brave New World*,[1] with its reproductive and genetic controls. His negative utopia offered a way to criticize several societal tendencies. However, for Huxley, developments in science and technology were *necessary* but *not sufficient* to create that negative utopia. By themselves they could not create the "Brave New World," for we as human beings can make choices for and against that world. Furthermore, Huxley did not simply reject the scientific and technological developments depicted in that world; he did not simply set an ideal of primitivism against such developments. For him there was a genuine dilemma, a real conflict of values, and he sought a third way (which he characterized in a paraphrase of the New Testament) of making technology serve humanity rather than having humanity serve technology.

Tiers or Levels of Moral Deliberation and Justification

The following chart presents several tiers or levels of moral deliberation and justification that are explicit or implicit in our responses to dilemmas. As long as it is not construed as offering a sharp dichotomy between facts and values, this chart may help us see several interactive factors that are involved in our deliberation about and justification of various actions. These tiers and levels are interrelated, not only in each column but across the columns. For example, an ethical theory might be grounded in theological, metaphysical, and anthropological convictions, and principles and rules will generate judgments about acts in situations as interpreted by agents.

Moral Beliefs	**Factual Beliefs**
Theory	Theological/Metaphysical Convictions
Principle(s)	Anthropological Convictions
Rules	Interpretation of the Situation
Particular Judgments	

The following case presents an illustration.[2] A father is reluctant to donate a kidney to try to save his dying five-year-old daughter who has had renal failure for three years, is not doing well on dialysis, and needs a kidney transplant. He has two kidneys, and after donating one, his remaining kidney could expand to perform roughly 80 to 90 percent of the capacity of both kidneys. He has a risk of 1 in 10,000 to 15,000 of dying from general anesthesia during the removal of the kidney. After receiving the information that he is a good match and that his kidney might save his daughter's life, the father decides that he does not want to donate.

Several factors influence this decision: (1) the father lacks the courage, (2) the daughter might be able to get a cadaver kidney, (3) her prognosis even after the transplantation of his donated kidney is uncertain, and (4) she has suffered a great deal already. However, the father asks the physician to tell the family that he is not a compatible donor, when in fact he is, because he worries that the truth would wreck the family. The physician decides that he cannot directly lie, but he finally agrees to say that "for medical reasons" the father cannot donate a kidney.

At least two problems exist in this case. One, did the father have an obligation to donate a kidney to his dying daughter? Second, did the physician act rightly in manipulating the truth in the circumstances? I will concentrate on the latter problem, which the physician viewed as a dilemma involving conflicting moral principles and values.

One possible approach to this case (and others) is to analyze the levels and tiers of moral deliberation and justification identified on the chart. The physician made a moral judgment that he should not lie, but he felt comfortable in saying that the father should not donate "for medical reasons." Those "reasons" could include psychological factors of the sort that prevented the father from donating.

On the one hand, regarding the judgment that he should not lie, the physician might well appeal to a rule, such as "It is wrong to lie." If asked to justify that rule, the physician might appeal to some more general principle, such as neighbor-love, or utility, or respect for persons.

On the other hand, he might ground his judgment against full disclosure in a rule of confidentiality—that is, the confidentiality of his relationship with the father took priority over full disclosure to family members—or in a principle of utility—the action would produce the greatest good for the greatest number. If asked for further justification, the physician might even offer a general theory about how all these elements—particular judgments, rules, and principles—fit together in a moral perspective.

Obviously, just focusing on moral beliefs is insufficient. As the right side of the chart suggests, the physician is applying moral theories, principles, and rules to actions in a situation; and he has to interpret that situation. This interpretation includes the medical facts and the probable benefits and harms of different courses of actions for the daughter, the father, and the family. For example, the father's concern about wrecking the family may be misplaced. Perhaps the family is already wrecked, in view of the evidence that many families fall apart under the severe pressures of caring for a seriously ill child over years. Perhaps no hope exists to salvage the family. The physician also has to consider whether transplanting a kidney from the father would offer the daughter a reasonable chance of benefit, and whether he should try to persuade the reluctant father to donate.

The physician's interpretation of the father's action may well depend on his fundamental beliefs about human nature. For example, if the physician believes that human beings are basically sinful, then he is likely to view the father's reluctance to donate a kidney as based on self-interest, rather than parental love.

With such an interpretation he might attempt to persuade the father to donate, perhaps even by putting pressure on him and by refusing to manipulate the truth to the family. For example, he might say to the father: "I won't help you; you will have to explain the situation to your wife." The physician's interpretation might also depend on theological or metaphysical beliefs—such as, beliefs about what God is doing in the world and in this particular family.

All of these convictions may be important in the physician's interpretation of the situation and hence in his judgment about what he ought to do in this dilemma.

The preceding points are relevant whether the physician is religious or secular in orientation. That is, even a secular person has fundamental convictions that parallel or are functionally equivalent to the religious person's theological convictions. Obviously, religious traditions often differ from secular traditions in the moral principles and rules that they accept, but major differences exist within as well as across each category. Major differences often occur in the interpretations and weights assigned to various principles, rather than in the principles affirmed. Differences also show up in divergent interpretations of a situation in relation to different convictions about human nature and ultimate reality. These visions of human nature and ultimate reality are often decisive in ethical decision making.

Types of Ethical Theories

Bioethics—or as I prefer biomedical ethics—involves the application of general ethical principles and rules to science, medicine, and health care. Biomedical ethics is not a separate discipline, and it does not involve separate principles and rules. Instead, bioethical systems mirror general ethical theories that differ in part according to the *aspects* of human action they emphasize. Aspects of human action include 1) agents, 2) acts, 3) ends, and 4) consequences.

Let us consider the physician's and the father's actions in our paradigm case from each of these aspects. First, look at the physician as an *agent* and consider what his actions display about his moral character. Do they display virtue or vice? Consider the same question about the father. Does his refusal indicate that he is a loving father or a coward? The father's remarks suggest both themes: he thought that his daughter had suffered enough, and he admitted that he lacked the courage to donate.

Second, consider the physician's *acts* and ask whether certain features exist that make them right or wrong independently of other aspects of the father's action. For example, if an act involves lying, that feature is relevant regardless of the agent's character or the ends and the consequences of his actions.

Or consider the father's *actions* in terms of a breach of the duty of faithfulness to his daughter to whom he made a commitment by contributing to her conception and birth and development.

Finally, consider the actions of both the physician and the father in terms of their *ends* and *consequences*. Possible ends and consequences include saving or losing the daughter's life and preserving or wrecking the family. All of these aspects are relevant in the assessment of the father's and the physician's actions in this case.

However, ethical theories emphasize different aspects of human actions. A *consequentialist* theory judges acts according to their consequences. A *teleological* theory judges acts according to their ends. A *deontological* theory holds that some intrinsic or inherent features of acts—not simply their ends or consequences— make them right or wrong. A *virtue* theory holds that acts are assessed according to what they display about the agent (e.g., the agent's virtue or vice).

Any of these types of ethical theories or bioethical systems may be theological or secular. Many theological-ethical systems are oriented to the virtues (e.g., love and humility) and are deontological in that they view some acts as right or wrong regardless of consequences. Even these theological-ethical systems include ends and consequences of action. Any adequate system must include all of the aspects of human action.

The question remains, Which aspect should be primary and which secondary?

Major Ethical Principles and Rules

Significant, although by no means universal, agreement exists across traditions about several major ethical principles and rules. Much of the moral debate focuses on their *foundations* (e.g., divine revelation or natural law) and on their *implications* (e.g., what they imply for particular cases and which should have priority when they conflict), rather than on the principles and rules themselves. Several major principles and rules can be derived from various theological and secular systems and include:[3]

1. Do no harm (nonmaleficence)
2. Benefit others (beneficence)
3. Balance benefits and harms (proportionality or utility)
4. Respect persons (autonomy)
5. Distribute benefits and harms justly (justice)
6. Derivative rules: truthfulness, privacy, confidentiality, fidelity

Some of these principles and rules focus more on ends and consequences (e.g., utility); others depend more on inherent or intrinsic features of acts (e.g., respect for persons and truthfulness). All of them have correlative virtues.

I will briefly consider the content of these principles and rules before examining their applications in biomedical ethics. First, a fundamental principle that is widely recognized in our social life as well as in biomedical ethics is "do no harm." From this principle of nonmaleficence one can derive various rules such as the prohibition against killing people or treating them cruelly. This general principle appears in the Hippocratic tradition as "first of all, or at least, do no harm."

However, we would not be very interested in science, medicine, or health care if its only principle were that of nonmaleficence, because we could avoid harm from professionals and others by avoiding those relationships. We seek those relationships because of a second principle—beneficence or benefiting others. For example, the physician's commitment to our welfare, in conjunction with acquired knowledge and skills to promote our welfare, is the reason we seek medical attention.

Because the world is a very messy place, benefits without harms are impossible. Therefore, we are driven in the third place to a principle to balance benefits and harms. This third principle may be called proportionality or utility, and it focuses mainly, but not entirely, on the kinds of consequences that flow from actions.

The next two principles emphasize features of actions that are not reducible to their consequences: respect for persons and distributive justice. Within the Judeo-Christian tradition, the

[handwritten margin note: Prolonging death — is also cruelty?]

principle of respect for persons involves respecting persons as embodied; they are creatures who have been created in the image of God and who have the capacity for self-transcendence. Respecting persons means in part respecting their autonomous choices. But this principle will be inadequate by itself or even in conjunction with the others already identified, for it is also necessary to ask how benefits and harms will be distributed: Who will gain the benefits and who will bear the harms, costs, and burdens? These are questions of distributive justice. Finally, there are several derivative rules about truthfulness, privacy, confidentiality, and fidelity.

These principles and rules provide an ethical framework that can be recognized and appreciated, if not fully accepted, across several religious and secular traditions. However, debates will continue, not only about the foundations of these principles and rules, but also about their weight and meaning in relation to problems. For example, regarding their weight, if a genuine ethical dilemma exists with two or more principles crossing each other, which should have priority? And regarding their meaning, what will count as harms and benefits or as disrespect for persons?

Thus, even if consensus exists about these principles and rules, vigorous debate will continue about what they imply for actions and about which should take precedence in conflicts.

The Abortion Debate

In this brief survey I can only sketch how these different principles and rules are applied in controversial areas. As an example in application, I will focus on the debate about abortion. The following chart (Figure 1) identifies several of the major ethical options regarding judgments about acts (one's own or others'), judgments about appropriate laws, and judgments about public policies of allocation of funds for abortion.

Figure 1. Some Major Positions in the Abortion Debate

	Judgments About Acts	Judgments About Laws	Judgments About Allocation of Funds
I.	No moral issue. Fetus viewed as tissue.	Abortion on demand. Regulate for health of mother.	Accepts allocation for abortions as for other medical procedures.
II.	Abortion as a moral problem; needs justification because of potential human life, but can be justified.	May argue for laws recognizing special cases (e.g., therapeutic abortions or abortions after rape) or permitting abortions depending on time (e.g., first or second trimester). May suggest abortions on demand but also regulate for health of mother.	May argue for funding on grounds of fairness or equality.
III.	Abortion is equivalent to homicide because an innocent human life is taken.	Absolute prohibition but may allow some "therapeutic abortions"—not considered as abortions because of rule of double effect.	Opposes the use of public funds for abortion in order to save more lives and to avoid implication in immorality.
IV.	Fetus is potential human. Woman is human: beneficence Precept:	Law irrelevant · Woman/couple choice in consult. & health care provider	Funds allocation same as #1

If we start with judgments about acts, different judgments will usually presuppose different views of the status of the fetus. Hence, those judgments will depend ultimately on theological, metaphysical, and anthropological convictions. These convictions are vitally important in the way we apply the ethical principles about benefiting and not harming others, about respecting them, and about treating them justly.

The first position on judgments about acts of abortion denies that abortion raises any special moral issues, because the fetus is only tissue, comparable to an appendix. Hence, any moral issues that are raised by abortion are identical to those raised by any other medical procedure in response to human needs and desires—for instance, is the procedure safe and has the patient given her voluntary, informed consent? This position can be found in the writings of Joseph Fletcher, among others.

The second position views abortion as a moral problem in itself. Abortion is a moral problem because the fetus is at least a potential human being. Thus, the relevant moral principles have to be applied to actions involving life or death of a potential human being. This application generates a moral problem. For this second position, abortion requires justification, but it can sometimes be justified when principles conflict. In paraphrasing St. Augustine's comments on war, proponents of this position believe there can be "just and mournful" abortions. They differ about the conditions that have to be met to justify such abortions. Some would limit the circumstances to protection of the pregnant woman's life and health. Others would include rape and incest. Some would also recognize different stages of fetal development, justifying abortion more easily during the first trimester.

In the third position, fetal life is full human life from the moment of conception, and the same moral principles apply to judgments about actions that result in fetal death as to judgments about actions that result in the death of adults. Thus, for this position, which is affirmed by official Roman Catholic teachings and by various Protestant groups, abortion is always wrong as the direct taking of innocent human life. The official Roman Catholic position does accept what some traditions would call "abortions" in cases of removal of a cancerous uterus of a pregnant woman or an ectopic pregnancy. However, in those cases the fetal deaths are viewed as the indirect and unintended results of legitimate medical procedures under the rule of double effect.

The major positions in the abortion debate have primarily focused on what the principle of nonmaleficence implies for actions that result in death to the fetus, variously viewed as tissue, as potential human life, and as full human life. In the past fifteen years, however, feminists have offered another perspective on the abortion debate by suggesting that moral judgments about abortion should not rest only on the principle of nonmaleficence in conjunction with convictions about the status of the fetus. Rather, they contend, the principle of beneficence more fittingly characterizes the relationship between the pregnant woman and the fetus. In order to make their point, philosophers such as Judith Jarvis Thomson and Susan Nicholson have even granted for purposes of argument that the fetus is a human being from the moment of conception, but then they have asked what obligations of beneficence the pregnant woman has to the fetus as a human being.

First, on what grounds is the pregnant woman obligated to act beneficently toward the fetus by providing bodily life support? Even though we have obligations of beneficence to strangers, most of our obligations of beneficence rest on our previous commitments, promises, or assumption of roles. From this perspective, the woman who is pregnant as a result of rape, incest, deception, or exploitation may have no obligation, or only a limited obligation, of beneficence to the fetus.

Second, how far is the pregnant woman obligated to go in bearing risks, costs, and burdens to provide bodily life support to the fetus, even when the obligation of beneficence is based on consensual sexual activity? Our obligations of nonmaleficence may require that we assume major risks in order not to harm others. However, our obligations of beneficence usually do not require such risk-taking. Thus, many have argued, the pregnant woman is not obligated to bear major risks, costs, and burdens in order to save the fetus. Even though we might praise her if she chooses to do so, we should not blame her if she fails to do so.

Feminists have also asked us to consider whether we consistently make similar judgments about cases of bodily life support that are relatively similar in the *degree of voluntariness* of the relationship and in the *degree of risk* to the agent of beneficence. Do we, they ask, make the same judgments about the pregnant woman's obligation of beneficence to provide bodily life support to the fetus and about the father's obligation of beneficence to provide bodily life support by donating a kidney to his dying daughter (as in the case discussed earlier)?

Of course, in the Christian tradition, agape may impose strong obligations in both cases. Even in the Christian tradition, however, there has also been a tendency, detected by the feminist hermeneutics of suspicion, to impose differential obligations of beneficence, including self-sacrifice, on women. This occurs even if situations are very similar as they are in the case of the woman who is pregnant after consensual sexual intercourse and the case of the father who is a potential kidney donor. Feminists argue that the relationship of beneficence in both cases rests on the same voluntary acts and that the risks of providing bodily life support are comparable.

Moral judgments about individuals' acts of abortion (the left-hand column on Figure 1) do not necessarily imply particular judgments about laws and about public policies regarding the allocation of funds for abortions. However, there is a rough correlation. For the first position, which views abortion as raising no special moral issues, the only appropriate legislation would be designed to protect maternal health, not to protect the fetus, which has no moral standing because it is only tissue. Furthermore, public policies should allocate funds for abortions as for other medical procedures, because nothing is special or morally significant about abortions themselves.

Proponents of the second position view abortion as a moral problem but also as sometimes justifiable. These persons prefer any one of a wide range of possible options regarding legislation and public policy. Some support abortion on demand, while others defend laws that limit abortions to certain circumstances (e.g., rape, incest, or threats to maternal health) or stages of fetal development (e.g., the first trimester). Some defenders of the second position may also accept other regulations of abortion, for example, by requiring counseling and a waiting period. The second position often supports funding of abortion on grounds of fairness and equality for poor women.

The third position, which views abortion as homicide, tends to support restrictive and even prohibitive abortion laws. Proponents of this position recognize exceptions only in cases of threats to maternal health and perhaps in cases of rape or incest. This position generally opposes the use of public funds to support abortions in order to reduce the number of fetal (i.e., human) deaths and in order to avoid complicity in moral evil.

In general, the feminist position, which accepts the humanity of the fetus (at least for purposes of argument) but construes the pregnant woman's obligations under the principle of beneficence rather than the principle of nonmaleficence, supports laws and policies defended by the first position on the abortion chart, rather than those defended by the second and third positions.

[handwritten margin note: statement to avoid copout placement in Figure 1.]

However, considerable variety exists in this position.

In the movement from judgments about individual acts of abortion to judgments about laws or public policies, religious communities face major questions about their relations to the world. In particular, religious communities accepting the third position, or strong versions of the second position, have to consider when it is appropriate to seek state action through the criminal law or through the denial of public funds to prevent what they consider to be moral evil, as in the case of (some) abortions. In a pluralistic society it is important to consider the source of moral disagreement about abortions, as well as other matters. Religious communities must determine whether that disagreement stems from divergent theological, metaphysical, or anthropological convictions (e.g., about the status of the fetus) or from divergent moral principles and rules, including their meanings and weights.

Whatever the source of the disagreement over abortion, there is, I believe, only a dim prospect that a moral consensus will emerge. Religious communities will be compelled to continue to deliberate about their appropriate responses in these disputes about abortion in a pluralistic society.

Questions for Reflection and Discussion
1. Identify the four tiers of moral deliberations.
2. Which ethical theory category best fits your actions?
3. Identify the six major ethical principles common to many ethical theories. Can you prioritize this list?
4. In considering the diagram in Figure 1, which abortion position is most compatible with your view? What do you find objectionable in the alternate positions?
5. Under what circumstances, if any, do you find abortion clearly acceptable? Clearly unacceptable?

For Further Reading
Hauerwas, Stanley
1986 *Suffering Presence.* Notre Dame, Ind.: University of Notre Dame Press.
Lammers, Stephen E., and Allen Verhey
1987 *On Moral Medicine: Theological Perspectives on Medical Ethics.* Grand Rapids, Michigan: Eerdmans Publishing Co.

Chapter 7

Christian Communities and Biomedical Technologies

L. Gregory Jones

Gregory Jones
Ph.D. in theology and ethics, Duke University. Assistant professor of theology, Loyola College, Baltimore, Maryland.

MOST OF THE TIME when we talk about ethics in general, and biomedical issues in particular, we assume that the most important question is deciding what I, or—from a communitarian perspective—we, should do. After all, ethics is said to be about right actions, so the focus of our deliberations is on whether we should use a deontological sense of duty (i.e., a system of unalterable rules) or a utilitarian calculus (i.e., a system based on evaluating consequences) in deciding what we should do.

Given this assumption that we ought to focus only on decisions, it will perhaps strike you as strange that I begin by telling you not about decisions, but about how a tribe in Africa understands themselves and their world.[1] The tribe is called the Nuer. In many ways they are very gentle, good people who generally live in peace with each other and with their neighbors. However, they have the view that any child born obviously retarded or deformed is not a Nuer. Instead, the child is a hippopotamus. An elaborate mythology underwrites the belief that such a child is actually a hippopotamus. The mythology specifies the place and responsibilities of the various kinds of animals in the world. The Nuer feel strongly that different kinds best care for their own. So a deformed child is placed in the river to be cared for by its own kind—the hippopotamus. Now we may want to call this euthanasia, or even murder, but the Nuer think they are doing the only moral thing they can do if they are to act responsibly. For them a moral issue would emerge only if there was a parent who was so attached to this "hippopotamus" that he or she wanted to keep it.

Such a situation reminds us that we do not come to situations, issues, and actions *de novo*. Rather, we come with a distinctive way of seeing and describing our lives and the world, a way learned in particular communities as part of an ongoing tradition. Hence, when presented with a case such as the Nuer, it appears odd that we spend so much of our time dealing with what we pretend are "straightforward cases and issues." Instead we ought to attend to the logically prior—and, I will suggest, in many ways more important—task of understanding how we come to describe the issues in this way, rather than that.

Thus, it is in the context of the community—or more precisely, communities—that we learn, or fail to learn, what issues are deemed important, how they should be described, and finally what should be done about them. In order to explain why this is the case, I will divide my comments into two sections. In the first, I will describe the place of communities in our moral thinking, and specifically the place of Christian communities. In the second, I will attempt to describe how the narrative of the Christian tradition provides a distinctive perspective on particular biomedical issues related to the unborn.

Traditional Communities and Moral Reasoning

The place we need to begin is with the notion of community. These days, partly as a result of a perceived overemphasis on individualism in American culture, we are beginning to hear calls for a return to community, for a return to "communitarian values." So we see the enormous popularity of Robert Bellah and company's *Habits of the Heart: Individualism and Commitment in American Life*.[2] I certainly do not want to discount any effort to overcome the individualism that marks so much of Western—and particularly American—culture. But I distrust abstract appeals to "community" and "communitarian values" because they attempt to talk about *the* community as it is opposed to *the* individual.

It is not just "community" that is important, but the kind of communities that are at stake. They are communities that are the bearers of a tradition and possess a language to express the history of that tradition. They are communities determined to pass on to new generations the tradition and its distinctive ways of seeing the world because they are convinced that their vision is truthful.

As there are different and competing traditions of understanding and reasoning—not only across religions, but also between particular religions and secular understandings—so also there will be differences between communities. Also remember, just as differences between communities and across traditions make conversation necessary, similarities and overlaps make such conversation possible.

Before we can undertake conversation across traditions, we must understand the distinctive perspectives of the communities of which we are a part. I refer to communities in the plural out of the recognition that we all participate in diverse communities, not all of which are bearers of the same tradition. For example, those of us who are Americans are involved in many of the practices of American life. Those of us who are Christians are also involved in the practices of Christian life.

The problem does not necessarily lie in the fact that we participate in such diverse communities and traditions; inevitably we will do so. The problem occurs when we are unaware of the tensions between the traditions so that we allow other languages and ways of seeing the world to determine and shape our moral discourse, rather than having it shaped by our commitment to the God of Jesus Christ.

Therefore, we see the importance of being "baptized" into Christ, of being located in the tradition defined by the life, death, and resurrection of Jesus of Nazareth. To be baptized is to be given a new identity. The significance of this new identity is identified by Alasdair MacIntyre when he suggests that "I can only answer the question 'What am I to do?' if I can answer the prior question 'Of what story or stories do I find myself a part?'"[3]

Even so, baptism is at once a sacramental act of the church conferring upon us a new identity *and* an ongoing process of learning to "live into that baptism," of responding in newness of life through discipleship. Christian communities are essential, for each person needs the resources of other Christians as she continually "unlearns" the ways of those traditions that previously defined her identity and "learns" to see herself and the world Christianly.

The shared practices of Christian communities and continual encounters with biblical texts in community under the guidance of the Holy Spirit create such "unlearning" and "learning." As new situations and cultural contexts continually present new challenges to our vision and discipleship, we seek to discern how God would have us to live and what judgments God would have us to make.

So it is that Christian thinking about moral issues in general, and biomedical issues in particular, must be shaped by ongoing communal processes of discernment. And for that discernment, we need the continuity of traditions that enable the development and recovery of skills, habits, and language so we can "unlearn" the ways of the world and gradually—sometimes slowly, painfully, laboriously—learn the ways of Jesus.

I have identified the importance of communities for discipleship and for understanding how we reason and make moral judgments, because no area in our culture exists where the issues are so sharply posed as in our thinking about biomedical issues. So I turn now to an exploration of how Christian communities provide a distinctive perspective on biomedical technologies and the unborn.

Unlearning and Learning About Persons in Christian Communities

The discussion about the unborn in bioethics is usually couched in language more at home in the tradition of political liberalism than in the Christian tradition. For example, the question of abortion is frequently framed in the language of rights: Which has precedence, the rights of the pregnant woman or the rights of the fetus? As the result of trying to answer that first question, other questions attain prominence: When does human life begin? At what point does the fetus become a "person"?

That debates rage interminably about such issues reflects the moral chaos of American society. H. Tristram Engelhardt, one of the more prominent of America's ethicists concerned with biomedical questions, has attempted to provide an answer to the question of "personhood" in rigorously secular terms, terms in which he thinks as Americans we should all give our assent. In an attempt to find a solution to American "pluralism," Engelhardt relies on an understanding of the person that is "self-conscious, rational, free to choose, and in possession of a sense of moral concern."[4] Many of us Christians, as well as non-Christians, use this description when we are asked what it means to be a person. Engelhardt is giving conceptual muscle to the intuitions many of us unreflectively share.

I want to make two initial comments about Engelhardt's understanding of personhood. First, it is troubling to begin reflecting about those who are excluded from being persons. Infants (and of course fetuses), the severely senile and mentally handicapped, severely brain-damaged—all these groups are comprised of individuals who are not persons in Engelhardt's definition. Engelhardt acknowledges that we may give reasons for wanting to treat them as persons; but they are not, strictly speaking, to be considered "persons."

My second comment concerns how this understanding alters the shape of discussion about biomedical issues. Using his conception of personhood, Engelhardt claims that abortion is not a "serious moral issue"[5] and that infanticide is only questionably to be considered as immoral. Because infanticide has been practiced in diverse cultures, Engelhardt concludes that

> the moral fabric does not depend on condemning infanticide. The fabric seems to be quite able to sustain a highly advanced and intricate culture with notions of generosity and magnanimity, while not condemning the killing of newborns in general or deformed neonates in particular. As a result, it is difficult to mount a plausible, nonculturally biased, strong argument against infanticide. The best that can be produced is a speculative, circumstantial argument.[6]

Although many may agree that abortion should not be a serious moral issue, talk of the legitimacy of infanticide still seems to offend even rabid secularists—although they are not certain why.

Though many will not share Engelhardt's conclusions about abortion and infanticide, his conclusions seem to follow from his conception of personhood. That conception of personhood, I suggest, is fundamentally at odds with central Christian convictions. But that gets obscured because Christians too often allow debates about biomedical issues to be framed by people like Engelhardt and the conceptions of personhood that they presuppose.

Thus, in dealing with biomedical issues Christian communities need to enable the "unlearning" of these alien conceptions of personhood and the "learning" of Christian convictions. To do so, we need to understand how language about "personhood" relates to Christian communities and descriptions of Christian discipleship. Two examples, one drawn from Scripture and the other from the early church, will help to provide an outline for our thinking.

The first example is the parable of the Good Samaritan. Oliver O'Donovan has suggested that the account of "neighborhood" in this parable provides important resources for thinking about what it means to be a person.[7] In the first place the term *person* is clearly intended to be a universal term in the same sense that Jesus claimed about *neighbor*. Neither term can legitimately be used to exclude certain classes of human beings. That is perhaps the most obvious and least objectionable point.

In the second place "Jesus' story shows *how* we identify our neighbor; from our active engagement with him in caring for him, sympathizing with him, protecting him."[8] So, likewise, "we can recognize someone as a person only from a stance of *prior moral commitment* to treat him or her as a person, since the question of what constitutes a person can never be answered speculatively."[9] Thus, it is in and through our active engagement with another human being that we identify her as a person. We treat the other as a person and thus prove the other's personhood.

In the third place Jesus' story tells how a Jew learned who his neighbor was. The Jew did not learn to care for the Samaritan in need. Rather, he learned to be cared for in his need by the Samaritan. So, O'Donovan remarks, "We know someone as a person as that person is disclosed in his or her personal relations to us, that is, as we know ourselves to be not simply the subject of our own attention to the other, but to be the object of the other's attention to us."[10] This illustrates a reciprocal relationship. We do not simply confer personhood on another by how we treat her, but we *discover* her personhood in her personal relations with us.

What this suggests to the Christian, therefore, is that no "criteria of personhood" exist independently of, or prior to, *personal engagement.*[11] We do not know who persons are by *observing* their capacity for relationship. We know them *in* relationship, which is to say that we must abandon the "observer's" stance and commit ourselves to treating them *as* persons.

I will return to this account and its import for our thinking about biomedical technologies in a moment. Before doing so, however, I want to develop a second example, drawn from a lecture by James Tunstead Burtchaell, which illustrates how the early church actually embodied such an understanding of personhood. The early Christians shared with their Jewish heritage a commitment to reaching out to the alien and the poor, to the widow and the orphan. In addition, the new Christian faith set four prophetic imperatives before those who would live in the Spirit and fire of Christ, four disconcerting duties that would distance them from Jews and Romans alike.[12] In addition to the alien, they were commanded to love their enemies. In addition to concern for the poor, they were commanded to acknowledge slaves and masters as brothers and sisters in the Lord. In addition to concern for the widow, husbands and wives were to pledge themselves to equal fidelity.

The fourth imperative was that in addition to those children orphaned by their parents' deaths, they were to protect the infant—unborn or newborn. This imperative is expressed in *The Didache, The Instruction of the Twelve Apostles* (the oldest Christian document we possess outside the New Testament):

> You shall not commit murder; you shall not commit adultery; you shall not prey upon boys; you shall not fornicate; you shall not deal in magic; you shall not practice sorcery; *you shall not murder a child by abortion, or kill a newborn*; you shall not covet your neighbor's goods. You shall not break your oath; you shall not give perjured evidence; you shall not speak damagingly of others; you shall not bear a grudge.[13]

In the light of such convictions the early Christians were understandably offended when antagonists spread rumors that Christians killed infants to obtain blood for their Eucharistic rites. The Christians' concern for newborn and unborn infants in a society where people were willing to destroy the young by choice was precisely the contrast that set Christians apart from the pagans. Minucius Felix, a Roman attorney of African origin, draws the contrast sharply:

> There is a man I should now like to address, and that is the one who claims, or believes, that our initiations take place by means of the slaughter and blood of a baby. Do you think it possible to inflict fatal wounds on a baby so tender and tiny? That there could be anyone who

would butcher a newborn babe, hardly yet a human being, who would shed and drain its blood? The only person capable of believing this is one capable of actually perpetrating it. And, in fact, it is a practice of yours, I observe, to expose your own children to birds and wild beasts, or at times to smother and strangle them—a pitiful way to die; and there are women who swallow drugs to stifle in their womb the beginnings of a [person] on the way—committing infanticide even before they give birth to their infant.[14]

The testimony of other early Christians could be cited, but I think the point has been made. As Burtchaell states, there is a clear sense that the destruction of the child, unborn or newborn, is infamy for those who follow Christ.[15]

Three comments about the early church's witness on these matters need to be made. First, their convictions about abortion and infanticide did not represent an isolated doctrine. They were integral to the life of discipleship just as much as the injunctions about adultery, greed, and theft. These convictions were part of an integrated set of beliefs about the need to protect those who are most vulnerable to being subject to *inhuman* treatment: the slave, the enemy, the wife, and the newborn or unborn infant.

Second, the early church's witness reflects the embodiment of the kinds of convictions I described above with reference to the Good Samaritan. The four categories described were those who—in varying degrees and for varying reasons—were denied the status of "person" by the wider society. The Christians discovered the personhood of the humans who comprised these groups through their personal engagement with them, by treating these others *as* persons, by committing themselves to being *in* relationship with them.

Third, Engelhardt's vision of biomedical ethics is far from the early Christians' convictions about who constitutes a person. Modern language about "persons" originally had a humane purpose. Christian communities had failed to embody their own best insights and had refused to treat enemies, women, slaves, and others as persons. However, definitions of "persons" such as Engelhardt's no longer extend consideration; they restrict it and unfairly exclude people.

Whereas Engelhardt thinks that abortion is not a serious moral issue and that infanticide is only a culturally variant one, the early Christians saw these as destroying our responsibility to those in need of our protection and care. What underlies these widely divergent perspectives about the treatment of the unborn and newborn is not so much their different cultural settings as their different beliefs about who is a person. As Burtchaell's analysis suggests, the early Christians refused to speculate about or define what constitutes a person; they simply *showed* personhood through their engagement with others. Christians need to repent of those examples in our history in which we failed to *show* such concern to others. The solution is not to allow definitions of personhood to control our discipleship, but to recapture our own best insights in care for others, particularly the vulnerable.

These examples from Scripture and the early church teach us that Christian communities are essential to our thinking about biomedical issues. It is by being located in such communities, which are bearers of the Christian tradition, that we are enabled to "unlearn" our speculative "criteria of personhood" that lead us into interminable quandaries and also to "learn" that we discover "persons" by being in relationship with them.

Christian communities are essential for an even more important reason; that is, they change the terms in which the issues are framed. In Christian communities the important questions are no longer (1) the rights of the mother versus the rights of the fetus, (2) when life begins, or (3) who is a person. Rather, the important question becomes what kind of community we must be to welcome new life as a gift from God, especially when tragic and complex circumstances surround it.

I am aware that what I have said does not resolve any of the complex biomedical issues that we face. But it does change the focus of the conversation and thereby enables us to see the issues in a new light. To see how this is the case, I want to explore briefly the distinctive perspective of Christian communities on two issues: severely deformed infants and abortion.

One of the results of advances in medical technologies is that now it is possible to keep an ever increasing number of severely deformed infants alive through intervention. Dilemmas arise over whether medical intervention is optional or necessary. In particular, what attitude should we have toward these infants? In many cases respected medical ethicists argue that it is immoral to keep the child alive and acceptable to assist in its death because the child has no worth. This is not dissimilar to the logic of Engelhardt's position. In other words, the child's life is not worth living.

I want to suggest, adopting a distinction of David Kelsey's, that the idea of worth contains two different questions: whether this life is worth living, and whether this life is good or intrinsically valuable.[16] Often these two questions are conflated by saying that if life is not worth living, then by killing that life you are not destroying anything of value.

Christians ought to resist the conflation of the two different questions. Christians claim that life is good because fundamentally it is a gift from God, and hence our presumption is that such life is worthy of respect. We are to embody that conviction by relating to the infant *as* a person, by discovering the irreplaceable significance which that life represents. But saying that this life is good, and that the infant is to be treated as a person, does not necessarily mean that the life is worth living. It is quite conceivable that a decision to allow such an infant to die might, given the dehumanizing conditions of that life, be an expression of our relationship and a discovery of that infant's personhood and not a denial of it.

Such decisions can be made only on a case-by-case basis. The complexity of the cases provides us with a threefold reminder. First, the responsibility for keeping the distinctions between personhood and whether a life is worth living lies with all those concerned with the infant's life, including the medical personnel and Christian communities. Second, the process of discerning what should be done calls for communal discernment under the guidance of the Holy Spirit. Third, if a decision is made to allow the infant to die, the decision should be accompanied by a profound sense of loss; a person has died. The life may not have been worth living, but it was good because it was a gift from God. Christian communities should respond accordingly.

Because of the kind of communities we are called to be and because of the God to whom we witness, we are called to make decisions about treatment of severely deformed infants in these ways. We are called to develop similar responses when confronting the issue of abortion. The public policy issues about abortion have become polarized into "pro-life" or "pro-choice" positions. Even the most casual observer can see that the arguments pass by each other like ships in the night.

When framed within the context of Christian communities, however, both positions are rendered more intelligible and discovered to be the wrong ways of framing the issues. Christian communities share with so-called "pro-life" groups the conviction that we are to treat the fetus as a person, preparing to welcome that life with joy—even when it has been conceived in less than ideal circumstances. But unlike many pro-lifers, we recognize that treating the fetus as a person carries with it responsibilities that extend beyond birth.

Conversely, Christian communities share with so-called "pro-choice" groups the conviction that a person facing an abortion is actually faced with two decisions: the decision whether to abort or not and the decision to make good on that decision by living with it. Hence, Christian communities must be concerned to treat not only the fetus as a person, but also the parents as persons, as well. Hopefully, we can provide the kinds of communities and social settings that will enable such persons to see options other than abortion; after all, Christian faith reminds us that parenting is a vocation that belongs to the whole community.

Even so, one of the realities of our world is that when a person is faced with the decision of abortion, she may be isolated from communities and placed in a situation with so few options that an abortion may be tragically necessary. But unlike many pro-choicers, we refuse to see such choices as good. Even in a case where an abortion may be tragically permissible, it should be accompanied by a profound sense of loss. A person has died. Christian communities should respond accordingly.

We ought not think about abortion by allowing it to be framed by the tradition of political liberalism. Rather, we should seek to understand what kinds of skills, virtues, and habits of language we need to learn to sustain our convictions and our witness to the God of Jesus Christ. We must "unlearn" ways of seeing and describing ourselves and the world that are alien to Christian convictions and continually learn—by the power of the Holy Spirit—to see and describe ourselves and the world in a Christian way.

The preceding task calls for imagination, an imagination that refuses to allow ourselves to be captured by the fashions and assumptions of the day. Such an imagination is reflected in Will Willimon's account of a conversation among ministers.

One of the ministers said that he thought that abortion was immoral.

"Do you mean that you would ask a thirteen-year-old girl who got pregnant, God knows how, to raise a child by herself? Do you think that a thirteen-year-old is capable of being a mother?" one of his colleagues said....

"Well, no," replied the antiabortionist. "I suppose there would be some extreme circumstances in which abortion would be justified."

"So what's wrong with a thirteen-year-old having a baby?" asked another minister. He was a black minister, pastor of a large black congregation in our town. "We have young girls who have this happen to them. I have a fourteen-year-old in my congregation who had a baby last month. We're going to baptize the child next Sunday," he added.

"Do you really think that she is capable of raising a little baby?" another minister asked.

"Of course not," he replied. "No fourteen-year-old is capable of raising a baby. For that matter, not many thirty-year-olds are qualified. A baby's too difficult for any one person to raise by herself."

"So what do you do with babies?" they asked.

"Well, we baptize them so that we all raise them together. In the case of that fourteen-year-old, we have given her baby to a retired couple who have enough time and enough wisdom to raise children. They can then raise the mama along with her baby. That's the way we do it."[17]

This example is a reminder of how much we need to do to reduce the male promiscuity and irresponsibility that leaves so many pregnant women isolated. The example also focuses our attention on how our imagination can turn tragedy into the possibility for healing and growth.

Conclusion
Christian communities are essential for dealing with biomedical issues in a variety of ways. First, they provide the context for us to unlearn destructive habits of language and ways of seeing the world so that we can learn to see and describe ourselves and the world rightly. Second, they are the focus of our discernment in the power of the Holy Spirit about how we should live and what we should do. And third, they are the locus wherein we can think and act imaginatively to help us deal more humanely with the complex issues raised by our developing medical technologies.

Because of the distinctive way in which we see the world, describe ourselves, and understand our relations to God and to one another, Christian communities have the opportunity and the responsibility to change the terms of the conversation. We cannot afford to let the world define us or our issues. Nothing less is at stake than our witness to the truth revealed to us in Jesus Christ.

Questions for Reflection and Discussion

1. From a Christian perspective, should the individual or the community be primary in moral deliberations? Why?
2. How does Christian baptism affect bioethical decision making?
3. Describe Engelhardt's view of personhood. What are the strengths and weaknesses of this view?
4. What four practices separated the early Christians in the first century from their Roman and Jewish peers?
5. In your experience, has the Christian community been a significant factor in bioethical decision making? Should it be?
6. How can a community's "character" be of any help in facing bioethical decisions?
7. What is the character of your local community? Does its character provide any insight for decision making?

For Further Reading

Hauerwas, Stanley
    1986 *Suffering Presence*. Notre Dame, Ind.: University of Notre Dame Press.
Lammers, Stephen E., and Allen Verhey, eds.
    1987 *On Moral Medicine*. Grand Rapids: Wm. B. Eerdmans.
MacIntyre, Alasdair
    1977 "Can Medicine Dispense with a Theological Perspective on Human Nature?" In *Knowledge, Value, and Belief*, edited by H. Tristram Engelhardt and Daniel Callahan. Hastings-on-Hudson, N.Y.: The Hastings Center. Pages 25-43.
O'Donovan, Oliver
    1984 *Begotten or Made?* Oxford: Clarendon Press.
Ramsey, Paul
    1978 *Ethics at the Edges of Life*. New Haven, Conn.: Yale University Press.
Shannon, Thomas A.
    1985 *What Are They Saying About Genetic Engineering?* New York: Paulist Press.
Shelp, Earl, ed.
    1985 *Theology and Bioethics*. Dordrecht: D. Reidel.

Vance, Richard
1986 "Medical Ethics in the Absence of a Moral Consensus." *Books and Religion* 14 (Dec.): 5, 13.
Werpehowski, William
1985 "The Promise and Pathos of the Abortion Debate." *Horizons* 12 (Fall): 284-310.

Chapter 8

Historical Perspectives

Michael J. Gorman

Michael Gorman
M.Div., Ph.D. in New Testament ethics, Princeton Theological Seminary. Assistant director, Council for Religious Independent Schools.

SEVERAL YEARS AGO I participated in a debate about abortion with a professor of philosophy at a small Friends college in the Midwest. The debate was quite congenial but rather frustrating for participants and audience alike. Perhaps this was because neither the philosopher nor I had really identified the most fundamental differences between us.

During the question-and-answer sessions after the formal debate, however, one astute student asked the philosophy professor a very significant question: "What, in your view, is the *status* of the fetus?" The philosopher's response? "A significant piece of tissue." That question and answer quickly clarified the differences between us, and the rest of the evening consisted of an invigorating discussion on the status of the fetus.

For thousands of years people have been discussing the nature, or ontological status, of the unborn; for millennia they have been assigning value to it. Although modern technology has brought about new issues and complicated old ones, we ignore the opinions and practices of past generations only to our detriment. Especially is this the case for Christians, who acknowledge the working of the Spirit across time and space and who therefore ought to take Christian tradition very seriously. Some theologians and philosophers have drawn directly on the past in developing their own perspectives. Furthermore, a study[1] (though a poor one) of past perspectives on the unborn and abortion was influential in the U.S. Supreme Court's 1973 *Roe v. Wade* decision.

To trace the variety of attitudes, both Christian and non-Christian, toward the unborn throughout history would require a massive volume. This chapter must therefore limit itself to an in-depth look at one particularly relevant time period and to a brief survey of some other times and places.

Until recent decades no place or era in Western civilization had dealt with the status of the unborn or the practice of abortion more than did the peoples of ancient Greece, Rome, and Palestine. The major contemporary issues and perspectives surrounding the unborn and abortion were already raised by the peoples of these ancient lands. In this world the Christian church was born and first developed its own perspectives on the issues surrounding human development in the womb. These early, pre-Constantinian Christian perspectives are significant for all Christians, but especially for Christians of Anabaptist heritage and persuasion. Anabaptists have drawn heavily upon the pre-Constantinian church in developing their ethics, especially on issues of violence and peace.

The texts and practices that we will examine generally address the status of the fetus in the context of only one specific bioethical issue, abortion. However, it is possible that other contemporary issues may also be implicitly addressed. What were the prevailing attitudes toward the unborn and abortion in the ancient world? How did the early church respond to these attitudes?

Views of the Fetus and Abortion in Antiquity

In the ancient world contraception was an unreliable mixture of guesswork and magic. Therefore, the most common techniques of birth control were abortion and infanticide. Both of these practices were usually considered to be parental rights.

Antiquity's two most influential and respected philosophers,

Plato and Aristotle, approved of abortion and even demanded it in certain cases. Plato believed the unborn was a living being with a soul. Yet in his ideal *Republic,* Plato required abortion in cases of pregnancy in women under the age of 20 and over 40.[2] Plato also required abortion in cases of bigamy, adultery, incest, and premarital sex. The rationale behind this seemingly arbitrary pronouncement on the value of a living human being is simple: For Plato, women bear children "to the State."[3] The state's ideals, goals, and needs take precedence over the life and rights of the unborn (as well as the newborn) and the rights of their mothers. Plato's goal of developing the perfect state necessitated a program of eugenics grounded in this utilitarian view of the individual. According to Plato, the state should encourage the killing of unborn or newborn children who have a high risk of mental or physical deficiency.

Like Plato, Aristotle had plans for an ideal state. Aristotle believed that the state would have to regulate both the quantity and quality of children in order to produce the finest individuals and hence the finest state. Therefore, Aristotle approved of the infanticide of deformed children as a means of birth control. However, if local custom opposed infanticide, abortion could be used as a substitute, although it was preferable to be done early in the pregnancy before the time of ensoulment.[4] Aristotle believed that the male fetus received its essentially human (either sensible or rational) soul at 40 days of gestation, the female fetus at 90 days.[5] After the time of ensoulment, the unborn is a living human being, he thought. Thus, Aristotle's overall preference was for early abortion, which would not be the killing of a human being. Undoubtedly, because he approved of eugenic infanticide, Aristotle would have supported eugenic abortion if a technology had been available to detect deformed fetuses.

The notions of Aristotle and Plato, though reflective of and influential in shaping the dominant mood of the Greco-Roman world, were not left unchallenged in ancient philosophy. The Pythagoreans, who believed in the transmigration of souls, believed that ensoulment took place at conception and, therefore, that abortion was the taking of a human life. Pythagorean influence has been suggested in the famous Hippocratic Oath, which includes a promise not to give an abortive drug to a patient.

The Stoics, who believed that everything should be done in harmony with rational nature, rejected infanticide as an unnatural practice because Nature would have us raise, not kill, our children. Although the Stoics believed that the fetus is a part of its mother and thus becomes an individual only at birth when it takes its first breath, they apparently still rejected abortion as an act as unnatural as infanticide.[6] The Stoics' popular philosophical archenemies, the Epicureans, practiced infanticide and abortion.

Opposition to abortion did come occasionally from other corners of the Greco-Roman world. Some condemnations reflect a view of bloodshed as an act that renders the agent ritually impure. Others appear to reflect profound horror at abortion as an act of murder.

Greek, and especially Roman law, however, viewed the fetus as a part of the mother with few or no moral or legal rights.[7] Along with the woman herself, the fetus was technically the property of the father. Early in Roman history the father was free to force abortion at will, and any abortion chosen by a woman without her husband's approval was viewed as an offense against him. In neither case was the act of abortion seen as an injustice committed against the fetus or the woman.

During the period of the Roman Empire, custom softened the father's power of life and death, but an abortion against the father's will was still perceived as a crime against the father, family name, race, and state—but not the fetus or woman. When Rome enacted its first laws against abortion (in the early third century A.D. under Christian influence), the act was still not a crime against fetus or mother. Instead, abortion was a "scandalous" act of a wife "depriving her husband of children without being punished."[8]

Greek and Roman physicians were split into two or three camps regarding the status of the fetus and abortion. A few, influenced by Pythagorean teachings and a strict interpretation of the Hippocratic Oath, had a high view of fetal life and opposed abortion in all cases. Most were willing to perform abortions, at least to save the mother's life, and some probably did them for any reason. Many midwives also performed abortions. Ancient gynecologists have not generally left records of their philosophical speculations. Undoubtedly, gynecologists who performed abortions either believed that the fetus did not possess a soul, that it was not a person but a part of the woman and therefore had no rights; or they believed that the needs and rights of the father, mother, or state took precedence over the rights of the fetus.

Abortion, then, was a common and accepted phenomenon in the Greco-Roman world—except among one group of people, the Jews. The Jews opposed abortion, except to save the life of the mother. This opposition to abortion is especially remarkable because almost all Jewish authorities agreed with Roman law in assigning to the fetus the legal status of being a part of the mother with few or no legal rights. But being rooted in the Hebrew Scriptures, Jewish opinion on the status of the fetus also acknowledged that the unborn was the creation of God.

Although the rabbis could not agree on such subjects as when the unborn received its soul, whether it was legally entitled to an inheritance should the father die before its birth, what legal and religious obligations parents had in the case of miscarriage, and so on, they did agree that the fetus had the moral or ontological status of "creation of God." Every Jewish writer who addressed the subject of deliberate abortion condemned it with a forceful "no." For example, Philo condemned abortion as a violation of the commandment against murder.[9] Similarly, the historian Josephus wrote that the Law forbids abortion, which he equated with infanticide.[10] Popular Jewish writings condemned the pagan practices of abortion and exposure of the newborn.

These various ancient views of the status of the fetus and abortion can now be summarized in three ideas: (1) their views of the status of the unborn, (2) the unborn's value and the basis of that value, and (3) the morality of abortion. People in antiquity believed that the unborn becomes truly human at a variety of stages in its development—conception, 40 or 90 days of gestation, birth, and perhaps even after birth. The criteria for determining humanity also varied, with possession of a soul as the chief criterion. In other words, philosophical import was attributed to biological development; moral status was a function of psychological and biological status.

However, even the attainment of a certain stage of development was often deemed insufficient for unborn, or even newborn, life to have value. The value of life was determined primarily on a utilitarian basis, either individualistic or social. That is, the value of the fetus was assigned by a controlling power, either the father or the state. The prevailing view in antiquity, then, was that a fetal "right-to-life" is nonexistent. The right to control or extinguish fetal life belongs to the powerful males in society (fathers and rulers). Some exceptions to this dominant perspective existed. The Pythagoreans, Stoics, and Jews believed that the presence of a soul, the laws of nature, or the image and work of God, respectively, made fetal life inviolable. Such views however, were not shared by the majority, nor by the law.

Abortion, therefore, was almost universally a right of the father and/or the state, and an unapproved abortion by a woman was an offense against those same powers. Abortion was *not* an act of violence committed against the fetus, nor against the woman. Into this world of values and beliefs about the fetus and abortion the Christian church was born.

Early Christian Attitudes

More than a dozen Christian documents from the end of the first to the end of the third century A.D. discuss abortion, and each one—without exception—condemns the practice. This unanimous voice of early Christian writings includes some of the most popular and important documents of the era, often considered by those who read them to be inspired Scripture, even though none was finally included in the New Testament canon.

Several examples of these texts include the following. "Thou shalt not murder a child by abortion" was a text that was contained in two early second-century guides to Christian life and worship.[11] "The fetus in the womb . . . is an object of God's care" and "We say that women who induce abortions are murderers, and will have to give account of it to God" are two comments that reflect the position of Athenagoras, a great apologist of the late second century.[12] The late-second-century theologian Tertullian wrote, "In our case, murder being once for all forbidden, we may not destroy even the fetus in the womb. To hinder a birth is merely a speedier homicide."[13] "There are women who ... [are] committing infanticide before they give birth to the infant," writes Minucius Felix in the early third century.[14]

Four themes are repeated in these and other early Christian texts on the unborn and abortion. First, the unborn is the creation of God and therefore a human being, a person, a neighbor. Second, abortion is murder. Third, the judgment of God falls on those guilty of abortion. Finally, opposition to abortion is part of a larger Christian ethic of nonviolence and love.

First, then, we consider the status of the unborn in early Christianity. The *Didache* and the *Epistle of Barnabas* include their prohibition of abortion in a discussion of the practical meaning of the command to "love your neighbor as yourself" (or, as *Barnabas* has it, "more than yourself"). Thus, these two documents, which adopt, yet radicalize, Jewish ethical traditions, view the fetus not as a part of its mother but as a child and a neighbor.

At the end of the second century Clement of Alexandria developed the Stoic notion of conforming to the laws of nature. He argued that the unborn and newborn should not be killed because they are the "designs of providence." Athenagoras claimed that the fetus was the "object of God's care." At about the same time, Tertullian, who had been trained as a lawyer, took Roman law to task concerning its view of the fetus when he wrote that the fetus is already a person "while as yet the human being derives blood from other parts of the [mother's] body for its sustenance."[15] In other words, contrary to Roman and even Jewish law, Tertullian made the significant claim that dependence on the mother does not make the fetus merely a part of the mother. He appealed to the experience of pregnancy ("the playful stirring of life within"), to the biblical references to God forming prophets in their mothers' wombs, and to the scriptural accounts of the prebirth activity of Jesus and John the Baptist in their mother's wombs (Luke 1:41, 46) as proofs of his belief in the personhood of the unborn.[16]

Noticeably absent from the earliest Christian references to the unborn and abortion is any distinction between formed and unformed, or ensouled and nonensouled, fetuses. All abortions were deemed homicides. The absence of such distinctions is especially remarkable because the early Christians' Old Testament (the Greek Septuagint, or LXX), under the influence of Greek philosophy, had mistranslated the Hebrew of Exodus 21:22-23. This mistranslation had erroneously introduced the notion of formed and unformed fetuses into the text, implying by the different penalties assigned that only the abortion of a formed fetus is murder. (The Hebrew words "no harm ... harm" were translated as "no form ... form.") Thus the LXX could easily have been used to distinguish human from nonhuman fetuses and homicidal from nonhomicidal abortions. Yet the early Christians, even the well-educated ones, did not do so.

By the late fourth century these distinctions had become quite common, however; the issue of fetal formation and ensoulment became a central concern of theologians influenced by Aristotle. The position of the earliest Christians, however, was straightforward: All unborn human beings are created by God and must be considered from a moral point of view to be true human beings, or "persons," whose deliberately induced death is murder.

The second early Christian theme, that abortion is murder, is based on the early Christian view of the unborn. Abortion is explicitly called murder during this early period by the *Didache*, the *Epistle of Barnabas*, Clement of Alexandria, Athenagoras, Tertullian, and Minucius Felix.

The conviction that abortion is murder logically yielded the third theme, that the judgment of God falls on those guilty of abortion. They will suffer the consequences of their sin.

Thus, early Christian attitudes toward the unborn and abortion differed radically from prevailing pagan notions and practices. Christians rejected the Roman definition of the fetus as merely part of the mother's body under the father's power to keep or destroy. Their opposition to abortion developed in Jewish-Christian communities where God's creative activity in the womb was respected and where social injustice and innocent bloodshed were abhorred. This Jewish perspective on the fetus and abortion became more radical and formed a new theological and ethical context in the early Christian church. The sacredness of unborn life took on deeper meaning in light of Christ; respect for the womb was increased because the early Christians believed in the incarnation and reverently read the Gospel stories of Jesus' conception, development in utero, and birth.

This deepened respect for the unborn was placed in a larger context. The fourth theme suggests that the Christian view of the unborn and abortion was part of a holistic, consistent Christian ethic of love and nonviolence.

The ministry and teachings of Jesus led early Christians to practice mercy and justice toward all defenseless people, especially children, whether newborn or unborn. Jesus' teachings and examples also caused them to oppose all forms of violence: killing in war, watching gladiator fights, and punishing by crucifixion. Furthermore, they vehemently opposed the common practices of exposing the newborn and aborting the unborn. The early Christians interpreted the practices of their society as acts of power over, rather than compassion for, the weak; they believed that their contemporaries had chosen bloodshed over love.

Abortion, then, was a sin of violence. To believe in the personhood of the unborn and to oppose abortion was one manifestation of Christian concern for the poor and weak, one consequence of their devotion to a Lord and Savior who had been the "fruit of Mary's womb," and one expression of their decision to forsake bloodshed and follow Jesus. This unified nonviolent ethic of love was most succinctly expressed by Athenagoras, who claimed that Christians had given up performing or watching any act of violence: "We are altogether consistent in our conduct."[17] The early Christian writers who condemned abortion also condemned other forms of bloodshed, including warfare.

To summarize, four themes about the unborn and abortion exist in the earliest Christian literature: (1) the unborn are God's workmanship, human beings ("persons"), our neighbors; (2) abortion is murder; (3) those who abort are guilty before God; and (4) opposition to abortion is one manifestation of a nonviolent, compassionate lifestyle.

To these four a fifth theme—more implicit than the others—may now be added. Although the early Christians did not use the language of "rights," their attitude toward the unborn and abortion was, in effect, the establishment of a new, basic human right—the right not to be killed, the right to life. In commenting on this implicit right in early Christian teaching, classical scholar John Rist notes, "It was almost universally held in antiquity that a child has no right to life" simply because it had been conceived or even born.[18] For the ancients, value was acquired either by developing intelligence or by being accepted by the family and society. For the Christians, however, the value of the fetus was grounded solely and completely in its relationship to God. The fetus had a God-given right not to be killed.

The Unborn and the Post-Constantinian Church

In the early fourth century Constantine the Great initiated the "Christianization" of the Roman Empire. At this time and throughout the following centuries of the Middle Ages, Christians continued to hold their belief in the sanctity of the unborn and opposed abortion. In the fourth and fifth centuries, for instance, the great theologians and preachers Basil, Chrysostom, and Ambrose gave eloquent expression to the established views of the unborn and abortion. At the same time they evidenced compassion and sensitivity to women who had aborted, offering them forgiveness and new life in Christ. However, four major developments in Christian perspectives on the unborn and abortion took place during the twelve centuries between the rise of Constantine and the time of the Protestant Reformation.

The first major development was the acceptance by some church leaders of a distinction between the formed and the unformed unborn—that is, those with and without a soul. The issue at hand was this: Does the unformed or unhumanlike embryo have a soul, and if it does not, is its abortion something less than homicide? Although the issue of the time of ensoulment had been raised by Christian theologians as early as the second century, many believed that ensoulment occurred at birth. For other Christians, however, their lack of interest in or uncertainty about the time of ensoulment did not affect their estimation of the unborn or their view of all abortions as murder.

Three kinds of evidence—biological, philosophical, and biblical—led some theologians to conclude that the unformed unborn had no soul, was not alive, and was not human. As we have noted, ancient embryology placed the formation of the embryo into a recognizable form at about 40 days of gestation for males and 80 or 90 days for females. Some ancient philosophers, such as Aristotle, had argued that upon becoming "formed," the embryo received its distinctively human soul and became truly human. This moment was known as ensoulment or animation (from Latin *anima*, "soul"). It was under the influence of Aristotle's philosophy that the Greek translation of the Old Testament (the Septuagint) mistakenly introduced this concept of formed and unformed into the text of Exodus. Those who were influenced by these three perspectives on the unborn still thought early abortion was a serious sin, but not murder.

The first evidence of this view in the church comes from Basil the Great, who in 374 rejected the distinction.[19] Augustine gave it more serious consideration, however, and his writings on the unborn—as on all subjects—had a great impact on subsequent centuries.

Believing that sex is only for procreation, not pleasure, Augustine condemned contraception, sterility, abortion, and infanticide as damnable transgressions of the law of procreation.[20] Although he viewed each of these as manifestations of "unbridled desire and the impulse to violence," he did not erase the moral differences between these sins. Abortion and infanticide were clearly in the literal category of "killing" for him. Augustine's views on the status of the embryo and on early abortion, however, appear to have fluctuated throughout his lifetime.[21] Although he says the unborn are "living" and although he asserts that God creates and nourishes all unborn including the embryo, the offspring of prostitutes, and the deformed, he also accepts the formed/unformed distinction. He argues that we can know with certainty that the soul is present in the unborn only after formation. Therefore, abortion of the unborn, though immoral, is not homicide. Augustine admits, however, the *possibility* that the unborn receive their soul prior to formation. This epistemological uncertainty keeps Augustine from saying too firmly that the unformed embryo is not human and that its abortion is not homicide.[22]

With this position on the unformed unborn, or embryo, Augustine, along with his contemporary Jerome, began a tradition of Catholic Christian thought that eventually became the dominant one. Following in this Aristotelian-Augustinian tradition also was the great medieval theologian Thomas Aquinas, whose main interest in the status of the unborn was whether they needed baptism for salvation when spontaneously aborted. This Aristotelian-Augustinian-Thomistic tradition, though preserving profound respect for the unborn and opposing abortion, saw significant philosophical and moral significance in the biological development of the unborn. This tradition remained the dominant Catholic perspective until its reversal in the 19th century to the pre-Constantinian view of no distinctions in the moral status of the unborn.

During the Middle Ages the second major development in connection with the theological evaluation of the status of the fetus was the initiation of debate among church leaders about the act of abortion as a crime to be penalized by church law. Beginning in the fourth century, Christian leaders, especially bishops assembled in councils, began to legislate penalties for all mortal sins, including abortion. The collected pronouncements of councils, bishops, and popes—pronouncements known as canon law—were not intended to determine the morality of certain acts but to assess penalties for acts assumed to be sinful. The ensuing legal tradition on abortion is evidence of a continuous official opposition to abortion as a serious sin. The concern of church leaders now was primarily pastoral, not ethical or philosophical.

Despite constant condemnation by church leaders, abortion made its way into the Christian church early in its history. Assuming the grave immorality of abortion, what appropriate penance would the church's leaders select for this act of violence that so often grew out of adultery? Until the tenth century A.D., canon law treated abortion as murder and made no distinctions between formed and unformed fetuses. Although at first the penalty for abortion was excommunication, the standard penalty quickly became 10 years of penance. Penalties were sometimes given to physicians and other accomplices, as well as to the women who had aborted.

At the same time that canon law was developing, unofficial systems of private penance and penitential books were being organized by monks and missionaries in Europe. Especially in the north, some of these Christian leaders assigned different penalties for the unformed, formed, and quickened (moving) fetus, often stating that abortion of the unformed was not murder. In the south, however, which was traditionally stricter, the distinctions of formed/unformed were generally not made.

At the height of the Middle Ages the formed/unformed distinction began to gain nearly universal acceptance in both legal and theological texts. In 1140 the distinction was included in Gratian's *Decretum,* a significant systemization of canon law. In 1157 the distinction also appeared in Peter Lombard's *Sentences,* which became the standard theology text for many subsequent generations. The formed/unformed, homicide/nonhomicide distinction was maintained also in the decretals, or universal church laws, of Pope Gregory IX in 1234, even though the decretals also labeled all antiprocreative acts as "murder." Similarly, some theologians and moralists argued that therapeutic abortion of a non-ensouled fetus was permissible because the fetus was not a human being and the abortion would benefit the mother.

The accepted theological, legal, and pastoral view of the fetus and of abortion at the end of the Middle Ages may be summarized as follows:

(1) the unborn receive their distinctively human souls, thereby becoming truly human, at 40 (for males) or 80/90 (for females) days of gestation;

(2) induced abortion is homicide if the fetus is formed and ensouled, and it is a serious, though lesser, sin if the fetus is not formed and ensouled;

(3) induced abortion is punishable by church law, with the required penance varying somewhat depending on the status of the fetus and local custom; and

(4) therapeutic abortion may be permissible if the fetus does not yet possess its soul.

Although the issue of ensoulment affected the precise legal status of abortion, this idea never diminished the seriousness of abortion or condoned the act in any way.

A third development during the Middle Ages was pastoral, as well as missionary, in nature. Beginning in the late fourth century under the leadership of both bishops and monks, orphanages and foundling homes (for abandoned and exposed children) were established throughout the Christian world. From its birth the Christian church had been characterized by its compassion for children. Even the earliest Christians frequently rescued abandoned children and raised them in a Christian family. The foundling homes became visible symbols of Christian compassion for unwanted children in the communities of Europe and the East. Although the effect of such institutions on popular attitudes and practices cannot be measured precisely, undoubtedly the existence of foundling homes had some deterring effect on the practice of abortion and encouraged women and couples to give birth rather than abort. These homes also influenced attitudes toward the value of children, both born and unborn.[23]

The important final and most subtle development in the Middle Ages stems from the "Christianization" of the Roman Empire that began with Constantine. The acceptance of a holy war or just war mentality in the church caused a necessary divorce of the issue of abortion from its original connection to all other forms of violence. Although the church continually viewed abortion as an act of lethal violence and condemned sex for any reason other than procreation, it accepted violence in war as a legitimate Christian enterprise. Abortion was treated primarily in the context of sexual sin, rather than in the context of violence and social injustice. The original Christian vision of no violence, no killing, no warfare, and no abortion was lost.

Protestants and Catholics During and After the Reformation

Although the Protestant reformers said little about the unborn and abortion, they echoed the established Christian regard for the unborn and condemned abortion. Martin Luther, Philip Melanchthon, and John Calvin believed that at conception the human soul was either passed on from the parents (Luther) or created by God (Melanchthon, Calvin). Although Luther did not address the issue of abortion, he believed the fetus to be "wholly the work of God alone."[24] Calvin twice mentioned and condemned abortion, once in a brief comment on the biblical story of Onan (in which he also condemned coitus interruptus) and once in his exposition of Exodus 21:22-23. In that context Calvin rejected the formed/unformed distinction and considered all abortions to be horrible forms of homicide: "If it seems more horrible to kill a man in his own house than in a field, it ought surely to be deemed more atrocious to destroy a fetus in the womb before it comes to light."[25]

To my knowledge, no references to abortion exist in the early Anabaptist writings. The few references to abortion from the English Reformation condemn abortion as infanticide, murder, or (with Calvin) invasion of a place of refuge where the workmanship of God resides. John W. Weemse, one English preacher who wrote at some length on the fetus, referred to the womb as the workshop of God and to the unborn as creatures already in the image of God. In interpreting Exodus 21:22-23 he argued that the text protects the life of the child even before its formation, and he called all abortions "murder." He did, however, accept a lesser legal penalty for the abortion of the unformed unborn.[26]

Those Protestants of the late 16th and 17th centuries who wrote about abortion condemned it sometimes more vehemently than their Catholic contemporaries. These Protestants generally rejected the formed/unformed, homicide/nonhomicide distinction. One important source for their anti-abortion arguments was the second-century theologian Tertullian, who had argued that the fetus is a separate person from its mother and that abortion is homicide. Some of these Protestants made special criticism of the Roman concept that had taken hold among many legal authorities—that the fetus is a part of the mother that can be controlled or destroyed by the father.

Protestantism in the succeeding centuries—until the 20th— paid relatively little attention to questions of fetal life and abortion. When abortion was discussed, it was condemned, though often in a very superficial way. Many Protestant physicians and clergy, however, were silent on the issues. This silence was often interpreted by lay people as tacit approval of abortion. Some Protestants lamented this lack of concern and chastised Protestantism for being behind Catholicism in the task of protecting human life. Harvard historian George H. Williams attempted to account for the general Protestant silence on fetal value and abortion. He suggested that Protestants, in their zeal for the principle of *sola scriptura*, had absolutely no knowledge of the early fathers' stance nor of the long tradition that had developed from it.[27]

In contrast to Protestant theologians, during and after the Protestant Reformation Catholic moral theologians and lawyers continued to discuss and examine the issues raised during the Middle Ages: the relation of contraception to abortion, the status of the fetus and of its abortion before ensoulment, the possibility of therapeutic abortion, and appropriate penalties for women and physicians involved in abortion. Because papal decrees of the late 16th century condemned both abortion and contraception but did not deal directly with therapeutic abortion, debate about this subject was especially lively.

Perhaps the most important development in Catholic circles, however, was the serious questioning of the biological and philosophical validity of the traditional theory of ensoulment at 40 or 80 days. Both science and philosophy attacked this notion of "delayed animation" and stressed the idea of continuity in embryonic development of both body and soul. Yet, while some theologians argued that ensoulment occurred at conception, others appealed to the Septuagint of Exodus 21:22-23 and to longstanding tradition in order to maintain that the nonanimated, unformed embryo was not made in the image of God and was not a human being. (In this context, the issue of the baptism of the embryo appeared again.) Still others argued that ensoulment occurs at birth. Although most people holding these views did not approve of nontherapeutic induced abortion, some did approve of it. In 1679, therefore, the Holy Office of Pope Innocent XI officially condemned several interpretations of the ensoulment issue. Two views with some degree of popularity were condemned: 1) that abortion of the unanimated embryo could be not only permitted but advocated, because the embryo is not human; and 2) that abortion is never homicide (because ensoulment occurs at birth).

Two centuries later, in 1869, Pope Pius IX faced a growing scientific and philosophical emphasis on continuity in embryonic development. No longer was it believed that a radical biological change or infusion of the soul occurred at some point to alter the essence of the embryo. This followed a corresponding movement in the church away from Aristotle, the Septuagint, and Augustine and back to the earliest fathers' position on the human status of the fetus from conception. Consequently, the pope condemned all abortions and pronounced excommunication as the penalty for the participants. Official Catholic teaching since that time has banned all induced abortions, including direct therapeutic abortion. (To be sure, that position has not gone unchallenged, as many Catholics have espoused new understandings of personal conscience and church authority.) Thus, the Roman Catholic church's present belief that abortion is homicide because the unborn is a human being from the moment of its conception represents an overthrow of the Aristotle-inspired position of Augustine and others. This change came about primarily because of studies in many fields that emphasized the continuity of life in the unborn from conception to birth.

The difference between Catholic interest in the unborn and Protestant apathy was manifested not only in theology, but also in missions. A prime example is China, where 19th-century Protestant missionaries decried the common practices of abortion and infanticide but initially did little in response. Catholic missionaries, on the other hand, began establishing homes for foundlings. As the Protestants themselves admitted, they lagged far behind the Catholics in this kind of work,[28] though some Protestants did maintain such homes.

Conclusions and Directions

From the preceding study the following conclusions have emerged:

1) Throughout its history (until quite recently), the Christian church has consistently regarded the unborn as the special handiwork of God, a being separate from its mother. Deliberate abortion has always been a serious sin and often an act of murder.

2) Although the church has discussed the precise status of the fetus and the meaning of abortion in many contexts and for many reasons, these discussions have always been grounded in the basic beliefs in the sanctity of the unborn and the immorality of abortion. Concern for the fetus has been the hallmark of Christian discussion on fetal development and death. To call the histo-

ry of the Christian stance against abortion a matter of "relative indifference" that was "episodic" or fragmentary and founded largely on negative views of sex[29] does not do justice to the almost unchanging fundamental perspectives within the Christian church for 19 centuries. Nor does it represent fairly the explicitly stated concerns in many of the texts that present these perspectives.

3) In the first centuries of the church, Christians believed that the unborn are human beings—neighbors or "persons"—at every stage of development, and that all abortions are homicides. This perspective was one part of the church's lifestyle of compassion and nonviolence as it rejected the practices of bloodshed in the Greco-Roman world.

4) Under the influence of ancient embryology, Greek dualistic philosophy, and an erroneous translation of Exodus 21:22-23, the dominant Catholic position came to distinguish formed and unformed, ensouled and nonensouled, and human and nonhuman unborn.

5) The dominant Catholic view was eventually overthrown as the result of advances in embryology, renewed study of Scripture and especially the writings of the church fathers, and corresponding changes in theology. The formed/unformed view was always the minority view in Protestant circles, although Protestants were generally far less concerned about the issues than were Catholics. Both Protestants and Catholics sometimes appealed to Tertullian for support of the contention that the fetus is an independent being.

6) Christian responses to the issues of fetal life and abortion have not been simply theological and ethical, but also pastoral. Three main pastoral responses over the centuries have included penance as permanent separation, penance as discipline and anticipated restoration, and provision of practical help by taking in otherwise unwanted children.

One scholar has correctly noted that recent "medical advance and social changes have caused to be heard sentiments and arguments [about the status of the fetus and abortion] which, to the historian of the Church in the Graeco-Roman world, have a curiously familiar ring."[30] He is referring especially to the way in which the Roman father's power of life and death over the unborn has been transferred in our world to the woman. Many other parallels exist, such as the legal and popular view of the fetus as a part of its "host"-woman, the search for criteria of humanity of personhood, the attempt to define humanity in terms of biological development, the desire to be rid of deformed babies, and so on. What is striking about church history, however, is that the Christian church has constantly said something straightforward and simple in the midst of its own participation in such debates: The unborn is God's special creation and must not be treated as anything less.

Perhaps more striking, however, is the way the earliest Christian view—that all unborn are inviolable, fully human beings, separate creatures from the women on whom they depend—resurfaced when modern biology discovered continuity in fetal development and when theology returned to Scripture and the church's pre-Constantinian writings. Given both our biological knowledge and our world's attempt to define the unborn as appendixlike tissues that are part of the woman's body over which she has control, the position of the early church ought to commend itself to us.

In the recent debate about the status of the unborn the governing philosophical assumption has been that in order to be a "person" the fetus must attain some quality of biological, psychological, or intellectual development. The language used to describe this attained status may be popular (human being), philosophical (person), or religious (image of God). My contention is, however, that the search for criteria of personhood in Christian circles is fundamentally flawed because it is a vestige of inaccurate, premodern science; Aristotelian, dualistic philosophy; and ignorance of early Christian teaching and practice.

For those who willingly admit that abortion is the killing of a human being or a person, abortion in certain situations is often defended in the same manner as is warfare—justifiable killing of another human being.[31] Such a defense rests on the validity for Christians of a just war or just lethal violence theory. This theory is at odds with the shalom of the kingdom of God inaugurated by Jesus, the teachings of the early church, and the most central Anabaptist principles.[32]

The original and essential Christian vision is that the unborn are to be viewed and treated as persons—as neighbors. This perspective of respect, compassion, and nonviolence toward the human embryo and fetus must be the foundation of all considerations of bioethical matters surrounding human conception and development. What Christians may not practice, promote, or even tolerate is any attitude or action that treats the unborn merely as tissue, even medically beneficial tissue. Neither may the unborn be viewed as persons, whether potential or actual, whose life may be disposed of when it is unwanted or abnormal (the "quality of life" perspective). Rather, the Christian vision of compassion and community leads us to active caring for all unborn human beings and to equally active concern for women who have unwanted pregnancies or unwanted children. As a position of peace and compassion, rather than bloodshed, violence, and disdain for the defenseless, this vision ought especially to commend itself to those who follow in the way of Jesus.

Questions for Reflection and Discussion

1. Should the unborn be treated as a person, as someone with value and rights?
2. How should Christians understand the meaning of personhood?
3. Is abortion an act of violence and a negative use of power to be rejected by people who practice an ethic of love and nonviolence?
4. What active responses are called for by an Anabaptist understanding of personhood when women have unwanted pregnancies?
5. What were the important categories of ethical discussion regarding abortion in the early church?

For Further Reading

Amundsen, Darrel W.
   1978 "History of Medical Ethics: Medieval Europe: Fourth to Sixteenth Century." In *Encyclopedia of Bioethics*, edited by Warren T. Reich. Vol. 3, 938-51. New York: Free Press.
Bonner, G.
   1985 "Abortion and Early Christian Thought." In *Abortion and the Sanctity of Human Life*, edited by J. H. Channer. Exeter: Paternoster. Available in the U.S. from Attic Press, Greenwood, S.C.
Carrick, Paul
   1985 *Medical Ethics in Antiquity*. Dordrecht, Holland: D. Reidel.
Connery, John R.
   1977 *Abortion: The Development of the Roman Catholic Perspective*. Chicago: Loyola University.
Gorman, Michael J.
   1982 *Abortion and the Early Church: Christian, Jewish and Pagan Attitudes in the Greco-Roman World*. Downers Grove, Ill.: InterVarsity.

1986 "Shalom and the Unborn." *Transformation,* 3(1):26-33.

Grisez, Germain G.
1970 *Abortion: The Myths, the Realities, and the Arguments.* New York: Corpus. See especially chapter IV, "Religious Views of Abortion," 117-84.

Harrison, Beverly Wildung
1983 *Our Right to Choose: Toward a New Ethic of Abortion.* Boston: Beacon. See especially chapter 5, "The History of Christian Teaching on Abortion Reconceived," 119-53.

Huser, Roger John
1942 *Crime of Abortion in Canon Law: An Historical Synopsis and Commentary.* Washington, D.C.: Catholic University Press.

Nelson, James B.
1978 "Abortion: Protestant Perspectives." In *Encyclopedia of Bioethics,* edited by Warren T. Reich. Vol. 1, 13-16. New York: Free Press.

Noonan, John T., Jr.
1970 "An Almost Absolute Value in History." In *The Morality of Abortion: Legal and Historical Perspectives*, edited by John T. Noonan, Jr., 1-59. Cambridge, Mass.: Belknap.

1986 (original 1965) *Contraception: A History of Its Treatment by the Catholic Theologians and Canonists.* Enl. ed. Cambridge, Mass.: Belknap.

Chapter 9

Maternal Perspectives

Anne Krabill Hershberger

Anne Krabill Hershberger
M.S. in maternity nursing, Wayne State University. Received a 1981-82 Lilly Foundation Faculty Open Fellowship to study bioethics at the Kennedy Institute of Ethics, Georgetown University, Washington, D.C. Associate professor of nursing at Goshen College, Goshen, Indiana.

BEFORE I EXPERIENCED pregnancy personally more than twenty years ago, I was exposed to some experiences in my maternity nursing practice that raised my curiosity about how mothers perceived their unborn babies. On one occasion during my graduate work, I was assisting at a birth. When the baby finally arrived, the mother shouted, "It's a baby! It's a baby!" She said this so often that the attending physician finally said, "What did you expect? An elephant?" I began to wonder, what do pregnant women expect and what are the images and perceptions they carry along with the growing fetus during their pregnancies? My comments are based on personal memories of being pregnant, on interactions with many pregnant women in my professional work, and on a variety of research studies.

Before focusing on how the mother perceives the unborn, a prior consideration in today's world is, "Who is the mother?" Is it the one who provides the ovum? The one who carries the fetus to birth? The one who contracted to raise the baby once it is here? The one who selected a frozen embryo (not her own) to be implanted in her uterus?

In biblical times King Solomon found a way to identify the real mother when two women were claiming one child. He determined that it was the one who did not want to see the baby hurt. We all are searching for the wisdom of Solomon for today's decisions. I have a feeling even King Solomon with all his wisdom might be puzzled by some of the dilemmas we face today.

The mother's attitude and behavior is key to fetal well-being and is an integral part of finding a course of action in the incredible ethical dilemmas surrounding issues at the beginning of life. Maternal perceptions of the unborn will differ, certainly, among individuals and also in different situations. I have chosen to discuss some common maternal perceptions of fetuses that are carried and desired, of fetuses that are not desired, and of fetuses that are not present but are desperately desired. I will then attempt to relate how these perceptions affect decision making.

Pregnancy, whether planned or not, is a significant event in a woman's life. Pregnancy may begin in an atmosphere of love, fear, hate, or indifference. Very little is known about the influence of these early behaviors and emotions on the development of later ties between mother and fetus. What is known is that ties do develop and increase as pregnancy progresses.[1]

According to Kemp and Page, "Pregnancy is the time when a woman literally begins to share her body with another being and this event produces profound changes in the way a woman views herself and her future relationship with her unknown offspring."[2] When a woman becomes pregnant, she identifies with the fetus and begins to view it as an extension of herself. Perceiving the fetus as part of herself, the woman attaches to it psychologically. The fetus is something no one can take from her. At the outset, however, there is no object of attachment. Only the idea of a child, as a possibility, exists. As Rubin says, "During pregnancy there is the idea of a child, but not an identifiable child. The existence and presence of the child is known indirectly by its mass, gravitational pull, and movement. Until the identity of the child can be ascertained after childbirth, there are only hypotheses of this child based on images and fantasies evoked by other models of childhood."[3]

Initially, the pregnant woman tends to look to models around her and how they have dealt with and responded to the same experience. Rubin has called this the replicative stage. In this stage, models of children are probabilistic; the child could be "like" this child or "like" that child. In fantasy, however, the woman sees her wished-for child—her own.[4] Fantasies occur in dream work, as well as during the day. Pleasurable fantasies generate hope, whereas unpleasant fantasies create anxiety.

The stimulus for these fantasies during the first three months of pregnancy is only an event, or rather, a nonevent—the lack of menstrual periods.[5] After quickening (when the baby's movements are first felt by the mother), the unborn baby is more real as an independent being and will often be named and given personality traits. The first experience of feeling the baby move is an event to be remembered. I still remember where I was sitting and what maternity dress I was wearing during a faculty meeting when this momentous occasion first occurred to me more than twenty years ago. (I wonder what my facial expression communicated to the speaker at that time.) This event heightens attachment considerably and even unwanted babies may begin to be accepted.

By the end of the second trimester of the pregnancy, the pregnant woman becomes very aware of the baby and attaches much value to him or her. She knows she possesses something very dear and important that gives her considerable pleasure and pride.[6] With continued input from the baby within, the mother's fantasies tend toward the idyllic. Rubin has described a typical fantasied image of this period as a "light-haired, light-complexioned child, regardless of parental coloring, of about six months in size, floating peacefully in space, very much like Michelangelo's pure cherubs. A woman's creative image of her wished-for child is that of an angel."[7]

The baby that a pregnant woman envisions in her fantasies is often older than a newborn. The mother imagines giving food to the child in a kind of communion that binds them even closer together. Sometimes the observation of baby clothing stimulates a fantasy of what her baby might wear—playclothes, ruffles. In the fantasy signs and clues to the gender of the child are sought. It is impossible to be the mother of an either/or child or one of indeterminate size, shape, and appearance. Dressing a child in fantasy is a series of explorations of the child in size, shape, and gender.[8] According to Rubin, "There is a playfulness, stimulated and reinforced by the growing and movement of the baby within. The mother may grasp a protruding leg, 'spank' the baby on the bottom, talk to it and find that the baby provides a comfortable ledge to support her folded hands or arms."[9]

Many pregnant women admit that they fear their fantasies will be thwarted in some way. Especially in the third trimester of pregnancy, fantasies of the child become subordinated by fantasies of "how it will be" in labor and birth. Fear and dread of delivery coexist with a wish for the child and relief from the burdensome pregnancy.[10] Concern for both self and baby is high. What endangers one endangers both. In the name of protecting their fetuses, some pregnant women do things they find impossible when not pregnant, such as refraining from smoking or using alcohol and drugs.

When the mother experiences some problem or threat, her immediate response is, "What will this do to my baby?" I have a vivid memory of this from an experience late in my second pregnancy. I was in our basement inserting an electrical plug into a receptacle that was a part of a ceiling light. This ceiling light had a suspended metal chain that served as the switch. The chain, unknown to me, became entangled between the prongs of the plug. As I inserted the plug, an electrical shock went through my body. I was stunned, of course, but my very first thought was, "My baby is in fluid, and fluid conducts electricity!" When that baby did not move during the next number of hours, I drove to the physician's office and asked one of the nurses to listen for the fetal heart rate. Immediately my fears were alleviated. At the moment of birth parents almost always ask, "Is he or she alright?"

Technology provides further insight into maternal perceptions of the unborn. We have heard that a picture is worth a thousand words. Now ultrasound technology permits parents to view the fetus and his or her movements on a monitor. Studies show that viewing the fetus accelerates the mother's bonding process with the fetus. In response to the question, "How do you feel about seeing what is inside you?" a mother answered, "It certainly makes you think twice about abortion!" When asked to say more, she told of the surprise she felt on viewing the fetal form, especially on seeing the fetus move: "I feel that it is human. It belongs to me. I couldn't have an abortion now."[11] Viewing the fetal form in the late first or early mid-trimester of pregnancy, before movement is felt by the mother, may also influence the resolution of any ambivalence toward the pregnancy itself in favor of the fetus. Ultrasound examinations may thus result in fewer abortions and more desired pregnancies.

As mentioned earlier, pregnancies begin in a variety of emotional milieu. The termination of pregnancies also elicits a variety of emotions. When the baby arrives, even in ideal circumstances of being wanted and of being healthy, parents may experience a momentary period of grief for the baby that did not come—the baby of their fantasies. In the unfortunate case when the baby is not perfectly formed, this grief is more acute and prolonged. The mother resists disengaging from the wished-for baby and from being the mother of the baby of her fantasies.

What I have described so far are the more usual maternal perceptions of the unborn. Some circumstances, however, cause the pregnant woman to have very different perceptions. In the case of a very young pregnant girl, an adolescent, her major focus is that of being an acceptable daughter, not a mother. Formation of a maternal identity in relation to this child and assumption of other maternal tasks do not occur.[12] The mother may be alienated from her parents and friends and may see the baby as a cure for her loneliness, someone who will love her without question. In her immaturity she tends to see the baby as a doll or plaything and not perceive the major responsibilities inherent in parenthood. On the other hand, she may see the pregnancy as a ploy to "catch her man." For single and divorced women the fetus may be perceived negatively and the woman may avoid bonding. However, the widowed woman tends to treasure the fetus as a gift from her late husband. Her bereavement is more acute in childbearing and childrearing, but the attachment to the child may be more intense than usual.

In about 10 to 20 percent of all pregnancies a significant possibility of fetal death, abnormality, or life-threatening illness is present. In such high-risk pregnancies the mother may avoid attachment to her fetus during the prenatal period.[13] She may reject feelings of concern and affection for the fetus because of a fear that the fetus will not survive. However, postponing psychological attachment until after diagnostic tests show the fetus is healthy or until the fetus is of viable age makes maternal-fetal bonding more difficult.[14] Women who do not want to be pregnant and later have a spontaneous abortion often experience real grief. Even following elective abortions, the grief reactions of these women give further evidence of the strong maternal-fetal attachments that develop during pregnancy. Despite popular myths, abortion as a solution is very difficult. The experience of a child, even in the abstract sense and without the pleasures of pregnancy, changes the woman's self.[15] Abortion and placing the child for adoption are traumatizing events, not easily undertaken and never forgotten. Stress during pregnancy appears to interfere with the developing maternal-fetal relationship, but it does not appear to negate the relationship.

About 10 to 15 percent of married couples in the U.S. experience the pain of infertility.[16] Dealing with infertility involves many stresses. Diagnosis of the infertility problem may involve temperature readings before rising each day to determine as accurately as possible when ovulation is occurring in the woman's menstrual cycle. In addition, the timing of sexual intercourse must be carefully scheduled to increase the likelihood of a pregnancy. A couple may be embarrassed by the need to reveal the most intimate aspects of the marriage relationship to health care professionals, persons outside the relationship. Through all of this, the wished-for baby becomes predominant in the woman's life, thereby putting all other plans and activities secondary to her efforts to produce a baby. Inability to conceive a child may cause a woman to avoid situations where she will be near babies—the pain is too great. The woman sees herself as having the potential to be a much better mother than many mothers who have babies. She tends to believe that having a baby of her own would solve all of life's problems. In other words, the baby she desires becomes bigger than life.

From these insights on how a woman perceives the unborn when the fetus is desired, not desired, or absent but very much desired, we can make some deductions. First, a woman does not take pregnancy lightly. Second, a fetus is more than a growth of tissue; it is special in the mother's perception. Third, decisions surrounding each pregnancy involve two key subjects—the mother and the fetus. Fourth, even when circumstances are not ideal for the pregnancy, a significant relationship exists between the mother and her fetus that deepens over time. Fifth, even when the fetus is destroyed, a relationship has existed that brings about grief and pain. Sixth, when a woman is unable to have a desired baby, her desire may become the overwhelming focus of her life.

These deductions express attitudes of concern and caring for the unborn. However, something is happening in our society that is confusing our understanding of what it means to care. Our increasing technological sophistication is allowing us to diagnose some fetal problems. Thus, parents can be warned that their baby will be born with a genetically induced condition that will prevent the baby from living a normal life.

What does that strong maternal-fetal relationship, that powerful maternal urge to protect the fetus, call for in this case? More importantly, what is a Christian's response? We all know that this world would be a much poorer place if only perfectly formed, nonimpaired people were allowed to live here. Even so, the question remains—is it right to knowingly bring a baby that may need to suffer and have no potential for relationship into the world?

Even when no fetal abnormality exists, questions arise. When pregnancy occurs in a woman who is at a point in her life that prevents her from emotionally, physically, or financially being able to care for a baby and she perceives personal devastation if she allows the pregnancy to continue, whose well-being takes priority—the mother's or the fetus'?

The new reproductive technologies hold much hope for the infertile couple. Technology such as in vitro fertilization allows a woman's ovum to meet her husband's sperm in a petri dish instead of her body when their path to meeting in the woman's fallopian tubes is blocked. Collaborative reproductive techniques in which a third party is needed to produce a baby also present hope to infertile couples.[17] These techniques include artificial insemination by donor when the husband's sperm are insufficient or ineffective in bringing about conception. Alternatively, the couple may hire a surrogate mother to receive the husband's sperm artificially, become pregnant, and return the baby to the biological father and his wife after giving birth to the baby.

Many people concerned about the ethical ramifications of these techniques say that in vitro fertilization is a helpful procedure for infertile couples and ought to be celebrated as a demonstration of God's gift of creativity to us. In describing in vitro fertilization LeRoy Walters used the metaphor of a physician providing a helicopter to transport an egg from a woman's ovary to her uterus when the natural bridge is out.[18] Some people, however, see an ethical dilemma because some fertilized ova are unavoidably destroyed in the laboratory. Some of these fertilized ova will not have a chance at life; but without them, none would have that chance.

Ethical problems are raised with collaborative reproductive techniques, as well. These have to do with the nature and meaning of marriage and parenthood. A third person enters the exclusive marriage relationship producing a radical asymmetry in the husband's and wife's relationship with the child. The donor of sperm and the surrogate mother do not assume responsibility for their offspring—they procreate without commitment. Even when their motivation stems from wanting to help a childless couple, limits to altruism exist. We do not rob banks to help the poor or kill ourselves to donate a heart or kidney to those who need transplants.[19] Neither should we jeopardize the marriage bond or one's personal integrity to produce a child. Just because collaborative reproduction works does not mean that we need to use it. I tend to agree with Edward D. Schneider when he says that the psychological risks inherent in collaborative reproduction are important enough to cause Christians to lean toward avoiding them.[20]

The unborn are on a biological continuum as are maternal perceptions of the unborn. Some dilemmas occur later on the continuum when the unborn should have stayed unborn longer. These babies come earlier than expected and consequently are of very low birth weight. Amazingly, today babies weighing 700 grams (1.54 pounds) can survive through neonatal intensive care and technology. This progress has a dark side, however. These babies have enormous risks of developing major physical problems, including brain damage, because of their immaturity.

Many parents who dearly love and want their tiny babies come to the point of begging the neonatologists to stop the high-tech treatment and let their baby die in peace. They care so much that they do not want their baby to suffer any longer. As a responsible society and as a community of Christians we also need to ask, "Is it right to spend more than two hundred thousand dollars to produce one 700 gram survivor with a high risk of morbidity through aggressive high-technology treatment, while hundreds of normal children in the same city have poor nutrition, poor health care, and poor educational opportunities?"

I am not suggesting that we do away with all technology in maternity care, although the risks and benefits must constantly be weighed. I am suggesting that we use an ethic of caring to serve as the basis for our decisions and that we carefully determine, with the help of God and our Christian friends, what caring means in individual situations.

I believe caring means directing our resources toward preventing problems in the first place: good prenatal care and nutrition for all pregnant women; avoidance of harmful habits that can harm the fetus (smoking, alcohol, drugs); a lifestyle that avoids exposure to sexually transmitted diseases that can endanger the fetus; and a lifestyle that prevents conception of unwanted babies.

When our prevention efforts are inadequate, problems exist, and simple answers are not forthcoming, we need to use our God-given powers to identify and weigh the options. This is where the Christian community enters. We can be helpful to each other by listening, asking hard questions, praying, and becoming knowledgeable about appropriate options.

We as Christian people are aligned with the Creator and have experienced a reshaping of our motivations to be like God's motivation. I believe that God's way is to individualize our approach in each case by carefully weighing all available information in a caring group and doing what seems to be the most loving thing to do. I recognize that this may be difficult to discern and that in our humanness some mistakes will surely be made. I believe that God expects us to treat all of God's human creation with compassion, love, and dignity—not necessarily with all the technology available. This kind of caring is what maternal perspectives of the unborn support.

As Christians we have a relationship with a God of compassion who gave us dominion over creation, who controls history from beginning to end, who promises a better life after death, who allows us to make choices, who gives us reasoning powers and creative abilities, and who expects us to use them. God also has given us each other in the Christian community to work through decisions together. May God give us the courage to proceed with confidence, hope, and love energized by our faith.

Questions for Reflection and Discussion
1. Is it morally right to bring a baby into the world if technology has demonstrated that it will be so abnormal that it can never form a relationship and will suffer severely? How might the mother's feelings of attachment affect this decision?
2. Whose needs take priority when the mother is unable physically, psychologically, and financially to care for the baby she has conceived?

3. Should pregnant women have an ultrasound examination to see if the fetus is normal? What are the implications of the resulting knowledge?
4. How does our modern society encourage or discourage maternal and paternal bonding to the unborn child? Does the church influence these patterns?

For Further Reading

Fletcher, John C., and Mark I. Evans
    1983 "Maternal Bonding in Early Fetal Ultrasound Examinations." *The New England Journal of Medicine* 308 (Feb. 17): 392-3.
Kemp, Virginia, and Cecilia Page
    1987 "Maternal Prenatal Attachment in Normal and High-risk Pregnancies." *Journal of Obstetrics, Gynecology, and Neonatal Nursing* 16 (May/June): 179-84.
Mahoney, Maurice J.
    1978 "Fetal-Maternal Relationship." In *Encyclopedia of Bioethics*, edited by Warren T. Reich. New York: Macmillan and Free Press.
Robertson, John A.
    1983 "Surrogate Mothers: Not So Novel After All." *The Hastings Center Report* 13 (Oct.): 29-34.
Rubin, Reva
    1984 *Maternal Identity and the Maternal Experience.* New York: Springer Publishing Company, Inc.
Schneider, Edward D., ed.
    1985 *Questions About the Beginning of Life.* Minneapolis: Augsburg Publishing House.
Walters, LeRoy, Jr.
    1983 "A Christian Response to Genetic Engineering." *Gospel Herald* 76 (April 12): 260-1.

Chapter 10

Psychological Perspectives

Enos D. and Ruth K. Martin

Enos Martin
*M.D., Pennsylvania
State University. Co-
director of sexual dys-
functions clinic, assis-
tant director of inpa-
tient psychiatric unit,
and associate professor
of psychiatry, Pennsyl-
vania State University
College of Medicine,
Hershey, Pennsylvania.*

Ruth Martin
*B.S. in secondary ed-
ucation, Shippensburg
State College. Student
in master's program in
community psychology,
Pennsylvania State Uni-
versity, University Park,
Pennsylvania.*

INITIAL DEBATE regarding the use of
reproductive technologies often focuses
on their potential for adverse psychological effects on the individual. After more
experience with the technology, negative
individual psychological effects are declared to be limited and not prohibitive of
its continued usage. However, whether or
not individuals suffer specific psychological harm from these technologies, the
church and society at large are greatly affected by their psychological impact, and
both struggle with the moral and ethical
dilemmas posed by the application of
these technologies.

For example, recent research suggests that the adverse psychological effects on the woman getting an abortion
are minimal.[1] However, the anxiety, anger,
and even violence demonstrated in the
current abortion debate suggest that psychological factors remain of critical importance in this discussion.[2] Furthermore,
the psychological factors currently associated with the abortion controversy affect

154

the society at large and not just the woman (or couple) and fetus involved. These societal psychological issues are not as easily defined with psychological tests and psychiatric interviews as are individual psychological reactions. Consequently, these societal psychological issues may be easily minimized or ignored and the inaccurate conclusion drawn that neither individual nor societal psychological factors are significant in deciding whether or not a given reproductive technology should be used.

This chapter will discuss the psychological significance of the stages of the reproductive process—generativity, conception, fertility, pregnancy, and childbirth—to both the couple involved and the church community. It will also detail some psychological implications of the technological interventions now available at each of the above reproductive stages both from the church community's, as well as the individual couple's, perspective.

Generativity—Its Psychological Meaning
to the Couple and the Community

Childbearing has deep psychological significance. People often look askance at the couple who decides not to generate children. A minister confided to a colleague that he was very upset with a local lay counselor because he had advised a couple not to have children. The minister felt this advice was destructive because the generation of children gives meaning to the life of the couple and the church community. In support of this attitude, Erik Erikson states that an important developmental task of adult life is generativity.[3]

Feeling good about who one is and what one has to contribute leads to the desire to generate, to give. Desiring children is often an indication that the couple feels they have something to pass on to the next generation. Persons who feel they did not receive enough love from their own parents or did not receive the right kind of parenting may decide they do not have the energy or the interest to give to children.

Desiring to generate children may also be an indication that the couple feels positively about the value and stability of the community. Couples who believe that the world is an evil place and becoming worse, or a place not likely to last much longer, may decide not to bring children into the world. A young businessman asserted to his friends that he and his wife did not plan to have children because "the danger of nuclear war during our lifetime is too great." However, other couples are willing to take this risk because they basically trust life.

Some persons wish to be productive and creative but do not choose to have children. Their decision to forego children does not arise out of fear of parenting or fear of life. Rather, they affirm life and contribute to it in other ways. The apostle Paul said, "An unmarried man is concerned . . . how he can please the Lord. . . . [A] married man is concerned . . . how he can please his wife—and his interests are divided. . . . I am saying this for your own good not to restrict you, but that you may live in a right way in undivided devotion to the Lord."[4] Paul, although he indicates that marriage and family life are appropriate for the Christian, makes clear that he chooses to be generative through total involvement in the Lord's work.

For the Christian the question of first importance is not "Am I open to generativity through marriage and family life?" but rather "Am I open to being generative and productive in my relationship with God?" To answer this question in the affirmative means to "seek first God's kingdom and God's righteousness."[5] It means to feel good about who we are and what we have in Christ and to desire to pass Christ's life on to others. It also means to be convinced that life in the church is durable and is a safe place to invest our life energies.

Having answered, "Am I being responsive to God's will?" the Christian is ready for the next question: "Will my being generative and productive for God include marriage?"

To Marry or Not to Marry

Throughout history the church and Western civilization have encouraged marriage between a man and a woman as the proper setting for sexual activity, conception, and childbearing. Although sexual activity, pregnancy, and childbearing sometimes occurred outside the marriage relationship, they were considered sinful by the church and illicit by society at large. If a young person wished to be sexually active and to rear children, marriage was the obvious choice; if not, then a life of singleness with celibacy was the approved choice.

In recent years these basic patterns of society have undergone dramatic changes. The number of couples living together outside of marriage in the United States quadrupled from 500,000 couples in 1970 to two million couples in 1985.[6] Single-parent families quadrupled from 234,000 in 1970 to 902,000 in 1979. This increase appeared to be largely due to the increase in births to single mothers and not to the increase in divorce. Births to single mothers increased 36 percent from 398,000 in 1970 to 543,900 in 1978.[7] In 1985 there were 828,174 births to unmarried women, which accounted for 7.3 percent of total births.[8] Because these changes affect increasing numbers of individuals and families, the social stigma against these options is not as great as it once was.

Other more radical changes are affecting the way we think about marriage and family. These changes include such variations on the traditional family theme as the legal adoption of children by lesbian couples or the bearing of children by lesbian couples through the use of artificial insemination by donor (AID).

Society presents these variant lifestyles to the young person with little to indicate that one lifestyle is any more or any less preferable than another. The media tend to seek out the unusual because of its interest value. Because the media give significant time to the alternative sexual and marital arrangements without editorial comment, some may infer that an aberrant lifestyle is as defensible, or even as desirable, as a traditional monogamous heterosexual marriage.

The unguided person may not realize the lifetime implications of choosing one option over another. Like a person reading a foreign menu, one makes a choice and takes the consequences, unaware of its potential for good or ill. A person can choose to have sex without marriage, relationship, or responsibility. A woman can choose to bear a child without sex, without marriage, or without an adult relationship.

Faced with these options, many delay making a marital commitment and choose, rather, to live together unmarried. Psychologically, these couples often fear the loss of control implied by a marital commitment or the embarrassment if they should fail after a public commitment. They often see this unmarried state as a short-term arrangement designed to test the feasibility of a permanent relationship. They do not intend to bring children into this relationship. If a child is conceived and the relationship is considered strong enough, they may decide to marry. Otherwise, they may get an abortion or decide to split up with one of the parents, usually the mother, raising the child alone.

Insecurity often plagues the relationship of couples living together without marriage. One partner may be reluctant to mention or deal with conflictual issues for fear of upsetting the other partner and leading to the termination of the relationship. One may become unduly jealous of the other, yet be unable to confront the partner. Thus, important issues are left unresolved and may become the nucleus of conflict that eventually destroys the relationship. As one young man stated after going through three or four such relationships: "There is no way to have a satisfying, intimate relationship without a promise."

One would hypothesize that children raised outside the security of a stable home with committed heterosexual parents would be at a disadvantage psychologically in terms of self-esteem, sense of security, and gender identity. Studies do indicate that the single-parent family has increased tensions. Single parents tend to be more socially isolated, experience more stressful life changes, and have less stable and supportive social networks than do married couples.[9]

Children raised by lesbian couples seem to be as well adjusted psychologically as those raised in single-parent families. Of course, lesbian couples and singles, like heterosexual couples, differ in their capacity to attend to the psychological needs of the child. The research to date suggests that the quality of family relationships and the pattern of upbringing are more important than the sexual orientation of the mother in determining how a child will develop. However, good longitudinal studies of the effects of a lesbian household on the personality of the child are not yet available.[10]

Ultimately, the church cannot depend on psychological studies to tell members how best to live a life. Psychological studies can shed light on health and pathology, but they may be quite limited in their ability to determine what is the optimal way to live a life. Based on divine revelation and the wisdom of the church over the centuries, we believe that a loving, committed heterosexual marriage is the best context in which to raise children. Although other contexts may allow the development of children without discernible psychopathology, this does not put these other options on the same ethical level with the heterosexual marriage. Our young people deserve to hear a clear word from the church that all options are not equally desirable or right from a Christian perspective.

Conception: To Conceive or Not to Conceive a Child

As discussed above, marital sexuality and procreation formerly were tied very closely together. Currently, however, technology provides the couple with a variety of ways to separate sexual intercourse from conception. For years many religious groups were ambivalent, if not negative, regarding the moral desirability of using contraceptives. Most religious objections have been put aside in response to some form of the dominion argument: because God has given us dominion over creation, we have the right, even the responsibility, to exercise that dominion in determining when and whether to have children. Therefore, the couple is faced with the issue: to conceive or not to conceive.

Many couples decide to postpone conception in favor of focusing on their relationship for the first years of marriage. In order to enjoy a satisfying sexual relationship without fear of conception, they need to use contraceptives.

Some couples are ambivalent regarding the use of contraceptives. If a person feels uncomfortable about or guilty regarding his or her sexuality, the use of a contraceptive may increase this guilt because it allows pleasure without consequences or responsibility. Also, to the extent that conception proves sound male and female functioning, not conceiving leaves the question open as to whether one is really "made right."

For those who choose to use contraceptives, a variety of methods are available. Each has its advantages and disadvantages medically. From a psychological standpoint a number of factors need to be considered.[11] First, which partner is willing to take the initiative or exercise control in the use of contraception? Some women like the pill or the diaphragm because either of these gives them the control over conception. However, they may later come to resent the responsibility or the risk of the contraceptives they are using. Of course, the successful use of the condom requires the male's cooperation and places some of the responsibility for contraception on him. Some men resist this, while others like to be in charge of this aspect of the relationship. If the woman develops side effects from using the pill or IUD, she may resent having to prevent a pregnancy while her husband does nothing but satisfy his own needs.

In deciding on a contraceptive a couple should consider their respective personality characteristics. A woman who has difficulty with schedules should not take the pill because its effectiveness is based on taking the pill at the proper time. A woman whose sense of identity and self-control is uncertain should avoid the pill because taking it, she may feel she is being regulated by a foreign substance.

The use of the diaphragm requires that the woman be comfortable with her body because inserting it requires touching. In addition, the diaphragm requires planning ahead for a sexual encounter unless the insertion of the diaphragm is made a part of the foreplay itself. Some people feel this planning ahead takes away the spontaneity of the sexual encounter.

The use of the rhythm method or withdrawal requires strong impulse control and the ability to delay gratification. Persons who are impulsive should avoid these methods if they wish to successfully avoid conception. Furthermore, the failure rate is high with these techniques.

The condom gives the husband the choice and the responsibility in the sexual encounter. It is readily available and protects from venereal disease. Yet many do not prefer this contraceptive, feeling it decreases sensation. In the future new male contraceptives may become available, thus increasing the man's responsibility for contraception. However, at the moment, the burden for ensuring contraception rests for the most part on the woman.

In contrast to most other methods, the IUD, if it has no side effects, can be forgotten by both partners after it is in place. Some, of course, will not use the IUD for ethical reasons because it is believed to prevent the fertilized egg from implanting.

Some may initially believe that the community is little affected by the couple's decision to conceive or not to conceive a child. However, the cumulative effect of many couples delaying conception means that couples in general will be older when they bear children and, with the later hour on the female biological time clock, will have fewer children. Statistics also show that teenage pregnancies are increasing.[12] The net result of these two phenomena for society is that those least capable of effectively rearing children are having more children, while those more capable emotionally, financially, and culturally are having fewer children. Thus, what appears to be a private matter has potentially profound effects on the community.

Infertility: To Be Able or Not to Be Able to Have a Child

To be fertile, to be able to bear a child, has a complexity of psychological meanings for the couple.[13] For both the male and the female, fertility indicates that anatomically and physiologically the couple is "normal"; it is a confirmation of masculinity and femininity. The prospective father is often teased by his friends, "Well, now we know you are a real man." Women often wonder whether they are "made right." Female genitalia are internal and not available for external inspection as are the genitalia of men. Thus, to become pregnant is a potent testimony to the intact feminine body of the prospective mother. In both the male and female, self-esteem is enhanced by the awareness of properly functioning bodies.

Fertility is also a confirmation for many couples of having reached adulthood. From early childhood many individuals fantasize about growing up and having a child as Mother and Dad did. Fertility, the realization of that fantasy, allows the couple to identify with the parents. In addition, fertility can be the expression of a drive to create or to insure a type of immortality where one's life and influence will live on after one's death.

For others pregnancy is a way of compensating for a loss. A couple who loses a child is often asked by relatives and friends: "You will have another, won't you?" Sometimes the couple even gives the "replacement child" the same name as the deceased child, thus signaling to the family and community that this child has a special role to fill in the home.

Fertility can also have negative psychological implications. Pregnancy can be the way for an unwed teenager to rebel against a restrictive home setting; or it can be an accident, an unwelcome consequence of a night of pleasure by two irresponsible people. For others pregnancy can be a way to hold on to a shaky relationship by "giving us something more in common." Some who are reluctant to enter the middle years and end their reproductive capabilities may conceive a child to postpone entering the next phase of life and leaving the present phase.

If fertility is the joy of a dream come true, infertility is the agony of a nightmare lived out day and night. Infertility is defined as the failure to achieve a successful pregnancy following a year of regular sexual activity without contraception. One in ten couples has difficulty in becoming fertile.

Causes of infertility can be either organic or nonorganic. About 70 percent of the couples with infertility have an identifiable organic cause for their infertility. About 15 percent of infertile couples have no clear organic cause for the infertility.[14] However, having no clear organic cause and having a psychological cause for the infertility are not synonymous. Not having a clear organic cause may reflect the lack of appropriate technology to identify the cause, rather than the true absence of an organic factor. Determination of psychogenic infertility should not be a simple diagnosis by exclusion, but should meet certain criteria. Mai recommends that in order to make the diagnosis of psychogenic infertility the following factors should be present: (1) sexual intercourse and an initially expressed desire for pregnancy; (2) reluctance expressed by one or both partners to become parents as evidenced by subsequent interview data; and (3) a clear mechanism that prevents conception such as the failure to ejaculate.[15] These criteria may seem rather rigid and extreme. Yet, adherence to these criteria will enable both the couple and their physician to actively pursue organic factors, rather than prematurely blaming infertility on psychogenic factors alone.

Such criteria and sophisticated technology that evaluate the cause of infertility have reduced cases of infertility assessed to be psychogenically caused from 40 percent to 5 percent.[16] However, abnormalities in hormones, transmitters, and releasing substances do not rule out psychological factors in infertility. In fact, we now know that most of the neuroendocrine functions of the reproductive process are influenced by the emotional and intrapsychic state of the infertile person. Furthermore, even azoospermia and oligospermia in the male are influenced by psychogenic factors. Thus, in assessing the causes of infertility, one should evaluate all clients for the nature and degree of the psychological factors contributing to and complicating their infertility, regardless of the organic factors involved.

Attempts have been made to identify specific psychological conflicts that contribute to infertility. Such proposed conflicts include identification with a hostile mother and rejection of pregnancy, conflicts about femininity, and conflict between the fear and the desire to have a child. Of course, conflicts about sexuality can lead to impotence, painful intercourse, and infrequent coitus, which can directly relate to infertility.

Kaltreider, in a study of married, childless women who chose to be permanently sterilized, found that even though these women consciously rejected motherhood, psychological tests indicated that they feared that they were inadequate.[17] Further, she found that these women were underachievers professionally and avoided commitments in other areas of their lives. On the other hand, some women have unconscious resistance to motherhood, yet feel the need to comply with familial or societal demands. Although they express a wish to be fertile, they become infertile. Seemingly, the infertility is a defense to protect against the unconscious danger of having a child. Clinically, it is important to respect the defenses and not strip them away without helping the person deal with their implications. In some cases women with apparent defenses against fertility nevertheless conceive and then become suicidal.

The awareness of infertility can be a "major life crisis" for a couple. Reacting to it can cause emotional havoc in their marriage and sexual relationship.[18] Many infertile couples state that infertility was the most upsetting experience of their lives. Martin's in-depth study of 25 couples seeking artificial insemination by donor revealed that learning of and adjusting to their infertility was much more traumatic to the couples than adjusting to artificial insemination by donor (AID).[19] In fact, dealing with the intense feelings associated with infertility has a destructive effect on the marital relationship for some couples. For those who worked through or survived the stresses of the infertility itself, the decision for AID actually had a constructive influence on the relationship.

As a couple faces the reality of their infertility, the first decision they confront is whether or not to accept childlessness. Some choose childlessness because the alternatives, such as adoption, involve too much hassle or too much uncertainty. Others choose childlessness because they would rather not have a child at all if it cannot be their own flesh and blood. Some doubt their ability to genuinely love a child whom they have not conceived. Others feel that a child who is not their own natural child would be a constant reminder of their inability to conceive. Still others feel that a child not biologically their own might have undesirable character traits that would make it difficult to raise the child.[20]

Some who accept childlessness see it as an active option. They have come to terms with their infertility and choose to find fulfillment in life in ways other than through their own children. They may turn their creative drives into areas totally unrelated to children and find success and fulfillment. Some devout persons who cannot have natural children focus on having spiritual children. They involve themselves actively and effectively in the lives of many more people than if they had had their own children. As mentors, they enable young persons to make the transition from dependency on parents to a mature adulthood by way of a transitional mentor or protege relationship. In other cases the childless couple may supply parenting to persons deprived or neglected as children and in need of a corrective emotional experience with caring and available adults. So in various ways these childless couples produce and create new benefits for the communities in which they live, and many children not naturally their own "rise up and call them blessed."[21]

Not all couples who remain childless choose childlessness as an active option. Some resign themselves to childlessness by seeing it as a tragedy that they must bear. They may resentfully and grudgingly accept the burden, becoming angry at themselves, at one another, at God, and at life for depriving them of their one great wish to have children. Others continue to maintain hope that someday they will have a child. Partly because of biological uncertainties and technological advances, many couples are unsure about when it is best to accept childlessness and when they should continue to hope and explore options.

Infertile couples may not often speak with others of their burden; yet, those around them sense that their childlessness is a sensitive issue. Tragically, the community often lacks the sensitivity and courage to be helpful to these couples. Some couples begin to define themselves in terms of their childlessness. No matter what else they do in life, it is overshadowed by the awareness that "we could never have children." Again, the community that revolves around families with children often fails to be a truly Christian community for such couples.

Adoption as a choice. Adoption used to be the primary alternative to childlessness for the infertile couple. A *Psychology Today* survey in 1984 showed that 84 percent of the couples surveyed would choose adoption over the new technologies.[22] Adoption allows the infertile couple to carry out all the parenting functions of fertile couples and gives the satisfaction of passing on in a very intimate way one's values and ideals to the next generation. Adoptive parents learn experientially that the "real parents" are the ones who parent the child and not the ones who simply gave their genes to the child.

Adoption has many psychological implications. Adoptive parents at times have difficulty accepting what is not their own flesh and blood. They may tend to see any failures or limitations of the child as genetic. They may distance themselves from the child and his or her failures by an overemphasis on adoption, unnecessarily reminding the child and community that "this is our adopted child." On the other hand, some adoptive parents are overly concerned about protecting the child from the knowledge that he or she is adopted, as though this fact is a terrible reality that must never be acknowledged. If the child in this family does learn the truth of his or her origins, the child may overreact to this information as though it were truly the most distressing thing in the world. Parents are best advised neither to overemphasize, nor to deny the adoption. This is best accomplished if the parents themselves have accepted the child's origins as a significant but not all-important fact, realizing that the quality of their relationship with the child is now infinitely more important than who conceived and gave birth to the child.

If the child someday wants to seek or meet the natural parents, this should be handled matter-of-factly and without panic by the adoptive parents. They should realize that even though the child develops a relationship with the newly found natural parent, that relationship can never be more than a close friendship and can never rival in intensity and significance the relationship with the adoptive parents.

Of course, not all infertile couples prefer or are able to adopt. Because the number of abortions has dramatically increased, the number of children available for adoption has markedly decreased. Waiting lists for adoption are measured in terms of years. Adoption agencies are very selective; some otherwise qualified couples may not be given a child because of their age, or a couple may not be able to adopt as many children as they wish.[23] For a variety of reasons infertile couples who still want children may choose against adoption in favor of seeking a child by way of one of the newer technologies such as artificial insemination by husband, artificial insemination by donor, or in vitro fertilization.

Artificial insemination by husband (AIH). In a few cases the couple's infertility can be treated through artificial insemination by husband. For example, if the husband has a psychosexual dysfunction and cannot ejaculate during normal intercourse but can with masturbation, AIH could be used. Or if the husband has a low sperm count, his sperm can be concentrated and admin-

istered through AIH. When AIH is used, the sperm are by definition the husband's. His sperm are placed mechanically in the vagina, rather than through normal intercourse. Catholics have had
objections to the method because of their strictures against masturbation. A few others object to the artificial means of the insemination. Most, however, view this as a medical procedure that
enables a couple to conceive their own biological offspring with
minimal psychological effects.[24]

Artificial insemination by donor (AID). Unfortunately, most
infertile couples cannot benefit from AIH because the husband
either has no sperm or a very low sperm count that cannot be
remedied by this method. If the wife has no reproductive abnormality and the husband is the cause of the infertility, the couple
may be candidates for artificial insemination by donor. In this situation the sperm of an anonymous donor are mechanically placed
in the vagina of the recipient woman at the time in her menstrual
cycle when she is most likely to conceive. Approximately 250,000
couples have conceived and borne children by this method from
the years 1960 to 1980. Estimates suggest that 10,000 children
are born each year by AID.[25]

Initial reports about the psychological implications of AID
were negative. A psychiatrist who treated a number of women
who sought AID concluded that seeking AID was, in its own
right, a sign of psychological disturbance. Psychotherapists and
others speculated on the negative psychological implications of
bringing a foreigner—that is, the anonymous donor—into the marital relationship. Even though there was never a real relationship
with the donor by either the husband or the wife, the couple's
fantasy of the donor who had contributed his half to the genetic
makeup of the child when the natural husband was unable to do
so was felt to be psychologically destructive to the couple.[26]

Later psychological reports indicated that no neurotic conflicts were necessarily associated with seeking AID. In 1988 Martin and Zimmerman reported on their study of the psychological
characteristics of couples seeking AID.[27] They evaluated both the
husband and wife of each couple by using a structured interview
and the Minnesota Multiphasic Personality Inventory (MMPI).
The MMPI data were compared to that of a control group
matched for age and sex. The results indicated that these couples
seeking AID had fewer signs of pathology on the MMPI than did
the normal control group. Approximately 15 percent of the sub-

jects had signs of psychological disturbance sufficient to require a diagnosis of psychological illness. However, this is no greater than the incidence of psychopathology in the general population. The psychopathology in this sample included acute depression and anxiety, which appeared to have been triggered by the infertility. However, signs of preexisting psychological conflicts existed in most of these symptomatic couples. These researchers therefore concluded that seeking AID is not in itself indicative of psychopathology.

The MMPI item analysis and the psychiatric interview data were congruent in indicating that there was a strong family orientation in these couples seeking AID. The majority of the couples reported warm and supportive relationships between husband and wife. They also reported values strongly supportive of the family unit; for example, they were negative toward extramarital affairs and homosexuality for themselves. At the same time they were tolerant of people with differing values.

This study further demonstrated that even though seeking AID is not a sign of psychopathology, there are significant stresses associated with AID. However, most couples found dealing with the infertility more stressful than adjusting to AID. By the time the couple had worked through the stress of the infertility, they were ready to see the AID as offering something better than the pain of childlessness. "At least the AID child will be a part of one of us," many said. Also with AID the couple has the opportunity to experience pregnancy and delivery.

The stresses associated with AID include a continuation of some of the stresses of infertility. One of these stresses is the constant monitoring of body temperature to determine the optimal time to go to the clinic to receive the AID. Exposing one's private difficulties to yet another professional who never quite promises the desired child is another stress. Further, the concern exists that confidentiality will inadvertently be breached, and family and friends will learn of the infertility and the AID.

In addition, some stresses are unique to AID. Ethicists and psychiatrists assume that the most significant stress facing the couple is adjusting to the reality that a third party—a stranger—has been introduced into the most intimate area of the marital relationship and that this poses a threat to the sexually incompetent husband. However, the actual experience of couples seeking AID does not support these concerns. First, husbands generally do not withdraw from seeking AID. In Martin's study[28] the husband in many cases actually took the initiative in seeking AID. The wives in a number of cases had thought of AID but were reluctant to pursue it lest it be threatening to their husbands. They were relieved and gratified when the husbands took the initiative.

The husbands' involvement was not limited to suggesting the AID process. They supported their wives during the subsequent pregnancy and delivery. After the birth of the child, they actively involved themselves in the child's care even to the extent of getting up at night to help with feeding the infant. Wives reported their gratitude and surprise that the husbands were so supportive. "It was just like it was his own child," a number of wives said. Were the husbands denying their own negative feelings about AID by going out of their way to be involved? No evidence from the interviews or the testing suggested that the husbands were suppressing intense resentful feelings against the AID process. A further indication of the husbands' genuine acceptance of the AID child was their expressed desire in a number of cases to have more children by AID. These men stated that the genetic origin of the child was not in any way as important as the joy of having a child to parent.

All the couples in Martin's study[29] had been offered the option of having the husbands present for the insemination or actually doing the insemination with the assistance of the nurse. However, although most men accompanied their wives to the clinic, none elected to do the insemination and very few elected to be present in the room when the insemination was performed. The couples all stated that they wished to see the insemination as a medical procedure. As such, it was not a personal interaction where another man—the anonymous donor—was brought into the relationship.

Some ethicists have asserted that this procedure is adulterous in nature. However, the couples make every effort to depersonalize the AID procedure. Most of the couples in this study minimized or denied having any significant fantasies about the donor or desiring to meet the donor. Most were adamant that they wanted the donor to remain anonymous.

A unique finding among the AID couples was their strong desire to keep the AID secret from persons outside the marital unit—parents, extended family, and friends. In some cases even the delivering physician was not aware of the child's true parentage. In all cases the husband's name was entered on the birth certificate as the father of the AID child. In a minority of cases even the AID couple remained unsure of the parentage of the child because the husband's sperm was mixed with the donor's sperm.

Keeping the AID parentage a secret runs counter to recent societal emphasis on the right of adopted children to know their true parentage. The placing of the husband's name on the birth certificate and the brief or nonexistent records of the donor's history and characteristics offer minimal chance that AID children could ever trace their paternity.

By keeping the parentage a secret, the couple is prevented from turning to usual confidants, such as mothers and best friends, for support and advice. Rather, they are forced to find support and counsel from the spouse within the marriage. This forced communication at first may be difficult for some couples but in time develops improved communication skills and increased intimacy that actually strengthens the marital relationship. One couple said that dealing with the infertility and the decision for AID was "like a second set of wedding bands." Some evidence suggests that these marriages are actually more stable than others. One researcher reported that in 800 couples who received AID only one divorce occurred.[30]

The impact of having an important long-term family secret on the couple or the child is not known. In Martin's study[31] one woman pregnant by AID became seriously depressed after she watched a TV show where a woman born of AID angrily denounced the practice. This young mother-to-be became obsessed with how she would be able to relate to her child without somehow communicating that she had a dreadful secret. The woman became so depressed that she considered getting an abortion and later considered suicide. After intensive psychiatric treatment, she recovered from her depression and obsessions and bore a normal child. Because the first child had brought her and her husband so much pleasure, she later sought to conceive another child by AID.

We have considered the psychology of the AID couple but have not discussed the psychology of the child or the anonymous donor. In both situations only limited information is available. Early studies of children do not indicate any significant psychopathology. Studies of these children are needed. Anecdotal reports exist of children suffering marked psychological distress upon learning the truth about their parentage. One woman, upon learning from her father that she was really the child of an anonymous donor, mounted a vigorous campaign to locate her biological father, who "cared no more for his offspring than the twenty-five dollars he got for his ejaculate." This person was also behind a move to ban AID.

If little information exists on the child, even less exists on the donor. Some have speculated on the motives that cause donors to continually involve themselves in the AID programs. From self-report their motives include the humanitarian desire to help a childless couple, the desire to spread their superior genes, the desire to discover if they are fertile before they enter their own marriage, and the desire for money at no great personal inconvenience.

In summary, current information suggests that seeking AID is not a sign of psychopathology in itself. An apparent benefit of AID is the joy of having a child that is genetically part of at least one of the parents. Keeping the parentage secret has potential benefits, as well as problems. On the positive side, the couple's secret forces them to deal with one another without bringing in outsiders to help resolve their differences. This appears to strengthen the marital relationship as suggested by the low incidence of divorce in these couples. On the negative side it is not known in the long run what effects a secret or a deception will have on the couple or the child who may eventually sense that there is something hidden about his or her family history. Nor is it known what effects these secrets will have on society. If safeguards are not put in place regarding the number of children a given donor is allowed to father, consanguinity may eventually be a problem to society. Also, what does it do to a man to contribute to the conception of children without knowledge of or responsibility for his offspring? On the other side of the secrecy argument, how would knowledge of AID affect the child's sense of identity?

In vitro fertilization. If a couple's infertility is caused by pathology in the wife's reproductive system, they may be able to consider having a child by in vitro fertilization. The first successful in vitro fertilization—fertilization within a test tube—and embryo transfer procedure resulting in a successful pregnancy occurred in 1979. Since that time hundreds of pregnancies have been reported worldwide as a result of fertilizing the egg outside the woman's body with the husband's sperm and then transferring the fertilized egg to the woman's uterus. In most cases this procedure is sought by women who can produce normal eggs but in whom tubal pathology prevents the egg from traveling down the fallopian tube, uniting with the sperm, and subsequently being implanted in the uterus.

An important ethical dilemma centers on the significance of the fertilized egg.[32] The IVF procedure involves fertilizing a number of eggs, implanting the most viable ones, and discarding the remainder. This discarding of potential human life creates moral anxiety for some thoughtful persons. Is accepting the destruction of fertilized eggs the "slippery slope" that leads to accepting abortion in the first trimester, the second trimester, or even euthanasia? These complex moral questions may trigger psychological problems.

Initial studies of couples seeking IVF indicate that these couples are no more pathologic than normals. However, significant stress is associated with the IVF. Stresses include the long waiting list, the intense depression akin to that seen with a miscarriage if the procedure is unsuccessful, and for some the moral anxiety associated with discarding the surplus fertilized eggs.[33]

Surrogate mothering. Surrogate mothering involves the services of a third person for a fee. A surrogate mother allows the implantation of the wife's fertilized egg into her uterus or allows herself to be inseminated artificially by the husband's sperm and then carries the fetus to term for the couple. In both cases the surrogate mother is expected to turn the child over at birth to the couple.

Although surrogate mothering may seem to be just another reproductive technology that allows an infertile couple to have a child of their own or at least half their own, aspects of surrogate mothering make it more complex than the other technologies. Surrogate mothering involves an outside person in a more intimate way than any of the other technologies. This process cannot be kept anonymous as can artificial insemination by donor. The surrogate mother is asked to give herself for the nine-month gestation period, to go through the physical and emotional changes of pregnancy, and to give the child up after developing a relationship with the unborn child.

The complexity of the potential emotional consequences of

surrogate mothering strains the imagination. What are the likely psychological effects on the surrogate mother who needs to give up the child, on the couple if the surrogate does not give over the child, on the child as it tries to clarify its identity, and on society as it tries to protect the stability and integrity of family units? On the other hand, what woman would not have psychological distress after carrying a fetus for nine months and then giving it up? Do we really want a society where people are able to do such things and not suffer a negative psychological reaction?

A 1984 survey in *Psychology Today* showed that only 14 percent of the women surveyed would even consider surrogate mothering if they were infertile.[34] In 1984 the National Committee for Adoption said that surrogate mothering will "affect children and parents adversely and divert attention from the need of children to have permanent, stable, and secure homes and families."[35] In Great Britain the Warnock Commission's report to Parliament called for "strong criminal penalties for agencies and professionals who knowingly assist the establishment of a surrogate pregnancy."[36] Concerns have been expressed by some ethicists that normalizing surrogate mothering will lead to women being coerced to serve as surrogates just to get the money, the dehumanization of the surrogate as they learn to give up their own flesh and blood by design, and serious identity problems for the child.[37]

To Carry or Not to Carry the Child

Prior to the 1973 Supreme Court decision legalizing abortion, to carry or not to carry a pregnancy was not a legitimate question. Because abortions were illegal, most women upon learning that they were pregnant prepared themselves to at least endure, if not accept, the pregnancy. Now, a pregnant woman can terminate her pregnancy without legal obstacles in the first trimester.

Statistics show that the incidence of abortion is increasing. *The World Almanac* reports that 1,268,987 legal abortions were performed in the United States in 1983. Seventy-eight percent of these abortions were in unmarried women; 21 percent were in married women. Eighty-nine percent of these abortions were performed during the first trimester.[38]

Researchers, clinicians, and society in general want to know the psychological consequences to the woman having an abortion. Intuitively, one would expect that traumatically interrupting a natural process involving life would have a significant psychological impact on the woman involved.

Prior to 1964, research studies suggested that therapeutic abortion was almost always followed by psychiatric illness. Now researchers look back and point out that many of these studies had methodological problems: they were impressionistic, had small samples, or were unduly affected by the bias of the researcher.[39]

Later studies from 1964 to 1973 continued to examine the emotional consequences of therapeutic abortion. These studies reported that only a 10 percent minority of women suffered serious psychiatric complications such as severe neurosis, sexual dysfunction, psychotic decompensation, or suicide.[40]

Studies since the legalization of abortion in 1973 have continued to emphasize the positive psychological outcomes of therapeutic abortions. In 1985 Lazarus did a questionnaire survey on 292 patients who had had therapeutic abortions. He did his survey two weeks after elective abortion of a first trimester pregnancy. He reported that relief was the predominant emotion for 76 percent of the women. Guilt and depression occurred in about 15 percent. Only 10 percent described the overall experience as negative.[41]

Smith in his 1973 follow-up studies of women two years after their abortions found that only 6 percent of the women sought psychiatric treatment after the abortion. He concluded that the majority of women suffered no psychological scarring from the abortion.[42]

This group of researchers seems to agree that where women decide without significant ambivalence to terminate a pregnancy, they are not likely to experience serious psychiatric disturbance. On the other hand, sadness, guilt, or depression after an abortion is not unusual. This negative response is supposedly not permanent, nor does it progress to more serious pathology in most women.[43]

The research indicates that certain factors place a woman getting an abortion at greater risk for developing a negative psychological reaction. These factors include marked ambivalence about getting an abortion, abortion in the second trimester, and a history of previous psychiatric illness.

A significant factor in the psychological reaction to abortion is the degree to which the child was wanted or not wanted. Those women who definitely wanted a child or were very ambivalent about the abortion experienced more significant depression following the abortion.

Those women who experience a spontaneous abortion (miscarriage) have a higher incidence of depression than do those who elect a therapeutic abortion because these women usually wanted a child and are deeply distressed by their loss. They often feel helpless to have prevented the loss. Their distress is at times increased by well-meaning friends who encourage them to "get over it and try for another child." They need, rather, to know that the significant others in their lives realize that they have experienced a real loss in the miscarriage of the desired child.

Women who choose to abort a pregnancy for genetic or medical reasons often have more psychological complications than women who terminate the pregnancy for psychological reasons. These women often wanted the pregnancy but, because of suspected physical abnormalities or inherited disease, chose to abort.

Women seldom decide for abortion without some degree of ambivalence. They may in part want the child but because they are single, have limited financial resources, or are in an unstable relationship, they decide to terminate the pregnancy. Blumenfield reported that one-third of women seeking abortion gave clear evidence that they had also wanted a pregnancy but were in conflict about it.[44] Reports that contraceptives did not work are often rationalizations by the women to disguise the reality that in part they wanted to be pregnant.

Women who seek second trimester abortions often have greater ambivalence regarding their pregnancy and delay or procrastinate in seeking help. These women are often adolescents in conflict with their parents about an abortion. Older women who lack the support of their husbands for the decision may also delay getting the abortion till the second trimester.

Although most women have ambivalence about deciding for an abortion, the woman who gets abortions repeatedly appears to have marked ambivalence. In fact, 20 percent of all abortions are repeat abortions. These women have been unable to resolve the ambivalence about having a child and thus place themselves in the position to get pregnant again. As soon as they learn they are pregnant, the other side of the ambivalence comes into play, and they seek an abortion. These women seeking repeat abortions are more likely to have a poor self-image and more psychological distress following the abortion.

Another factor affecting whether or not a woman will have a negative psychological reaction to an abortion is the degree to which she is able to depersonalize the fetus. This is, of course, more easily done in the first trimester when she has as yet experienced few signs of pregnancy and when the pregnancy can be terminated with dilatation and curettage of the uterus (D and C).

By the second trimester more investment in the baby has occurred. The mother often uses the term "baby" and not "pregnancy" or "fetus" when speaking of her condition. In addition, the abortion techniques used in the second trimester are often more distressing to the woman. The injection of prostaglandin or saline requires 12-36 hours in a setting where the woman is likely to hear sounds of full-term babies being born. The procedure at this stage is likely to have more complications, such as pain leading to anger, hostility, and depression. Body parts of the fetus may be seen in association with the abortion process. Obviously, a woman who has begun a relationship with the developing fetus and who had at least in part wanted a child will have more regret and distress regarding an abortion than a woman who experiences an unwanted pregnancy and terminates the pregnancy in the first trimester.

Women who have negative psychological reactions to abortions are more likely to have had preexisting psychological problems. The more severe the postabortion disturbance, the more likely the woman suffered serious disturbance prior to the abortion. Abortion does not resolve or lessen severe psychiatric disorders. In fact, a person with schizophrenia may incorporate the abortion into her delusions and become worse.[45]

Much of the recent research minimizes the real significance and magnitude of the negative psychological consequences of abortion. Even if only 10 percent of women getting an abortion have serious psychological reactions, that amounts to over 100,000 women seriously affected by the consequence of an elective procedure annually in the United States. And every year at least that many more new cases of psychiatric dysfunction will be added to the statistics. If abortion were a surgical procedure associated with a large personal and social benefit, society could possibly tolerate a 5-10 percent rate of serious side effects. But if the procedure has no compelling value other than the desire, comfort, and convenience of the mother, is the price too high?

Some people would respond to this question by pointing to

the consequences of being denied an abortion. A 1980 review of studies done in Sweden, Scotland, and Czechoslovakia indicated that some women prevented from having an abortion gave up their children for adoption or sought illegal abortions. Those forced into parenting ("mandatory mothering") showed more unstable marriages and less involvement with child rearing. Unwanted children were also often the victims of child abuse and neglect.[46]

Yet in our country the incidence of child abuse has increased along with the incidence of abortion. The prevention or discouragement of abortion is not synonymous with insisting on "mandatory mothering." Traditionally, those not wishing to mother could find couples eager to adopt the unwanted child.

To Have or Not to Have a Perfect Child

In the past several decades it has become possible to diagnose debilitating inherited diseases in the fetus prior to delivery. The technique involves securing a sample of cells from the amniotic sac surrounding the developing fetus and chemically studying these cells for signs of genetic disease.

Genetic disease is a significant health care problem. Twenty-five percent of all hospital bed occupancy is related to genetic disease. Four to 5 percent of all live born children have genetic disorders at birth. Because abortion is now legal, if not entirely socially acceptable, the couple who learns that they are carrying a child with a genetic disease faces a dilemma of whether or not to carry to term a child who will suffer from a genetic disorder.[47]

The reaction of a couple to learning that their unborn child has a genetic disease is similar to the reaction of parents who learn that their child has a fatal disease. First, there is strong denial and shock, with the parent expressing disbelief. During this time medical personnel should not push more information on the couple but rather give them time to adjust to the new reality and the loss. As the couple develops the cognitive awareness of the genetic disease, they will become anxious to somehow restore a sense of well-being. When the reality of the disease fully sinks in, the parents may become bitter and hostile and eventually depressed. They may fluctuate back and forth through these various emotions as they adjust to the new reality.

The attitude of the physician is important in helping a couple deal with the knowledge that the unborn child has a genetic disease. Young women tend to be less anxious and more mystified by the implications of an inherited disease. Then they become severely anxious if real problems develop in their newborn.

Prior to the amniocentesis a pregnant couple who thinks they may have a child with a genetic disease needs to be actively involved in the decision-making process about whether or not to have the amniocentesis and whether or not they will have an abortion if the results are positive. Many couples can accept the idea of having an abortion in the abstract if the fetus has a serious genetic disease, but in the concrete reality they have severe difficulty actually deciding for the abortion of a wanted but imperfect pregnancy. Abortion goes against the history of personal caring and life promotion that the couple has always endorsed.

Following the abortion of a wanted child who has an inherited disease, 92 percent of mothers have depression. A mother can view a miscarriage as an unfortunate accident over which she had little, if any, control. But the abortion of a child with an inherited disease involves a parental decision. The mother may wonder, for example, "If I abort a fetus with Downs Syndrome, what does this say about the value of the life of my neighbor's living Downs Syndrome child?" The mother may also fear that she will never be able to have a normal child, and her self-esteem may be seriously affected by the knowledge of a genetically impaired child. Couples in this situation need much support and help to make the most informed decision possible and to live with the consequences.[48]

Although not presently practiced in humans, it is technically possible to alter the genetic makeup of the fertilized egg—to delete undesired traits and to select for desired traits. In the unlikely case that such gene selection ever becomes the norm, the couple would be faced with intolerable pressure to make the right decisions and the right selections to insure the best offspring. One could imagine that for some parents anxiety would paralyze their attempts to design the perfect child.

To Have One or Many Options

We have seen that what was once a single option—"to marry or not to marry"—has become many options: to conceive or not to conceive, to carry or not to carry the child, to have or not to have a perfect child. Along with the sense of limitless possibilities comes the conviction that because the options are available, we are entitled to pursue them regardless of the personal or societal cost: "If you want it, you are entitled to go for it."

Entitlement, the expectation of favorable treatment, is based on the multitude of conscious and unconscious, verbalized and nonverbalized expectations that undergird our everyday interactions. For example, a husband who has exchanged marriage vows of faithfulness feels entitled to his wife's monogamous love. If he learns she is unfaithful, he is angered because he did not receive what he felt entitled to. A person expresses a pathologic sense of entitlement when he or she consistently has unrealistic expectations for favorable treatment from others. For example, the person who assumes he or she should never have to wait in line illustrates narcissistic entitlement.

Because of recent technological changes that give humans more control over their environment and reduce the limits with which they have formerly lived, we have developed a sense of entitlement bordering on the pathologic. We feel entitled not to have to tolerate any limits or frustrations of our desires.

This entitlement is illustrated in our response to pain. We have long assumed that pain and suffering are unavoidable. No one could reasonably expect to live a life free of suffering, limits, disappointments, and frustrated desires. As one struggled with pain and suffering and the limits of the human condition, one gained deeper insights into life and greater strength of character. Paul, when suffering from his intractable thorn in the flesh, was encouraged by Christ with "My strength is made perfect in weakness."

This acceptance of limits has changed in our society. The development of anesthesia approximately 200 years ago and its subsequent refinements have enabled humans for the first time to consistently avoid serious pain. Concomitant technological advances lightened work and removed other former limitations.

Similarly, reproductive technology has made it possible to overcome many of the natural barriers to fertility and reproduction. The infertile couple often develops the sense that they are entitled to conceive and bear a child. If they are unable to bear a child, they are sometimes bitter and resentful toward one another, God, or the medical profession, all of whom have not given them what they deserve. This sense of entitlement causes the couple to pursue every avenue technologically available, regardless of the cost to themselves or society and regardless of the ethics of the option.

Entitlement can also lead to a sense of ingratitude for what one has. It can take away the joy and awe in life. Rather than being focused on what one has received with concomitant gratefulness, the entitled one is focused on what he or she did not receive but was entitled to, what others have but he or she does not. Paul said, "Godliness with contentment is great gain." But often today to be contented with one's lot in life and to find sublimated sources of satisfaction is considered a "cop-out," a betrayal of the expectation to "go for all you can get," and a passive acceptance of what is instead of an active choice to pursue what could be.

Many take the position that if something can be done, it should be done. If a person can choose the sex of his or her child, the person feels obligated to choose. Seemingly, humans have broken through the barrier to the technological supremacy first erected at the tower of Babel. Now by speaking one common technological language, humans are able to do what God had prevented for their good. Is everything humans can do good for them?

This question has, of course, been asked about many technological advances that we now take for granted. Has it been good for humans to drive automobiles, fly airplanes, and travel in space? On the other hand, do all technological advances have the same level of ethical and psychological significance? Does the psychological significance of flying in an airplane in any way compare to the psychological significance of the reproductive technologies? Even though psychological tests prove that a mother is not made neurotic by the use of these technologies, where is the test that can assess the soul of a people, the spirit, or the sense of identity at the deepest level? These are all judgments, matters of perspective and intuition.

Because we are in a technological society, we use technological means to address all our questions. A technological approach, however, cannot answer spiritual or moral questions about what ought to be. The technological approach can only say what *is* and what can be but not what *ought* to be.

For some this multiplicity of options becomes an overwhelming burden. Now instead of enjoying the mystery of life and the gifts of life, one is required to make decisions about issues that humans were never expected to decide from the time of creation until now—"for you cannot make one hair white or black." How can you really tell what color of eyes or what sex will be best for a child fifty years from now? God wanted to protect us from this kind of decision. God tried to protect us in the garden by limiting access to the tree of life and again at the tower of Babel by confusing the language. Our decisions are not a threat to God but to ourselves and our happiness.

Couples, under the pressure of the multiplicity of options, may do one of several things. They may become paralyzed with anxiety over which is the right decision, make an impulsive decision, or withdraw from all decisions, even appropriate ones. Those who become paralyzed with anxiety are overwhelmed with the implications of their decision making. Life will be different for the child and for the parents if they choose a boy over a girl. How shall they decide? Some agonize for a while over such issues and then make an impulsive decision. The impulsive decision may not even reflect the best judgment of which the couple is capable. Still other couples may be so overwhelmed by all these decisions that they avoid even appropriate decisions by taking a passive fatalistic stance of "whatever will happen will happen."

At the same time that the couple has needs, the community also has needs. The community needs stability, justice for all, and meaning. The community can allow many options if it can be assured of the stability of home and family and if it can be assured of justice for all. If the community cannot be assured of these things, then it needs to limit the options it allows its people.

Conclusion

In conclusion, couples faced with many reproductive options are served best if they have solid community support of their marriage and relationship, support that continues regardless of reproductive capability. Couples need a sense of limits to protect them from the anxiety of unlimited options. They need encouragement to find a balance between two extreme tendencies: on the one hand, the passive acceptance of whatever happens and, on the other hand, the aggressive demand for whatever they want. Couples need support to find the middle road of an active and creative response to life and its limitations, while considering personal and community needs. The community needs to give support and meaning to all persons—those with perfect and those with imperfect minds and bodies, those fertile and those infertile, and those with children and those without.

Only as we creatively accept and manage our limits can we grow to be mature. Dispensing with limits can lead to a narcissistic, self-indulgent, destructive society where safety and satisfaction for all life are threatened.

Questions for Reflection and Discussion

1. How should the church relate to people as they make choices about lifestyle and generativity, marriage, conception, fertility, pregnancy, and childbirth?
2. To what degree are you and your community affected by social norms that require fertility or childbearing to prove normality in one's sexual identity? How are you affected by social norms that indicate that children are needed to achieve immortality?
3. What are the psychological implications of a couple keeping AID secret from family and church support groups?
4. Will acceptance of in vitro fertilization with its destruction of fertilized eggs lead the church down a "slippery slope"?
5. Should society tolerate a 5-10% rate of serious psychological side effects of an elective procedure as seen in abortion?
6. What are the psychological, social, and spiritual implications for a society that tolerates abortion of normal or abnormal children? AID? Surrogate mothering?
7. Should humans use all the technology available to achieve their desires to have or not have children? Should they limit their options, their sense of "entitlement"?

For Further Reading

Behrman, S. J.
    1973 "Artificial Insemination," in *Progress in Fertility*, 2d ed., edited by S. J. Behrman. Boston: Little, Brown and Company.
Gadpaille, W. J.
    1975 *The Cycles of Sex.* New York: Charles Scribner's Sons.
Greenfield, D. and F. Haseltine
    1986 "Candidate Selection and Psychosocial Considerations of In-Vitro Fertilization Procedures." *Clinical Obstetrics and Gynecology* 29(1):119-26.
Keye, W. R.
    1984 "Psychosexual Responses to Infertility." *Clinical Obstetrics and Gynecology* 27(3):760-766.
Lazarus, A. and R. Stern
    1986 "Psychiatric Aspects of Pregnancy Termination." *Clinics in Obstetrics and Gynecology* 23(1):125-134.

Schneider, E. D., ed.
  1985 *Questions About the Beginning of Life*. Minneapolis: Augsburg
    Publishing House.
Shain, R. N.
  1986 "A Cross-Cultural History of Abortion." *Clinics in Obstetrics and
    Gynecology* 13(1):1-17.
Singer, P. and D. Wells
  1985 *Making Babies: The New Science and Ethics of Conception*. New
    York: Charles Scribner's Sons.
Stout, M. G.
  1985 *Without Child*. Grand Rapids, Mich.: Zondervan Publishing
    House.
Youngs, D. D. and A. A. Ehrhardt
  1980 *Psychosomatic Obstetrics and Gynecology*. New York: Appleton-
    Century-Crofts.

Chapter 11

Legal Perspectives

Kathryn Stoltzfus Fairfield

Kathryn Fairfield
J.D., Duke University.
Practicing attorney,
Harrisonburg, Virginia.

THE LAW IS the embodiment of the ethics of a society. Whether the U.S. Constitution, laws enacted by legislators, or court decisions made by judges, the law is not created in a vacuum or a law library. Rather, the law is a reflection of the social values of the community. To the extent that society's ethical values clash with those of the Christians within it, Christians may find the law to be unacceptable.

This chapter will address the law in two main areas where there is a lot of discussion and controversy: abortion and surrogate motherhood. I will seek to state what the law presently is, but because new decisions are imminent, I will illuminate some principles that can help to predict the future of the law in these areas. I will also touch briefly on several other issues such as in vitro fertilization, wrongful birth and wrongful life, and fetal rights.

Abortion

I believe that eventually the right of abortion will be limited to the first 16 or 18 weeks of gestation. Several developments lead me to this conclusion.

The 1973 landmark decision of *Roe v. Wade*[1] gave women the right to seek abortions as part of their constitutional right to privacy. Certain limitations on the states' rights to regulate and control abortions were included. In the first trimester (first three months of pregnancy), because early abortion is safer than childbirth, the states may not interfere with abortion, although certain health and medical exceptions remain. In the second trimester, the states can limit abortion only "in a way reasonably related to maternal health."[2] In the third trimester, states may regulate and even proscribe abortion.

The court based its third-trimester distinction on the fact that the fetus becomes viable, or able to survive outside of the womb, during the third trimester. Now that abortion is considered safer than childbirth beyond the first trimester (in fact up to the 21st week) and younger and younger fetuses can be aided to survive (even 23-week-old fetuses), a dilemma that is causing discomfort to pro-life and pro-choice advocates alike has arisen. Justice O'Connor has delineated the problem in her dissent in the case of *Akron v. Akron Center for Reproductive Health*.[3] She sees a collision of the trimesters occurring with the states unable to regulate abortion as long as abortion is safer than childbirth, yet having the right to proscribe abortion entirely as fetuses become viable at an ever earlier age.

Nancy Rhoden, a leading ethicist and legal scholar, deals with this problem and the related one of live births from abortions in her article, *Trimesters and Technology: Revamping Roe v. Wade*.[4] She suggests that the distinction between permitted and proscribed abortion should be "the ethical precept that late in gestation a fetus is so like a baby that elective abortion can be forbidden."[5] A specific time point late in gestation should be the criterion, rather than viability, even though we may have to work harder to decide what that particular time point is. Rhoden advocates choosing "a cut-off point which does not permit live births but which also does not deny second trimester abortions to the group most in need of them,"[6] such as poor, ill-educated, or minority teenagers. Under the prevailing *Roe v. Wade* standard, abortion can be chosen up until the 24th or 28th week; Rhoden

states it may not be unreasonable to require women to decide by
week 16,[7] although given present realities, abortion should not be
prohibited before week 20.[8] (She would advocate extending the
time abortion can be chosen if the fetus is severely defective).

Daniel Callahan, bioethicist and director of The Hastings
Center, an organization that deals with ethical issues, points to
some of the reasons that the abortion question is now so controversial in his article *How Technology Is Reframing the Abortion
Debate.*[9] The first reason concerns recent advances in neonatal
medicine. "How, many have asked, can one justify salvaging imperiled 22-week or 23-week or 24-week newborns, while accepting the abortion of perfectly healthy fetuses of the same age?"[10]
The second reason points to the use of the sonogram, which
makes very vivid the characteristics of well-developed, young fetuses. Third, embryological knowledge since *Roe v. Wade* has increased our awareness of the sophistication of the early developmental stages of the fetus. Fourth, late abortions can produce live
fetuses, which is demoralizing for pro-choice medical personnel.
Fifth, an increased awareness of environmental risks to fetuses,
maternal responsibility to the fetus, lawsuits for prenatal injuries,
and therapy that can treat impaired fetuses in utero seems incon-
sistent with ideas of abortion.

Callahan, who considers his public position to be conservative pro-choice, states that he has "a shadow self which does not
remain unaffected"[11] by what he has learned over the past de-
cade.

> It has raised my uneasiness a notch or two, made me less sympathetic
> to the rhetoric (and, I guess, feeling) of outrage toward the pro-life
> position that marks many of my pro-choice allies, and all the more in-
> sistent that the pro-choice perspective find room for an open airing of
> the morality of what should (I continue to hold) remain legally accept-
> able acts. The pro-choice movement in its most political manifestation
> is particularly vulnerable to the medical and scientific developments.
> It has never made sufficient room in its public stance for a serious
> consideration of the fetus. Simultaneously, by deliberately cultivating a
> supposedly neutral, therapeutic language toward the medical act of
> abortion—calling it a "procedure," a "termination of pregnancy," and
> so on—it mistakenly seems to think it can pacify and comfort the se-
> cret self, minimizing and denaturing some unmistakable realities.
> There is still time to rectify that error, time for pro-choice adherents
> to show themselves as willing in practice as in theory to concede the

moral uncertainty of abortion decisions. If that is not done, the combination of the new medical developments and too many secret selves for too long holding their doubts at bay may well begin shifting some public selves. In that event, the pro-choice movement will have done itself far more damage than those who try to stop it by bombing abortion clinics. The repression of self-doubts has an even more explosive potential than nitroglycerin.[12]

So far, attempts by state legislatures to limit abortion by enacting laws that require informed consent 24 hours before an abortion have not been permitted by the Supreme Court. The majority of the court has decided that requiring a woman to be informed of the possible detrimental effects and medical risks of abortion, the risks of carrying the child to term, the probable gestational age of the unborn child, the father's liability for child support, and the availability of medical assistance for childbirth and neonatal care before she can consent to an abortion unduly restricts her constitutional right to have an abortion.[13] The new composition of the court, however, with the recent Supreme Court appointments of Sandra Day O'Connor, Anthony Scalia, and Joseph Kennedy makes it likely that the next abortion case will begin to limit the right to abortion under *Roe v. Wade.*

I do not think that abortion will be banned altogether. I believe that the ethic of the larger community is that early abortion is acceptable and even necessary. I see our task as Anabaptist Christians to make the option of abortion one that needs no longer to be considered.

Fetal Rights

Cases involving fetal rights are increasing. In a number of situations women have been sued for negligence that resulted in harm done to the child they were carrying in utero. In other cases women were ordered against their wishes to submit to Caesarean sections when physicians believed normal childbirth could harm the women's fetuses.

These cases raise many questions. What moral duties do pregnant women owe fetuses? To what extent should the state be able to force women to act in the interests of their fetuses?[14] What is the impact on the right to abortion if fetal rights increase?

Wrongful Birth and Wrongful Life

Another relatively new area of the law is that represented by wrongful birth and wrongful life cases. In most states the parents can have a wrongful birth action arising out of a physician's negligence that results in pregnancy and childbirth, but damages are generally limited to the costs of the pregnancy itself. Courts are moving in the direction of allowing persons born with serious abnormalities caused by a physician's negligence to bring wrongful life actions. So far judges have disallowed awards for pain and suffering, limiting harm to actual medical expenses.[15]

Artificial Insemination and In Vitro Fertilization

The technologies of artificial insemination and in vitro fertilization raise many legal questions. The Uniform Parentage Act adopted by 42 states addresses itself mainly to the issues surrounding artificial insemination. The main clarification is in the area of the paternity of a child born as a result of artificial insemination: If the husband has consented to the artificial insemination of his wife by donor sperm, he is treated in law as the natural father of the child and the sperm donor has no rights. This act seems to reflect the common-sense views of society that a sperm bank donor should be required to remain anonymous and that a husband who has not consented to the artificial insemination should not be required to support the child in case of a marital breakup.

In vitro fertilization raises further questions about parentage. Is the mother the woman who provided the ovum for fertilization, or the woman who was implanted with the fertilized ovum and who carried and gave birth to the baby? Can the carrying mother change her mind about giving up the baby to the donating mother and prevail under current law regarding termination of parental rights? Will we see a case in which a child is declared to have two mothers, followed by a custody dispute involving who would provide the better care for the child? These issues need to be addressed by the law.

Surrogate Motherhood

The Baby M appeal[16] decided by the Supreme Court of New Jersey on February 3, 1988, overturned, in the main, the ill-conceived and seriously flawed lower-court decision rendered on March 31, 1987.[17] A brief introduction to relevant, generally accepted law will promote understanding of these decisions.

In adoption cases most states permit the termination of a mother's rights in her child only after a period of time has passed after the birth and she has received counseling and given her consent (barring termination of her rights because of unfitness as a mother). A child can be released for adoption only if these requirements have been followed. If the parents of a child are separated or unmarried, they are to be treated equally with respect to custodial rights. But the strong, well-established concept of what is in the best interests of the child determines who gets custody. The main factors that are considered in determining the best interests of a child are caretaking and bonding: Who has been the main caretaker of the child and to whom has the child bonded? Secondary considerations are such things as family income and prospects for the future.

The facts of the Baby M case are as follows. Mr. and Mrs. Stern, operating under the impression that a pregnancy by Mrs. Stern could cause her severe damage because of multiple sclerosis, entered into a written contract with Mrs. Whitehead and her husband. The couples agreed that Mrs. Whitehead would be artificially inseminated with Mr. Stern's sperm, carry the baby, surrender it at birth to Mr. Stern, and terminate her parental rights so that the baby could be adopted by Mrs. Stern. Mrs. Whitehead was called the "surrogate mother" and was to be paid $10,000 for her services.

Things proceeded as planned. Mrs. Whitehead became pregnant and gave birth to a baby girl. However, after the birth of the child, Mrs. Whitehead would not give up the baby. When ordered to do so by the court, she fled with the baby into hiding in Florida. She was found four months later and forced to give up the baby. During the trial the baby was placed in the temporary custody of the Sterns.

The law on termination of parental rights and adoption is based on our knowledge of the surprising strength of the human maternal bond. Even though a woman may have an unwanted pregnancy, carrying her baby, giving birth to her baby, and holding the baby for the first time normally make her want her baby and be unable to give it up.

In the *Baby M* case the lower court validated the surrogacy contract, terminated Mrs. Whitehead's maternal rights, and permitted the adoption of Baby M by Mrs. Stern without the consent of Mrs. Whitehead. In doing so the lower court ignored not only the statutory law on termination of parental rights and adoption, but flew in the face of the accumulated wisdom on how human beings operate and what traits we as a society want to encourage.

The high-court opinion of Chief Justice Wilentz of the Supreme Court of New Jersey was strong, well reasoned, and evidence of a good grasp of human psychological makeup. Chief Justice Wilentz invalidated the surrogacy contract, saying it was against the laws of termination of parental rights and adoption of New Jersey. He called the use of money for the purpose of achieving "the adoption of a child through private placement"[18] illegal and perhaps criminal. He emphasized that an agreement to surrender a child can be made only after birth and after the mother has been counseled. Wilentz went on to state that the contract was invalid, moreover, because it was against public policy: "The contract's basic premise, that the natural parents can decide in advance of birth which one is to have custody of the child, bears no relationship to the settled law that the child's best interests shall determine custody."[19] The public policy in this area is that a child is to be protected from unnecessary separation from the natural parents and that "the parent and child relationship extends equally to every child and to every parent, regardless of the marital status of the parents."[20] Finally, Wilentz declared the contract invalid because of its total disregard of the best interests of the child.

With the contract put aside, the issue still remained. Who should have custody of Baby M—Mrs. Whitehead as the mother (Mrs. Stern's adoption was declared invalid) or Mr. Stern as the father? The case was treated as any custody dispute between separated spouses. The standard here, as it always must be, was the best interests of the child. Here the major consideration was that Baby M had been with the Sterns and was bonded to them for nearly two years. The court recognized that the probable judicial error of the lower court that gave temporary custody to the Sterns while the case was being decided was critical here. But the court maintained correctly that "we must look to what those best interests *are, today,* even if some of the facts may have resulted in part from legal error. The child's interests come first: We will not punish it for judicial errors . . . ."[21] The court correctly decided that to take a two-year-old child from the only home it has known would be devastating and cruel. Thus, Mr. Stern was given custody of Baby M and Mrs. Whitehead was to have visitation to be determined by the lower court.

Chief Justice Wilentz was not content to overrule the lower court on the issue of the validity of the contract and to state that in the future no newborn will be taken from its mother during a custody dispute, except in an extreme case. He felt it necessary to try to correct the harsh evaluation of Mrs. Whitehead's conduct as given by the lower court. Although not condoning Mrs. Whitehead's conduct in fleeing with the child to Florida against the order of the court and threatening to kill herself and the baby if the Sterns persisted in trying to take the baby from her, Wilentz said, "She was guilty of a breach of contract, and indeed, she did break a very important promise, but we think it is expecting something well beyond normal human capabilities to suggest that this mother should have parted with her newly born infant without a struggle. Other than survival, what stronger force is there?"[22]

Justice Wilentz's opinion, in summary, reinforced the long-held community standards that gave rise to our laws on termination of parental rights and adoption. I believe that Justice Wilentz's opinion reflected the view of most people in our society on the issue of surrogate motherhood. I believe that our legislatures will enact laws based on the principles set forth in this opinion, with one minor variation. I think that legislation in this area will permit a woman to be paid to be a surrogate mother as long as she has the right to change her mind and keep her baby if she can show that this is in the best interests of the child. I believe that our society perceives that couples such as the Sterns have a right to be able to have a child that is biologically the child of at least one spouse. In addition, a woman should be able to choose to be a surrogate mother if she wishes. The Baby M case should serve as a very clear warning, however, that for most women it will not be realistic to plan to give up the child born as the result of a surrogacy arrangement.

Questions for Reflection and Discussion
1. What rights belong to the human and how will an increase in the fetus's legal rights affect the mother's abortion rights?
2. To what extent should the state be able to force women to act in the interests of their unborn child?
3. Should courts award damages in cases of physician negligence resulting in pregnancy?

4. Who is the mother of the child produced by in vitro fertilization if the carrying woman is not the one who produced the ovum?
5. Do you agree that a surrogate contract prior to the birth of the child should not be legally binding? That a child's best interest at the present moment, rather than parental rights, should come first in custody decisions?
6. Should surrogate mothering be made illegal? Why or why not? How will this decision affect society?

For Further Reading

Annas, George J.
   1986 "*Roe v. Wade* Reaffirmed, Again." *Hastings Center Report* 16 (5): 26-27.
Bartlett, Katharine T.
   1987 "Baby M: The Legal System Confronts Conflicting Human Values." *Duke Law Magazine* 5 (Summer): 4-8.
Johnson, Dawn
   1987 "A New Threat to Pregnant Women's Autonomy." *Hastings Center Report* 17 (4) (August): 33-40.
Law Week
   1986 *Thornburgh v. American College of Obstetricians and Gynecologists.* 51 L. W. 4618, June 10.
Rhoden, Nancy K.
   1984 "The New Neonatal Dilemma: Live Births from Late Abortions." *Georgetown Law Journal* 72 (June): 1451-1509.

   1985 "Treatment Dilemmas for Imperiled Newborns: Why Quality of Life Counts." *Southern California Law Review* 58 (6): 1283-1347.

   _____ and John D. Arras
   1985 "Withholding Treatment from Baby Doe: From Discrimination to Child Abuse." *Milbank Memorial Fund Quarterly/Health and Society* 63 (1): 18-51.

   1986 "The Judge in the Delivery Room: The Emergence of Court-Ordered Caesareans." *California Law Review* 74 (6): 1951-2030.

   1986 "Trimesters and Technology: Revamping *Roe v. Wade*." *Yale Law Journal* 95 (4): 639-697.
U. S. Reports
   1973 *Roe v. Wade*, 410 U.S. 113.

   1983 *Akron v. Akron Center for Reproductive Health*, 462 U.S. 416.

Chapter 12

Communal Responsibilities

Donald B. Kraybill

Donald Kraybill
Ph.D. in sociology, Temple University. Professor of sociology, Elizabethtown College, Elizabethtown, Pennsylvania.

MY BROTHER AND sister died of cystic fibrosis during their childhood in the early 1950s. Cystic fibrosis in that era was undetectable in pregnancy and, as today, was incurable after birth. At my sister's funeral I distinctly remember my father explaining the tragedy and comforting us with the words, "The Lord giveth and the Lord taketh away, blessed be the name of the Lord." God bestowed life, we were taught, and in due time and for reasons that often eluded us, God also took life away. In the early 1970s when I became a father, cystic fibrosis remained a threat. Thus, I was anxious about the birth of our children. Would they too be victimized by it, forcing my wife and me to suffer as my parents and siblings had suffered?

Today things are different. Physicians are able to detect the presence of cystic fibrosis in the fetus after conception. Parents are able to abort the child and thus avoid unnecessary anguish and suffering. Other forms of prenatal diagnosis will likely expand such therapeutic abortion options for many other congenital diseases, as well. A similar procedure can even be applied to test the sex of a child. If the fetus is a male and the parents want a female, they can abort and try again. With new advances in genetic engineering people may be able to control the sex of a child, as well as other characteristics of their offspring, at the time of conception. Genetic therapy may permit removing the cystic fibrosis-producing gene and replacing it with a healthy one. If long noses are notorious in the family pedigree, the nose-controlling gene might also be manipulated shortly after conception to yield a more modest nose.

Even more astonishing, the manipulation of sex cells or blastomeres could perpetuate a distinctive physical characteristic across future generations. These potential and likely scientific advances hold the promise of unbelievable happiness and horror, for while many genetic diseases might vanish, we might also be able to create any sort of human being we want.

The true terror is not the weird-looking creatures that we might create, but the usurpation of God's role in human creation. The genetic revolution threatens to snatch the procreative role away from God. No longer will we be able to say, "The Lord giveth and the Lord taketh away, blessed be the name of the Lord." The new litany will more likely read, "Humans give and humans take away, blessed be the name of science." The new technologies will toss innumerable bioethical dilemmas onto our laps in the coming years. Should we abort a fetus that will surely bring only suffering and agony? Is it really humane to permit such suffering when we can step in and prevent it? Should those who are sterile consider test tube fertilization to fulfill their dreams of parenthood? Even more vexing quandaries are sure to come.

Modernization, in brief, is a story of greater control, of humans exercising a tighter grip over their physical, and now even their genetic, environment. Birth control and now genetic manipulation and genetic therapy reflect the tightening grip of scientific control. The scientific advances are breathtaking in their sweeping advances. At the same moment they raise startling ethical and theological dilemmas.

First, as technological control increases, we are losing our grip on meaning and mystery. If humans begin to control the creative process—if we give and take life at our pleasure—how will we ever sustain the image of a Creator God? If we tamper with the genetic code and produce new forms of life—which we have already done by combining goats and sheep into "geeps"—will we still be able to proclaim that life is a "gift from God?" What will it mean for the new breed of genetically packaged children when they realize that they are merely the products of their parents' peculiar preferences and the scientific laboratory?

The divine givenness that anchors the soul of all of us is endangered by genetic manipulation. All of this foists a more sinister dilemma upon us. For as we increase our control over conception, we lose our grip on the bigger issues of meaning, belonging, and identity. What will happen to the cultural roots, the psychological identity, and the emotional moorings of persons who discover that they were purchased at a local sperm bank?

A second dilemma, an ethical lag, also encapsulates our quandary regarding these monumental advances. The speed of the recent scientific discoveries is astonishing. Since 1970, some 1,000 of the 50,000 or so genetic codes have been mapped, and the remaining 49,000 will likely be tagged as we enter the twenty-first century. This permits us to identify the genetic material that determines our physical features. We can already detect the genetic apparatus that controls some 200 of the more than 3,000 inherited diseases. In sharp contrast to this breathtaking speed, our moral codes have emerged over thousands of years in a context where the Lord truly did give and take away life.

We are thus caught in the lurch—in an ethical gap—as technology races far ahead of our ethical formulas of bygone years. Ironically, as the technological precision increases, the moral precision wanes. The old answers that prescribed the boundaries between right and wrong, good and evil, are suddenly blurred by the provocative questions stirred by the spiraling genetic technology. After four decades of playing theological catch-up with the nuclear age, we finally have realized that the old "just war" formula is archaic for fighting nuclear wars. Now we face a new game of ethical catch-up as we try to maintain stride with the technological leaps in genetic engineering.

The third dilemma is the enormous burden of choice that falls on the shoulders of the individual. Choice is the central tattoo on the fabric of modernity. The individual in modern culture is free to choose—liberated from the constraints and confines of cultural traditions and physical domination. The new technology multiplies our choices. Having a baby used to mean the joy and pain of letting nature have its own way. Few decisions were needed. We had little control over the process. Having a baby today is hard and serious work because it entails myriad decisions. When, where, and how shall it be done? Should a couple enter genetic counseling before or after pregnancy? Or should they, like previous generations, meander along in the twilight of fate and hope? Should a couple control the sex of their child. If sterile, should they seek in vitro fertilization? The options are not only many, but they are heavy because a couple might have only one, or at most two, children.

At the very moment in modern life when individuals are free to choose among a panoply of choices, they are also freed from meaningful social bonds in durable communities—bonds that could provide help and support in the midst of incessant decision making. Thus, the modern individual, faced with weighty life-and-death decisions, often faces them alone. The individual struggles in the terror of isolation, for the modern experience tends to unhook us from the grip of dependable groups.

The bioethical textbooks reinforce the individualistic model by focusing on the decision making of the "autonomous individual" who must act and make choices. The cool, detached professional follows professional protocol by providing the facts without bias and sketching out the options in order to permit "informed consent." The individual or couple may need to make heavy decisions, loaded with life-and-death consequences, in a matter of hours or minutes. The overarching bioethical dilemma is this: We increasingly face ultimate decisions, placed before us by the new genetic engineering, at the very moment that we are being stripped of communal support. Thus, moderns often struggle with the dilemmas alone or at best in the shadows of cool and necessarily detached professionals.

An Amish family recently lost a newborn child to a serious congenital defect. This was their second child lost to the same deformity. However, the couple keeps on trying, cooperating with mother nature, with the result of some healthy children. This traditional cultural setting offers little control, few options, no ethical gap, few choices, and little interest in taking charge of the giving and taking of life. Both their first and second tragedies were filled with meaning and belonging because the family was surrounded by a community that deeply cared and sprang into immediate action by providing culturally programmed forms of support in their time of grief.

By sharp contrast a modern urban couple planned the birth of their one and only child very carefully. They considered all the options proposed by a genetic counselor and, when faced with certain evidence of a serious genetic defect in their unborn child, they decided to abort the fetus. They shouldered the decision, as well as its consequent guilt, alone. The modern couple enjoyed the benefits of options and with extensive research, carefully charted their course. Here was planning, control, and liberated autonomy, but little mystery, no meaning, and no community. They not only elected to give and take life; they did it in the terror of their own privacy.

So how do we cope with these dilemmas that will surely intensify? We might resort to naive denial, doctrinaire clinging, or foolish flinging. We can engage in denial by arguing that scientists will never be able to do these things, that God will never let them. But that is to deny the evidence. We can bury our heads in theological sand and hope that the rapture will occur before we tinker too much with the genetic code. But if we look the other way, these things will surely come to pass by default in the same way that artificial birth control quietly invaded the lives of most Protestants and many Catholics in the past few decades.

If denial seems a bit too wimpish, we can also respond by clinging to old rules and ancient dogmas. We can embrace doctrinal orthodoxy and contend that the old answers are perfectly suitable for all the new questions. All humans want certainty in the midst of moral ambiguity. One of the easiest ways to get certainty is to reassert the bygone ethical codes and formulas despite their irrelevance for the new questions. Ethicists can recite with great fervor the old moral maxims for making good decisions—respect individual autonomy, do no injury, be as helpful as possible, act justly, and keep costs and benefits in proportion. Clinging to the old solutions may provide certainty, but surely not answers.

Instead of denying the new situation or clinging to old dogmas, we may be tempted to fling away our theological heritage in the face of this avalanche of genetic possibilities. We may be tempted to concede that religious precepts and values are obsolete—that the image of a Creator God is passé. We may be lured to acquiesce to a technological imperative and lamely conclude that science will have to come up with its own answers and that religious moralists should stop obstructing the progress of scientific research.

A more constructive response to all of this, one that flows from both our Christian and Anabaptist heritage, is to engage in communal discernment under the tutelage of the Holy Spirit. Dialogue, discussion, listening, and debate are the marks of this mode of response, rather than naive denial, doctrinaire clinging, or foolish flinging. As the people of God with an open ear to the Spirit of truth and a passion for shalom, we must reread the old Scriptures with new eyes and listen to them with new ears. This midway approach between doctrinaire legalism and flinging away our spiritual heritage entails openness and vulnerability, but not aimlessness. Rather, we are guided by the resources of Scripture, the wisdom of Christian friends, and the prompting of the Holy Spirit. This is a more holistic and humane approach than the prevailing model of "leaving it up to each individual," because here the dilemmas are wrestled with in the context of caring brothers and sisters who become partners in the decision, as well as in its consequences.

Many resources are at our disposal in this communal approach to bioethical dilemmas. Images of the kingdom of God, rooted in the synoptic Gospels, remind us that we are responsible not only for each other in this upside-down kingdom, but for our enemies as well. Jesus' own behavior modeled responsibility for the stigmatized, those discarded by the powerful on the human trash heap—the lepers, women, prostitutes, and Gentiles. The ethic of Christian responsibility pervades the Gospels and impels us to stand alongside those who are in the crucible of agonizing bioethical decisions. The image of the church as a body in the Pauline epistles reminds us that even in the midst of a technocracy, we are members one of another, connected and attached to a body through ligaments of responsibility and duty. In the Anabaptist story we learn that faithful discipleship must be applied to the practical issues of life and that members of the believers church engage in mutual aid and mutual accountability.

What, then, are our communal responsibilities as we cope with the new life-and-death possibilities that are being placed in our hands by the genetic revolution? Our first and fundamental obligation is to simply be the church—to embody the discerning, caring, forgiving community. That may sound trite and we may rarely actualize such a community in all its potential richness. To relinquish the vision, however, is to prostitute the very core of the Christian faith and to forfeit our own Anabaptist legacy.

The contemporary community of faith—the circle of signifi-cant others in our lives who join us in the common confession that Jesus Christ is Lord—is our fundamental resource for spiritu-al wisdom, judgment, and discernment in the midst of excrucia-ting bioethical quandaries. This network of Christian siblings may not always have specific answers for our questions, but they will encourage us to ask the right questions as we sort our way through the ethical maze. And they will be with us to mediate God's incarnate love. The most immoral thing we can do in this modern dilemma is to leave members of the body stranded alone under the heavy weight of bioethical choice. Our supreme re-sponsibility is simply to be the church, to be the caring com-munity that helps to shoulder the burden.

A variety of secondary responsibilities flow from our central mandate. Those in the midst of agonizing decisions bear the re-sponsibility to seek the counsel of their brothers and sisters in the community of faith. The American way considers conception, birth, and death as utterly private and personal issues, thus purg-ing them from the communal agenda. The privatization of bioethi-cal dilemmas obstructs in the most pervasive way our mandate of shared Christian responsibility in these matters. Widespread availability of "do-it-yourself" kits in local convenience stores for detecting the sex of unborn fetuses and for aborting them will surely accelerate the American propensity for privacy. To func-tion as a member of the Christian body means vulnerability, being willing to open our lives to the guidance and counsel of others.

Those not directly involved in bioethical dilemmas bear re-sponsibility to seek gentle ways of offering support. Bystanders can share the burden of decision. This is done, not in formal meetings by consensus or vote, but in dialogue, in conversation, and through a witness of presence. Genuine discernment, atten-tive to the special needs of the moment, sprouts from informal pockets of human concern that surround the one in need, rather than in large formal gatherings.

In our discerning conversations we should not assume a pre-packaged or even a single "morally right" outcome. Our focus, rather, should be on raising the helpful questions, offering sup-port, and providing new alternatives in seemingly deadlocked sit-uations. Rather than searching for simple moral guidelines that will spell out clear-cut solutions once and for all, we ought rather to keep asking, "Are we being the kind of community that embodies God's incarnate love, compassion, and service?" Thus, the focus of our effort is shifted from searching for the proper ethical criteria and worrying about the final outcome of the situation to asking, "What kind of a body, what sort of a kingdom, what type of a community are we creating to envelop the one(s) struggling with the dilemma?"

In this communal model the structure of decision making shifts away from the solitary individual to the circle of Christian siblings. Many of the standard ethical principles of no harm, justice, and so on will continue to be relevant; but the decision-making base is expanded and enlarged. To put it in other words, the number of agents in the process is multiplied.

If we pretend that we can develop an ethical system to adequately handle the new bioethical dilemmas that will surely be coming down the road, we will be sorely disappointed. If there is anything distinctively Anabaptist in our response to these mind-boggling quandaries of the genetic revolution, it is not that we will concoct a distinctive moral calculus. If there is anything unique to the Anabaptist mode of coping with these issues, it will be that we will persist in asking, "Are we as a community embodying the love and mind of Christ? Are we creating a dialogue between the issue and the Scriptures? Are we corporately seeking the guidance of the Holy Spirit?" The communal core of the Anabaptist legacy is preeminently relevant and durable in the face of uncertain bioethical choices.

The focus of the contemporary abortion debate, in true individualistic fashion, often revolves around the rights of the mother versus the rights of the unborn. In the context of Christian community we are responsible to enlarge and expand the scope of the questions beyond the rights of a single individual. For instance, "What is best for the extended family? What sort of memories will this experience create in the lives of all those involved? What is best for the community of faith? What will be the long-term effects of this decision over the years? Does this decision reflect the incarnate spirit of Christ? Are we as a community willing to support the implications of this decision with time and funds over the years?"

As we share together in bioethical dilemmas, we need to find ways not only for the community to carry the emotional and practical weight of decisions, but also more importantly for God to share the burden of decisions and their consequences along with the community. God has suffered and visited us in the person of Jesus Christ; he has been through the torture of Golgotha. He walks with us even today and shares the burden of our gravest decisions. As communities of faith, we need to find ways to confer God's blessing on the decisions that are made. We need to affirm them in God's name.

The church bears the responsibility to restore spiritual meaning in the midst of spiritually barren and technologically driven choices. Prayer, singing, Scripture reading, and special litanies shared in the context of the worshiping community offer ways to restore meaning and to invite God to stand with us in difficult times. In some circles we find a resurgence of the use of anointing for healing, not only of physical maladies, but of social and emotional ruptures, as well.

We must find corporate ways through rituals, litanies, ordinances, and other forms of worship to confer God's love and blessing on those in the throes of decision making. A pastor friend recently wrote a special "litany of release" for a family who decided to pull the plug on the respirator attached to a parent. This litany, shared at the patient's hospital bedside, provided divine closure and blessing to the family in their agonizing decision.

As individuals and as congregations, we can provide long-term support for the victims and survivors of the decisions, support for the healing of memories as well as for the care of unwanted and debilitated children. Some of our support will be direct and personal, whereas other aspects of it will be institutionalized in programs operated in the name of Christ. As organized bodies, denominations need not only to make position statements at their national conferences, but also to provide educational materials and programs that enable pastors and laity to prepare for the choices that the genetic revolution will increasingly place before us. Formal programs of pastoral training are needed to sensitize pastors to the religious questions and ethical issues embedded in the dilemmas that will penetrate the lives of parishioners. Congregations might consider designating members, such as elders, to be trained to assist other members who are sorting their way through the bioethical maze. The church ought to encourage members to consider professional careers in genetic counseling. Such persons could combine the latest technological advice with sensitive spiritual wisdom in roles that could benefit the church as well as the society at large.

This communal approach to Christian responsibility in bio-ethical dilemmas is fraught with some pitfalls. Apart from the guidance of the Holy Spirit, it can degenerate into a feckless exercise of like-minded people invoking the name of God to bless their vilest impulses. This communal approach can pit individuals against the community and exacerbate tensions. Moreover, too often the natural web of social relations needed to undergird communal discernment is not in place at the moment of crisis. However, when anchored in the kingdom story, informed by the Anabaptist legacy, and steered by the Holy Spirit, a communal approach to bioethical dilemmas offers the most humane strategy for coping with the new choices. In addition, this approach articulates a potent witness to God's presence in the midst of a genetic revolution.

Questions for Reflection and Discussion

1. Is it true that technological control results in loss of meaning and mystery in life?
2. What happens to a society's view of God and its self-understanding when technology is used to produce life or control the characteristics of life? Might not God "lose out" in some way?
3. Given our individualistic lifestyle, is communal discernment a likely response to today's bioethical dilemmas?
4. How does an ethic of responsibility affect decision making about the unborn?
5. Should the church be more concerned about helping people ask the right questions than about providing the right moral solutions? About being with those who struggle than about developing an adequate ethical system?
6. How can church worship be used to provide perspective on bioethical issues?
7. Is the current church able to take on the consequences of people's choices about children? What are some of the new ways in which the church should respond?

For Further Reading

Ames, David A., and Gracey, Colin B.
    1984 *Good Genes? Emerging Values for Science, Religion and Society.*
        Cincinnati, Ohio. Forward Movement Publications.
Annual Conference of the Church of the Brethren
    1987 "Genetic Engineering Statement." Elgin, Ill..

Kissinger, Warren S.
    1986 *Brethren Life and Thought*, 31 (4): Autumn. Special issue on ge-
        netic engineering.
Panel of Bioethical Concerns, National Council of Churches
    1984 *Genetic Engineering*. N.Y.: The Pilgrim Press.

Chapter 13

The Maze
of Bioethical
Dilemmas

Marlin E. Miller

Marlin Miller
Dr. of Theology, University of Heidelberg. Member of Inter-Mennonite Committee for New Confession of Faith, member of Society for Christian Ethics; president and professor of theology, Goshen Biblical Seminary, Elkhart, Indiana.

THIS TOPIC IS framed in terms of a metaphor—the image of a maze. A maze has a beginning and an end. Between the beginning and the end of a maze, numerous possible paths exist. Some ways initially appear promising but turn out after a short time to end against a wall. Others, after a longer time, also do not lead to the goal. Usually only one or a limited number of ways constitute the right path through the maze. Furthermore, the entire way remains invisible to the one seeking direction. This makes the choices at each juncture difficult and uncertain, unless the seeker has been given a map or at least some important clues. The pathway through the maze may thus be discovered by trial and error, by reading a map and following it correctly, or by ferreting out clues and interpreting them properly. Once the path has been found, it can be followed again with greater facility.

Contemporary biomedical technologies have created a maze of bioethical choices that seem to be uncharted on our maps and appear to have few relevant clues. Proceeding through the maze simply by trial and error is too costly in moral, as well as in social and financial, terms. My assignment for this presentation is to reflect with you regarding the content of the preceding chapters, to summarize the clues for revising and using our ethical maps, and to suggest a directional pathway through the maze of bioethical dilemmas. Proposing a directional pathway does not mean that the entire way has become fully visible and completely charted. Nevertheless, the foregoing chapters have provided a wealth of information and ethical perspectives that can help us along the way.

Finding a way through the bioethical maze includes clarifying the concepts and language we use. To begin with, we may too easily and indiscriminately resort to speaking about bioethical "dilemmas." A genuine dilemma is more than a complicated problem with many new dimensions for which we have little apparent precedent. In the field of logic a dilemma is an argument that presents an opponent with a choice between equally unfavorable or disagreeable alternatives. When our children were small, we presented them with choices between equally disagreeable alternatives, such as whether they wanted to go to bed right away or in ten minutes. An ethical dilemma would mean a choice between alternatives that are both morally questionable or morally wrong.

Doubtless, some of the choices made possible by recent developments in biomedical technology have extended the arena of bioethical dilemmas. But not every case constitutes a moral dilemma in the sense that we must choose between alternatives that morally are equally problematic. We would do well to distinguish between merely complicated issues that we do not yet understand and matters that constitute ethical dilemmas. For example, not everything that we have heard about abortion constitutes a moral dilemma. Although "therapeutic" abortions may frequently present us with genuine moral dilemmas, most of the abortions now performed in the United States have little to do with moral dilemmas.

Finding a way through the bioethical maze also involves orienting ourselves by our starting point and the way we have already come. In previous chapters, we have assumed that the Anabaptist heritage can help us address contemporary bioethical questions constructively. We are interested in having the clearest possible scientific and biotechnical information. We are concerned with assessing the resources available within the range of general theological and ethical considerations. In addition, we are also testing the degree to which an Anabaptist heritage contributes to tracing a directional pathway in the maze of bioethical dilemmas. Without disparaging the insights that may be available from other sources, we as a community carry a particular responsibility for ascertaining if an Anabaptist orientation provides a helpful or formative perspective on the maze. What have we concluded, or what may we conclude about this question?

Perhaps a word of caution about this nod to the ancestors is in order. Many contemporary Mennonites tend to label anything good as "Anabaptist." We have Anabaptist visions, Anabaptist interpretations of Scripture, Anabaptist tours to Europe, and Anabaptist lifestyles. I would hardly be surprised if someone were to begin marketing an Anabaptist deodorant (that radically reforms underarm wetness). Before that happens, we should clarify what we mean by "Anabaptist."

We cannot go back to the sixteenth-century Anabaptists for any direct guidance on bioethical dilemmas. No record exists that the sixteenth-century Anabaptists either wrote or testified in court about abortion and obviously not about in vitro fertilization. Gorman did not know about any such instance in the records. Burkholder did not find any. So unless further historical research demonstrates that these topics were discussed among sixteenth-century Anabaptists, we simply have to assume that we cannot look to them for any direct answers to our questions.

However, we apparently think that an Anabaptist perspective provides a helpful orientation for finding a pathway through the maze of bioethical dilemmas. Admittedly, this orientation also appears in other movements and is therefore not uniquely Anabaptist. Nonetheless, an Anabaptist emphasis on discipleship, on pacifism, and on community points a direction through the maze.

Kraybill has eloquently described the need for community in contemporary Western culture and society. Finding the way through the bioethical maze will depend particularly on participating in a Christian community—an alternative community of moral discernment where we discern God's will, learn to make moral choices, and cultivate a way of seeking and speaking about reality that provides mutual support and discipline. Echoes of that conviction are in Kraybill's, Hershberger's, and Jones's contributions, as well as in others.

What will it take to implement this emphasis on community? Who participates in this community? Are decisions about what constitutes a pathway through the moral dilemmas made only by the leaders of the Christian community? Are the professionals and experts in biomedical technology the decision makers? Should people who are existentially caught in biomedical dilemmas make the decisions? Or should the average people with common sense make decisions for the entire community?

The emphasis on Christian community as the place of moral discernment and decision making means that all persons—whether expert or not, whether theologian or not—who have made a common commitment to Jesus Christ assemble to determine the way through the maze. Becoming a genuine community of moral discernment would, however, require a much more sustained and comprehensive effort than a book containing a series of presentations. Other beginning steps have been taken in a series of hearings on biomedical questions sponsored by Mennonite Mutual Aid. Most Mennonite congregations and conferences still lack the kind of "binding and loosing" fellowship that takes the time and provides the place to address these kinds of issues and to follow through in a supportive and discipling fashion.

If we are going to accept the answer that an Anabaptist perspective calls for discerning communities to find and follow the path through the bioethical maze, we still do not have an easy job ahead of us. In fact, the job will be at least as difficult as designing any new or preserving any old moral codes, because we have a long way to go in becoming that kind of community. However, the challenge still stands! And the prospect promises more for finding the way through the maze than its alternatives of individualism and professional pluralism.

Making operational an Anabaptist emphasis on the church as the discerning community will also mean correcting a current Mennonite tendency to reduce moral community to a process of conversation. Particularly with reference to complex issues such as bioethical dilemmas, the temptation is to remain endlessly in process without adopting substantive community standards. The danger is one of being disoriented in the middle of the maze and assuming that as long as we keep moving, we are nearing the goal. Kraybill emphasized the importance of community and community process, rather than specific standards and answers that may be given and perpetuated without compassion and mutual support. If we take seriously an Anabaptist perspective on community and moral discernment, we need both the community process and Christian moral norms and standards.

We need to care for and clarify the language and concepts through which we perceive reality and make moral judgments, as well as to provide a context of compassion and personal support for people facing—or suffering from—difficult decisions. We should balance an emphasis on community process with cognitive guidelines and ethical norms. We would also do well to develop such guidelines and norms in the context of Christian community, without playing "community process" against ethical codes and standards that provide direction. At the same time we need to remain appropriately flexible.

In addition to an Anabaptist emphasis on community, the Christian tradition and particularly the scriptural foundations of the Christian tradition point a directional pathway through the bioethical maze. Burkholder, Hershberger, Gorman, Jones, and others said that Scripture teaches us to think of human life in relation to God, rather than as a reality that can be understood apart from God and defined only in reference to itself or to other empirical realities. Kraybill has described some of the difficulties of perceiving human life in relation to God. In the context of contemporary Western secular assumptions, traditional ways of seeing human life, health, and gender as gifts of God are undermined because we have become increasingly capable of controlling life through biotechnological means.

Ironically, modern technology may give us far less control than we think. Although it solves some problems, it creates new ones. Perhaps giftedness remains more a part of our mentality and understanding of life than secular Western thinkers are willing to admit. However that may be, the emphasis on understanding and living human life in relation to God is strongly grounded in Scripture and in the Word becoming flesh. Definitions of the human person that exclude this relation remain fundamentally distorted and unacceptable for discerning a way through the maze.

The Bible consistently includes the stranger, the slave, the orphan, the widow, the weak, and the defenseless in its understanding of the human person because God's compassion and justice extends particularly to them. Whenever we attempt to exclude such as these from what it means to be human and from being created in God's image, we are called to reorient our language to Scripture. Jones's comments on concepts of personhood illustrate this point poignantly. Further, as Gorman has reminded us, Christian moral discernment on the beginnings of human life is set in a broader picture during pre-Constantinian church history. Early Christians rejected abortion, which was widespread in the surrounding society, not as an isolated issue but as part of a broader orientation that rejected violence and war and emphasized the caring for the weak and the defenseless. They quite rightly found this broader orientation grounded in the Scriptures.

An occasional focus on a specific issue is helpful in order to gather information and to ascertain the implications and complexities of specific ethical situations. Such focusing, however, should not isolate one set of questions from the broader biblical understanding of life in relation to God. The beginning of life is certainly distinguishable from many other questions, but it is not an isolated issue for moral judgment. We need to see it in the context of a broader Christian commitment to the care of life as it is given and preserved by God and in cooperation with God. We may need to renew a holistic vision of human life even to answer the questions related to the beginning of life in contemporary American society. Caring for the lives of both unborn infants and enemy Iranians corresponds to a scriptural and, therefore Christian, perspective. I find nothing particularly Christian about opposing abortion and favoring war against the communists or the Iranians.

In addition to Christian community as the place of moral discernment and the biblical view of personhood, the language with which we understand and perceive reality can help us find—or hinder us in tracing—a pathway through the bioethical maze. Without going into detail, let us note that the Jones and Gorman chapters particularly address the importance of shaping and maintaining a conceptual language that is appropriate to the moral standards of Christian communities. The relevance of language for moral discernment may again be illustrated by the concept of human life and personhood.

We may all agree and acknowledge that the boundaries of life and the boundaries of personhood are ambiguous and cannot always be defined with great precision. Perhaps for these reasons as well as because scientific language dominates our culture, Christians tend, for example, to speak simply about "the fetus" or "the embryo." Why not speak in terms of "a human fetus" or "a human embryo"? After all "fetuses" and "embryos" are not generically indifferent, but exist only as human fetuses or rabbit fetuses or the like.

Furthermore, by speaking about the human embryo rather than simply the embryo, we would constantly remind ourselves that we are talking about a developing human life, rather than simply about developing organic life. That will not resolve all ethical complexities or all moral dilemmas. Such an approach would, however, point out an identifiable direction in a context where our primary language has almost unquestioningly become scientific and, by implication if not explicitly, morally neutral.

How do the foregoing considerations about community, Scripture, personhood, and language shape a Christian response to the specific bioethical dilemmas that have been discussed in this book? Do these considerations point a direction through the maze of bioethical dilemmas? Let us reconsider one or two dilemmas in illustrative fashion, rather than attempting to construct a complete catalog of issues and proposed answers.

One of the problems that may pose a moral dilemma is a high-risk pregnancy, that is, one that constitutes either a grave risk for the life of the mother or the human fetus or a high risk of abnormality in the human fetus. According to statistics reported by Hershberger, 10 to 20 percent of all pregnancies are high risk in one of these senses. High-risk pregnancies are, therefore, not all that rare. According to Overman, 3 percent of human beings are born with serious birth defects. What measures may be taken to reduce the dangers of high-risk pregnancies? What actions should be taken in relation to birth defects?

Although we have recognized that some abortion cases represent, at least in some measure, moral dilemmas rather than simply complicated problems, Christian moral considerations put the burden of proof on "therapeutic" abortion, rather than seeing it as a simple or self-evident solution. That burden includes emotional and psychological considerations, as well as the biblical bias to care especially for the weak and the defenseless.

Furthermore, amniocentesis and other biotechnical measures should be heavily weighted toward diagnostic and therapeutic uses, rather than those uses that might contribute to indiscriminate abortion or abortions that depend simply upon an individual's (or the parents') choice without broader consultation in the

Christian community and orientation by its moral standards. In any case the broader emphasis on community means that Christians are called to provide support and moral resources for those in the community who are facing genuine moral dilemmas.

Another instance that may sometimes constitute a bioethical dilemma is in vitro fertilization. For example, does a procedure that imposes a choice between destroying some fertilized human ova and not having a child amount to a moral dilemma? The question is not whether in vitro fertilization is possible or whether it will be used by anyone. The question is, rather, how Christians should respond and for what reasons.

Several people have suggested that we look at other options. Martin referred to a mentality of "entitlement" that informs contemporary middle-class American society. As Americans, we assume that we are "entitled" to health, education, and welfare, as well as whatever else we desire. The Christian community should learn to distinguish between legitimate desires and this mentality of entitlement.

Further, the alternatives that commend themselves to Christians will most likely differ from the options that seem self-evident to the mentality of entitlement. For those who have great difficulty or who find it impossible to bear children under normal circumstances, in vitro fertilization may not be the only option. With the support and encouragement of the Christian community, they might be called to a particular ministry where it will even be advantageous not to have children. Jesus once said that some would do well to remain single for the sake of the kingdom. Similarly, some could be called to remain childless for the sake of the kingdom and to do so without dishonor.

In addition to encouraging the exploration of other options, a distinction should be made between in vitro fertilization with or without third-party intervention. To be sure, some would argue that even without third-party intervention, in vitro fertilization constitutes a moral dilemma because some of the fertilized human ova may be destroyed. That is to say, incipient human life is destroyed for the sake of giving birth to a human life. However, according to statistics reported by Killian, approximately 60 percent of the embryos conceived arc lost by the sixth week of pregnancy. Thus, the "natural" processes of human procreation also "destroy" human embryos. If an analogy can be drawn between the loss of fertilized human ova with in vitro fertilization and natural human reproduction, the process of in vitro fertilization for a married couple does not constitute a moral dilemma.

In contrast, in vitro fertilization with third-party intervention, either in the form of a donor or in the form of a surrogate, introduces qualitatively new and different moral issues. Hershberger pointed out that psychological and social considerations fundamentally shape human identity, marriage, and family. Richard McCormick has, therefore, characterized surrogate motherhood as a "stillborn idea."[1]

Perhaps the suggestions of the joint Mennonite Church and General Conference Mennonite Church Study on Human Sexuality on this point merit review and revision. This study concluded that a Christian community could take the position that in vitro fertilization with a third party can be a blessing, but that a couple should carefully consider the various issues before reaching a decision. In contrast, I suggest that in the Christian community, in vitro fertilization *without* third-party intervention can be a blessing. However, introducing a donor or a surrogate mother would better be discouraged from a Christian perspective because of broader familial, marital, social, and psychological considerations.

Other issues have been raised in these chapters. Rather than attempting to summarize and assess them, I close by suggesting several matters that merit sustained attention and closer scrutiny. First, to return to the metaphor of the maze, what is the goal of the maze? We have devoted little attention to the purpose of moving through the bioethical maze. Are we trying to create a perfect humanity? Are we trying simply to make life more tolerable? Most likely, the future shaped by genetic engineering will be less positive than the optimists hope and less negative than the pessimists fear. In any case, what is the goal of all this?

Second, Killian posed the question about the relation between moral and research priorities. That is an important question lacking easy answers. Mennonites have tended to make moral issues out of other kinds of research, particularly research related to armaments and the military. The potential implications of biomedical research for human life and social relations are also far-reaching and call for ethical discernment.

Third, Burkholder and others have pointed toward other issues that are particularly important both from an Anabaptist perspective and in relation to the contemporary American debate on biotechnology. What is the relation between normative Christian ethics and public policy on abortion, biomedical research, and numerous other related issues? These chapters have quite rightly emphasized the distinctively Christian and Anabaptist perspectives that point a direction through the bioethical maze. Relatively little explicit attention has been given to the relation between distinctively Christian perspectives and public policy in a pluralistic society.

Finally, we have not sought to set the bioethical maze within the broader order of priorities for the Christian community. We have talked about the relevance of the Christian community for moral discernment and about its mission in the world. What are the church's priorities in relation to biomedical technology and issues such as abortion and in vitro fertilization? We are not able to do everything. Shall we focus on influencing public legislation, on providing community support for people in difficult situations, or on providing advice and counsel for professional people? The Mennonite Central Committee in Canada decided several years ago to develop a program that provides a support system to give alternatives to abortion, rather than trying first of all to influence public policy. Perhaps others will follow that lead.

In any case finding and following a directional pathway through the bioethical maze depends in part upon setting that maze in the broader context of the church's mission and priorities in today's world.

Questions for Reflection and Discussion

1. Is it true that most abortions in the U.S. today are done without regard for moral dilemmas?
2. How can professionals and nonprofessionals work together in church communities on bioethical dilemmas? What is the role of community leaders?
3. How can church communities provide support and flexibility while at the same time adopting standards and norms for ethical decisions?
4. What is the value of biotechnology to the church?
5. Should the church encourage limitations on research endeavors that create bioethical issues? Why or why not?
6. Should the church seek to influence public policy on bioethical questions? What are the implications of doing so?
7. What are the church's priorities in relation to the bioethical agenda?

For Further Reading

McCormick, Richard A.
   1987 "Surrogate Motherhood: A Stillborn Idea." *Second Opinion* 5:128-132.
Mennonite Church and General Conference Mennonite Church
   1985 *Human Sexuality in the Christian Life.* (General Conference Mennonite Church and the Mennonite Church.)

Notes

Chapter 1

1. All biblical citations throughout this article are taken from *The Holy Bible, Revised Standard Version Containing the Old and New Testaments with the Apocrypha/Deuterocanonical Books: An Ecumenical Edition* (New York: William Collins Sons & Co., 1973).

2. See also Deut. 28:1-14 and 30:1-10. The obverse of this blessing motif is found in the curses that are called down upon those who are disobedient to the voice of the Lord (Deut. 28:15-19; cf. vv. 47-57).

3. See also Gen. 20:18.

4. Consult the footnotes in the Revised Standard Version for the etymological links between the (Hebrew) names in question and their respective explanations.

5. Such a confession of faith can also precede the birth of the child. During Elizabeth's pregnancy prior to the birth of John the Baptist the narrator recounts that "for five months she hid herself, saying, 'Thus the Lord has done to me in the days when he looked upon me, to take away my reproach among men'" (Luke 1:24-25). In this instance the confession of faith appears to have no direct link to the name of the child. Cf. also Gen. 16:11 where, in reverse fashion, it is the angel of the Lord who announces to Hagar that "you shall call his name Ishmael; because the LORD has given heed to your affliction."

6. Cf. the statement of Paul in Romans 4:19: "[Abraham] did not weaken in faith when he considered his own body, which was as good as dead because he was about a hundred years old, or when he considered the barrenness of Sarah's womb. No distrust made him waver concerning the promise of God, but he grew strong in his faith as he gave glory to God, fully convinced that God was able to do what he had promised."

7. Gen. 21:1-2—Sarah; Gen. 20:17—the women of the house of Abimelech; Gen. 25:21—Rebekah; Gen. 30:22-23—Rachel; Judg. 13:24—the wife of Manoah; 1 Sam. 1:19-20—Hannah; Luke 1:24—Elizabeth.

8. See also Deut. 7:14-15.

9. See also Luke 21:23 and Matt. 24:19.

10. Cf. Rom 4:19.

11. See also Isa. 54:1//Gal. 4:27; Ps. 113:5-9; and 1 Sam. 2:2-8, where God is likewise portrayed as the one who transforms barrenness into the fruitfulness of childbearing.

12. Cf. 1 Chron. 22:6-10, where David later recounts the same event.

13. The narrative in which this birth prediction is embedded indicates that the child to be born is one who will appear in the time of Ahaz. Cf. Matt. 1:23, however, where this birth prediction is later reinterpreted as a prediction of the birth of Jesus.

14. Although this text is in fact a prophetic oracle and not a birth prediction *narrative* as such, it nevertheless serves the same purpose as the previously identified texts: to announce the birth of a child. In this case the announcement comes not to an individual but to all who hear Isaiah's oracle.

15. In this instance Eli does not *predict* the birth of a son to Hannah but rather *prays that the Lord will grant Hannah's own request* for a son. Nevertheless, in supporting Hannah's request and invoking the action of God, Eli's words have the impact of an actual birth prediction. As the narrative ends, both Hannah and the reader appear to be confirmed in the conviction that God *will answer* Hannah's request.

16. It would appear that in its original form and context the reference here is simply to a young woman; but see Matt. 1:23 for the alternate interpretation.

17. See footnote 16 above with reference to Isa. 7:14.

18. Cf. Gen. 17:1-21 and Gen. 18:1-15, where the time of Isaac's birth is specified in the same way.

19. This account is once again unique among the birth prediction narratives (see footnote 15 above) in that Samuel's vocation is identified for him by his mother and not by Eli. However, since Hannah is the one who initiates the discussion of the son to be born to her, she is also the one who speaks of the child's vocation.

20. Although 1 Kings 13:1-3 also predicts the birth of one who will be king, the focus of the prediction is on Josiah's character, rather than on his vocation.

21. Cf. the more general references to the action of God in "forming" individuals within the womb (Isa. 44:2, 24; Isa. 49:5; Jer. 1:4-5) and "bringing" or "taking" them from the womb (Job 10:18-19; Ps. 22:9-10; Ps. 71:4-6).

22. Cf. Luke 1:15, where these same prohibitions are laid upon John the Baptist. In this case, however, it is not specifically indicated that the prohibitions extend to Elizabeth.

23. Cf. Hos. 12:2-3.

24. Cf. the metaphorical formulation of Hos. 13:12-13, where the sin of Ephraim lies in the fact that "he does not present himself at the mouth of the womb."

25. Cf. Luke 1:15, where the angel states explicitly that John "will be filled with the Holy Spirit, even from his mother's womb."

26. See also 2 Kings 15:16.

27. Cf. Hos. 13:16, where this action is identified, in reverse fashion, as the judgment upon Samaria because of her sin.

28. See Michael J. Gorman, *Abortion and the Early Church: Christian, Jewish and Pagan Attitudes in the Greco-Roman World* (Downers Grove, Ill.: InterVarsity Press, 1982), 48.

Chapter 2

1. Daniel Callahan cited by James T. Burtchaell, *Rachel Weeping and Other Essays on Abortion* (Kansas City: Andrews and McMeel, Inc., 1982), 109.

2. See chapter one of Stanley Hauerwas, *Suffering Presence: Theological Reflections on Medicine, the Mentally Handicapped, and the Church* (Notre Dame, Ind.: University of Notre Dame Press, 1986),

3. For detailed biblical analysis, see the article on "Life," Otto A. Piper, *The Interpreter's Dictionary of the Bible*, Vol. III (New York: Abingdon Press, 1962), 125-130.

4. Paul D. Simmons, *Birth and Death: Bioethical Decision-Making* (Philadelphia: Westminster, 1983), 60.

5. James F. Childress and John Macquarrie, eds., "Natural Law," *The Westminster Dictionary of Christian Ethics* (Philadelphia: Westminster Press, 1986), 412-414.

6. Stanley Hauerwas, *Vision and Virtue* (Notre Dame, Ind.: Fides Press, 1974), 133.

7. Paul D. Simmons, *Birth and Death* (Philadelphia: Westminster Press, 1983), 81f. and 172ff. (The vitality/humanity distinction is credited to Jürgen Moltmann.)

8. We are not here probing the nature and essence of God, but rather the manner of God's revelation, with the particular reference to ethical norms.

9. Richard A. McCormick, "Bioethics and Method: Where Do We Start?" *On Moral Medicine: Theological Perspectives in Medical Ethics*, Stephen E. Lammers and Allen Verhey, eds., (Grand Rapids: Eerdmans, 1987), 49.

10. John Macquarrie, as quoted by McCormick, 1987, 49.

11. Hauerwas, *Suffering Presence*, 1986, 143.

12. Ronald L. Numbers and Darrel W. Amundsen, eds., *Caring and Curing* (New York: Macmillan, 1986), 284. (The book is a project of Lutheran General Health Care System and Park Ridge Center.)

13. J. Denny Weaver, *Becoming Anabaptist* (Scottdale, Pa.: Herald Press, 1987), 120-121.

14. *Abortion, A Summary Statement* (Scottdale, Pa.: Mennonite Publishing House, 1976).

15. See George Brenneman, "Abortion: Review of Mennonite Literature, 1970-1977," *Mennonite Quarterly Review* 53 (April 1979): 160-172.

16. J. Howard Kauffman and Leland Harder, *Anabaptists Four Centuries Later* (Scottdale, Pa.: Herald Press, 1975), 180-181.

17. Kauffman and Harder, 1975, 180-181.

18. The 1972 survey put opposition to war among all Mennonites at 73%; for the Mennonite Church the figure was 87%. Kauffman and Harder, 1975, 133.

19. See Ted Koontz, "Hard Choices: Abortion and War," *The Mennonite* (February 28, 1978): 132-34.

20. John H. Yoder, "The Biblical Evaluation of Human Life" (paper presented at a seminar on "A Theology of Life and Human Values," sponsored by Mennonite Mutual Aid, Chicago, Ill., May 1973), 6.

21. This issue is a recurrent theme in the writings of Stanley Hauerwas: see *Vision and Virtue*, 1974; *A Community of Character*, 1981; and *Suffering Presence*, 1986.

Chapter 6

1. Aldous Huxley, *Brave New World* (New York: Harper and Row, 1979).

2. This case is drawn from Melvin D. Levine, Lee Scott, and William J. Curran, "Ethics Rounds in a Children's Medical Center: Evaluation of a Hospital-Based Program for Continuing Education in Medical Ethics," *Pediatrics* 60 (August 1977): 205.

3. Tom L. Beauchamp and James F. Childress, *Principles of Biomedical Ethics*, 2d ed. (New York: Oxford University Press, 1983).

Chapter 7

1. Cf. Mary Douglass, *Purity and Danger* (London: Routledge and Kegan Paul, 1966), 39.

2. Robert Bellah, *et al.*, *Habits of the Heart* (Berkeley, Calif.: Univ. of California Press, 1985).

3. Alasdair MacIntyre, *After Virtue*, 2d ed. (Notre Dame, Ind.: Univ. of Notre Dame Press, 1984), 216.

4. H. Tristram Engelhardt, Jr., *The Foundations of Bioethics* (New York: Oxford Univ. Press, 1986), 105.

5. Englehardt, 242.

6. Englehardt, 229.

7. Cf. Oliver O'Donovan, "Again: Who Is a Person?" in *Abortion and the Sanctity of Human Life*, ed. J. H. Channer (Exeter: The Paternoster Press, 1985), 123-137.

8. O'Donovan, 125-126.

9. O'Donovan, 126.

10. O'Donovan

11. O'Donovan, 127.

12. James Tunstead Burtchaell, "Opening Statement in Debate," *Commonweal* 114 (Nov. 20, 1987): 663.

13. *Didache* 2:2-3, cited in Burtchaell, ibid., 663. Emphasis is mine.

14. Marcus Minucius Felix, *Octavius* 30:1-2, cited in Burtchaell, ibid., 663-664.

15. Burtchaell, "Opening Statement in Debate," 668.

16. David Kelsey, "Theological Reflections on Birth," Tate-Willson lecture delivered at Southern Methodist University (Dallas, Tex.), February 13, 1986.

17. William H. Willimon, *What's Right with the Church?* (New York: Harper and Row, 1985), 65.

Chapter 8

1. Noted and criticized in Harold O. J. Brown, "What the Supreme Court Didn't Know," *Human Life Review* 1, No. 2 (Spring 1975):5-21.

2. Plato *Republic* V. 460-62.

3. *Republic* V. 461.

4. Aristotle *Politics* 7. 41. 10 [=1335b].

5. Aristotle *Historia animalum* 7. 3.

6. For a different interpretation of the evidence see Paul Carrick, *Medical Ethics in Antiquity* (Dordrecht, Holland: D. Reidel, 1985), 119-123.

7. Justinian *Digest* 25. 4. 1. 1; 35. 2. 9. 1; 38. 8. 1. 8.

8. Justinian *Digest* 47. 11.

9. Philo *Special Laws* 3. 108-9.

10. Josephus *Against Apion* 2. 202.

11. *Didache* 2. 2 and the *Epistle of Barnabas* 19. 5.

12. Athenagoras *Plea* 35.

13. Tertullian *Apology* 9. 6.

14. Minucius Felix *Octavius* 30. 2.

15. Tertullian *Apology* 9. 6.

16. Tertullian *De anima* 25. 3; 26. 4-5.

17. Anthenagoras *Plea* 35.

18. John M. Rist, *Human Value: A Study in Ancient Philosophical Ethics* (Leiden, Holland: E. J. Brill, 1982), 142.

19. Basil *Letter* 188.2.

20. E. g., Augustine *De nuptiis et concupiscentia* 1. 15-17.

21. Germain G. Grisez, *Abortion: The Myths, the Realities, and the Arguments* (New York: Corpus, 1970), 145-148; Michael J. Gorman, *Abortion and the Early Church: Christian, Jewish and Pagan Attitudes in the Greco-Roman World* (Downers Grove, Ill.: InterVarsity Press, 1982), 70-72.

22. Augustine *Enchiridion* 23: 85-86.

23. On this subject see John Boswell, *The Kingdom of Strangers: The Abandonment of Children in Western Europe from Late Antiquity to the Renaissance* (New York: Pantheon 1988). Boswell's reconstruction of social customs is much more convincing than his integration of attitudes toward these customs.

24. Martin Luther *Works* 45: 333.

25. John Calvin *Commentary on Exodus*, ad loc.

26. Grisez, *Abortion*, 158-59. I am indebted to Grisez for his discussion of post-Reformation developments, on which much of the following section depends.

27. George Hunston Williams, "Religious Residues and Presuppositions in the American Debate on Abortion," *Theological Studies* 31(1970):42.

28. *China Centenary Missionary Conference Records* (New York: American Tract Society, 1907), 151.

29. Beverly Wildung Harrison, *Our Right to Choose: Toward a New Ethic of Abortion* (Boston: Beacon, 1983), 127, 129, 152, et passim.

30. B. Bonner, "Abortion and Early Christian Thought," in *Abortion and the Sanctity of Human Life*, J. H. Channer, ed. (Exeter: Paternoster, 1985), 11.

31. F. Forrester Church, "A Just War Theory for Abortion," *Christian Century* Vol. 104 (Aug. 26-Sept. 2, 1987): 733-34.

32. Michael J. Gorman, "Shalom and the Unborn," *Transformation* 3 (1986):26-33.

Chapter 9

1. Maurice J. Mahoney, "Fetal-Maternal Relationship," in *Encyclopedia of Bioethics*, ed. Warren T. Reich (New York: Macmillan and Free Press, 1978), 485.

2. Virginia Kemp and Cecilia Page, "Maternal Prenatal Attachment in Normal and High-risk Pregnancies," *Journal of Obstetrics, Gynecology, and Neonatal Nursing* 16 (May/June 1987): 180.

3. Reva Rubin, *Maternal Identity and the Maternal Experience* (New York: Springer Publishing Company, Inc., 1984), 53.

4. Rubin, 45.

5. Rubin, 54.

6. Rubin

7. Rubin, 45.

8. Rubin

9. Rubin, 46.

10. Rubin, 47.

11. John C. Fletcher and Mark I. Evans, "Maternal Bonding in Early Fetal Ultrasound Examinations," *The New England Journal of Medicine* 308 (17 Feb. 1983): 392.

12. Rubin, *Maternal Identity*, 60.

13. Kemp and Page, "Maternal Prenatal Attachment," 180.

14. Mahoney, "Fetal-Maternal Relationship," 486.

15. Rubin, *Maternal Identity*, 60.

16. Edward D. Schneider, ed., *Questions About the Beginning of Life* (Minneapolis: Augsburg Publishing House, 1985), 9.

17. John A. Robertson, "Surrogate Mothers: Not So Novel After All," *The Hastings Center Report* 13 (Oct. 1983): 28.

18. LeRoy Walters, Jr., "A Christian Response to Genetic Engineering," *Gospel Herald* 76 (12 April 1983): 261.

19. Schneider, *Questions*, 66.

20. Schneider, 70.

Chapter 10

1. Arthur Lazarus and Roy Stern, "Psychiatric Aspects of Pregnancy Termination," *Clinics in Obstetrics and Gynecology* 13:9(March, 1986):132.

2. Rochelle N. Shain, "A Cross-Cultural History of Abortion," *Clinics in Obstetrics and Gynecology* 13:1 (March, 1986):15.

3. Eric Erikson, *Childhood and Society* (New York: W. W. Norton, 1963)195.

4. 1 Corinthians 7:32-35, *New International Version of the Bible.*

5. Matthew 6:32.

6. Hoffman, M. S., ed., *The World Almanac and Book of Facts 1988* (New York: Pharos Books, 1987), 814.

7. Marsha Weinraub and Barbara M. Wolf, "Effects of Stress and Social Supports on Mother-Child Interactions in Single- and Two-Parent Families," *Child Development* 54(1983):1297.

8. Hoffman, 812.

9. Weinraub and Wolf, 1309.

10. Susan Golombok, Ann Spenser, and Michael Rutter, "Children in Lesbian

and Single-Parent Households: Psychological and Psychiatric Appraisal," *Journal of Child Psychology and Psychiatry* 24:4(1983):570.

11. Notman, Malkah T., "Fertility, Infertility, and Sexuality," In Nadelson, Carol C. and Marcotte, David B. (Eds.) *Treatment Interventions in Human Sexuality.* (New York: Plenum Press, 1983), 225.

12. D. D. Youngs and A. A. Ehrhardt, *Psychosomatic Obstetrics and Gynecology* (New York: Appleton-Century-Crofts, 1980), 200.

13. Warren J. Gadpaille, *The Cycles of Sex* (New York: Charles Scribner's Sons, 1975), 380. See also Notman, 215-217.

14. Lorraine Dennerstein and Carol Morse, "New Clinical Issues in In Vitro Fertilization," *Clinics in Obstetrics and Gynecology* 12:4(December, 1985):836.

15. Dennerstein and Morse, 837.

16. Youngs and Ehrhardt, 250.

17. Youngs and Ehrhardt, 244.

18. Dorothy Greenfeld and Florence Haseltine, "Candidate Selection and Psychosocial Considerations of In-Vitro Fertilization Procedures," *Clinical Obstetrics and Gynecology*, 29:1(March, 1986):123.

19. Enos D. Martin and Heidi Zimmerman, "Couples Seeking Artificial Insemination by Donor: Clinical Characteristics and Personality Patterns." (Submitted for publication, 1989.)

20. Martha Stout, *Without Child* (Grand Rapids, Mich.: Zondervan Publishing House, 1985), 85-86.

21. Stout, 95-100.

22. D. Neff, "How Not to Have a Baby," *Christianity Today* 31:6(1987):34.

23. Stout, 104-105.

24. Peter Singer and Deane Wells, *Making Babies: The New Science and Ethics of Conception* (New York: Charles Scribner's Sons 1985), 42.

25. A. Clamar, "Psychological Implications of Donor Insemination," *Journal of Psychoanalysis* 40(1980):183.

26. G. Gerstel, "Psychoanalytic View of Artificial Donor Insemination," *American Journal of Psychotherapy*, 17(1963):64.

27. Martin and Zimmerman.

28. Martin and Zimmerman.

29. Martin and Zimmerman.

30. S. J. Behrman, "Artificial Insemination." In Behrman, S. J. and Robert W. Kistner (Eds.), *Progress in Fertility*, Second Edition (Boston: Little, Brown and Company, 1973), 781.

31. Martin and Zimmerman.

32. D. Gareth Jones, *Brave New People* (Grand Rapids, Mich.: William B. Eerdman Publishing Company, 1985) 108. See also Dennerstein and Morse, 836.

33. W. I. H. Johnston, K. Oke, A. Speirs, G. A. Clarke, J. McBain, C. Bayly, J. Hunt, and G. N. Clarke, "Patient Selection for *In Vitro* Fertilization: Physical and Psychological Aspects," In Seppala, M. and Edwards, R. G. (Eds.), *In Vitro Fertilization and Embryo Transfer* (Annals of the New York Academy of Sciences, 1985), 498-500.

34. Hoffman, 818.

35. Lazarus and Stern, 125.

36. Lazarus and Stern, 125.

37. Lazarus and Stern, 127.

38. Lazarus and Stern, 127.

39. Lazarus and Stern, 129.

40. Lazarus and Stern, 129.

41. Lazarus and Stern, 129.

42. Lazarus and Stern, 130.

43. Neff, 34.

44. Neff, 34.

45. Neff, 34.

46. Neff, 35.

47. Youngs and Ehrhardt, 130.

48. Youngs and Ehrhardt, 142.

Chapter 11

1. *Roe v. Wade*, 410 U.S. 113 (1973).

2. *Roe v. Wade*, 163-164.

3. *Akron v. Akron Center for Reproductive Health*, 462 U.S. 416 (1983).

4. Nancy K. Rhoden, "Trimesters and Technology: Revamping *Roe v. Wade*," *Yale Law Journal* 95 (March 1986): 639.

5. Rhoden, 643.

6. Nancy K. Rhoden, "The New Neonatal Dilemma: Live Births from Late Abortions," *Georgetown Law Journal* 72 (June 1984): 1506.

7. Rhoden, 1506.

8. Rhoden, 1507.

9. Daniel Callahan, "How Technology Is Reframing the Abortion Debate," *Hastings Center Report* 16 (February 1986): 33.

10. Callahan, 34.

11. Callahan, 41.

12. Callahan, 41.

13. *Thornburgh v. American College of Obstetricians and Gynecologists*, 51 L.W. 4618 (June 10, 1986).

14. Dawn Johnsen, "A New Threat to Pregnant Women's Autonomy," *Hastings Center Report* 17 (August 1987): 35.

15. *Becker v. Swartz*, 46 N. Y. 2d 401, 386 N. E. 2d 807 (1987), *Procanike v. Cillo*, 97 N. J. 339, 478 A. 2d 755.

16. *In the Matter of Baby "M"* 525 A. 2d 1128 (N. J. Super Ch. 1987).

17. *In the Matter of Baby "M"* 537 A. 2d 1227 (N. J. 1988).

18. *In the Matter of Baby "M"*, 1240.

19. *In the Matter of Baby "M"*, 1246.

20. *In the Matter of Baby "M"*, 1247 (quoting N. J. S. A. 9:17-40).

21. *In the Matter of Baby "M"*, 1258 (emphasis in original).

22. *In the Matter of Baby "M"*, 1259.

Chapter 13

1. Richard A. McCormick, "Surrogate Motherhood: A Stillborn Idea," *Second Opinion* 5: 128-132.

Index